IN HIS FIRST COOKBOOK, Kwame Onwuachi—"the most important chef in America" (*San Francisco Chronicle*)—shares the dishes of his America, dishes that show the true diversity of American food.

Featuring more than 125 recipes, *My America* is a celebration of the food of the African diaspora, as handed down through Onwuachi's own family history, spanning Nigeria to the Caribbean, the American South to the Bronx, and beyond. From Nigerian Jollof Rice, Puerto Rican Red Bean Sofrito, and Trinidadian Channa (Chickpea Curry) to Jambalaya, Baby Back Ribs, and Red Velvet Cake, these are Onwuachi's spins on global home recipes that represent the best of the patchwork that is American cuisine. Interwoven throughout the book are stories of Onwuachi's travels, illuminating the connections between food and place, and food and culture. The result is a deeply personal tribute to the food of "a land that belongs to you and yours and to me and mine."

ALSO BY KWAME ONWUACHI

Notes from a Young Black Chef

(with Joshua David Stein)

MY AMERICA

MY AMERICA

RECIPES FROM A
YOUNG BLACK CHEF

KWAME ONWUACHI

WITH JOSHUA DAVID STEIN

Photographs by Clay Williams

ALFRED A. KNOPF · New York

2022

THIS IS A BORZOI BOOK
PUBLISHED BY ALFRED A. KNOPF

Copyright © 2022 by Kwame Onwuachi
Photographs © 2022 by Clay Williams

Text design by Cassandra J. Pappas
Front-of-jacket photograph by Clay Williams
Jacket lettering by Stephanie Ross
Jacket design by Kelly Blair
Recipe testing by Caroline Lange
Recipe development by David Paz-Grusin

Manufactured in China
Published May 17, 2022
Second Printing, June 2022

I dedicate this book to my mother, Jewel Robinson,

for gracing my hand with the spirit of our ancestors.

When a dish tells a story it has a soul;

you are not only cooking to achieve perfect seasoning,

but you are also cooking to share a memory and an anecdote.

Thank you, Mom, for keeping our history alive.

CONTENTS

GREENS AND OTHER VEGETABLES 69

LEGUMES AND TUBERS 95

SEAFOOD AND SHELLFISH 117

POULTRY 161

MEAT 187

BREADS, PASTRIES, AND DESSERTS 233

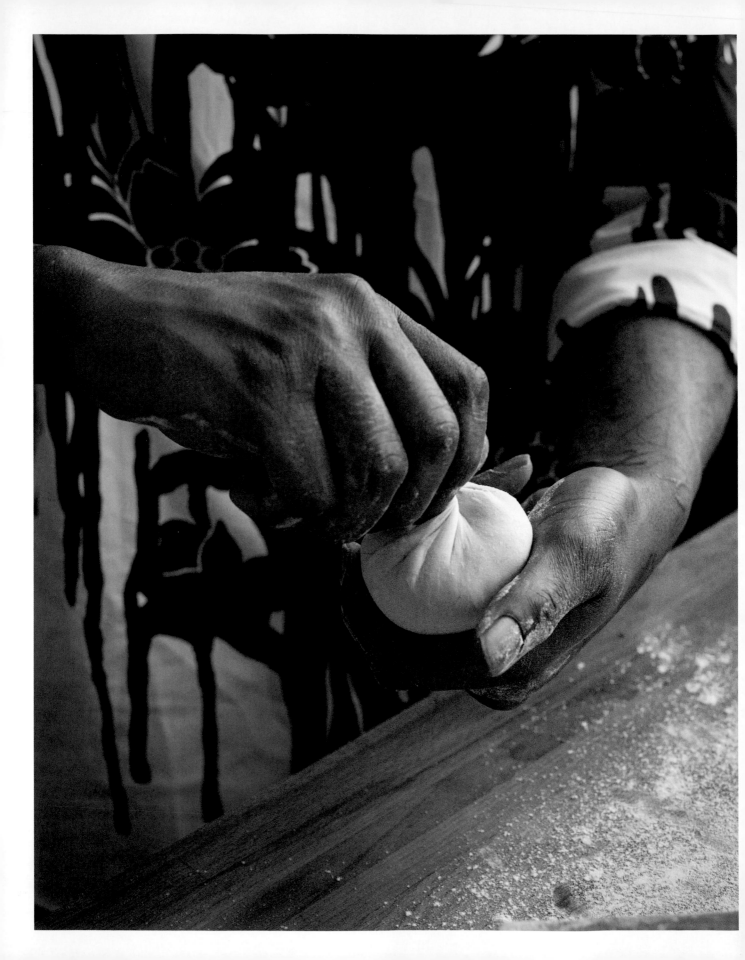

INTRODUCTION

Show me an America made of apple pie and hot dogs, baseball and Chevrolet and I won't recognize it. That's a foreign land to me. Maybe that's someone's America but it isn't mine. Waves of grain and purple mountain majesty are part of this country of course, a chorus perhaps, or maybe the hook. But the verse is tighter, more compact, maybe less catchy but at least real. My America is full of internal rhymes, studded with a thousand languages, references, allusions, bits snatched from here or there, some bits shared, but mostly taken. It's a country of countless flavors and endless adaptation, an America that didn't just arise but was built on something. This book is from that America, my America.

The Bronx, where I grew up, is a borough of blocks, parks, bricks, and people. The only one of the five boroughs that isn't an island, the Bronx contains multitudes: the Jamaicans of Gun Hill Road, where my father, himself half Jamaican and half Nigerian, lives; the West Indians from Wakefield; the Puerto Ricans and Dominicans of the South Side, where I lived with my mother and sister; and countless more. With language, with music, with fashion, and, most importantly, with food, they proudly proclaim that though they belong there they are from elsewhere. Jamaican corner bakeries sell hardo bread and jerk chicken, beef patties and coco bread. Closet-sized Trinidadian roti shops are fragrant with curries, channa, and paratha. Puerto Rican and Dominican cooks stand behind the steam of lechon and pernil and in front of rotisseries where chickens are crisping. In our own home, what my mom cooked was part of another sort of story, the food of the American South and its Black sons and daughters. Crawfish étouffée, jambalaya, and potatoes tinged with russet-red house spice told of her own family's lineage, embroidered into the southern coast of Louisiana and Texas, then north with the Great Migration.

As a not-yet chef, I consumed all of these cultures with gusto. My world opened up at the table. My mother, a talented chef and caterer, showed her love through cooking, she and I side by side at the stove. As I grew up and gradually, after a lot of wayward adventures, made my own way in the kitchen, I held on to the feeling of cooking next to her and the flavors with which I grew up. And I kept adding to that repertoire as the years went on. Food was, and continues to be, how I make sense of the world.

When I was ten years old, my mom sent me to live with my paternal grandfather in Nigeria to "learn respect." The experience exposed me to novel flavors and ingredients, a new culture, and an approach to food much closer to the earth. If we wanted a chicken, we killed a chicken. If we wanted yams, we grew yams. Later on, I spent time living with my mother in Baton Rouge, Louisiana, tasting the source code for so much of what she cooked for me as a kid. I worked as a chef on a cleanup boat in the Gulf of Mexico, where I saw firsthand how much food can serve as a reminder of home.

But by the time I entered culinary school, I had mentally cordoned off the food I loved from the food I wanted to make professionally. The fine-dining kitchen was a universe of clean cuts, fluorescent light, precise technique, luxury ingredients, and far-flung flavors, so foreign to my own experience that I was immediately enchanted. I wanted to be part of this well-heeled universe, and the fact that nobody looked like me and few looked like they liked me didn't get in the way. Nor did the fact that when I returned to the Bronx or to Harlem, feeble with exhaustion after a fourteen-hour shift, the food that sustained me, that gave me joy, that let me know I was home, had nothing to do with the wizardry of downtown. I sustained myself on pollo asado, red beans and rice, egusi stew, Senegalese thieboudienne, and chicken yassa.

Meanwhile, at the Culinary Institute of America, my fellow students and I were put through the paces of French tradition. The techniques, the sauces, the ingredients, the language, the white hats, the clean toque, the *Oui, chef*—all this formed a pyramid with France at the top. Like anyone learning a foreign language, I found the process exciting. And I learned how to form words, then sentences, and eventually stories with these techniques. But whose stories was I trying to tell?

Like any chef who deserves the title, I wanted to express myself through my cooking, but I thought the language to do that was, and would always be, the Western, that is the white, culinary idiom. Experiences in fine-dining kitchens only helped that thought colonize my mind further.

When I finally did open my own restaurant, a short-lived venture called the Shaw Bijou in Washington, D.C., I went to great lengths to tell my own story, the story of my childhood and my travels, expressed in true decadence. The halal chicken and rice I ate growing up became a rice chip with lamb sweetbread glazed in chicken jus. Jerk chicken became jerk duck prosciutto with a pistachio tuile. Butterfingers became mignardise at the end of the meal. The menu nodded to my time in the Bronx, to my mother, to my dad, to my Jamaican aunties and Louisiana cousins. But it was an autobiography—of one man, me—and looking back on it in hindsight, it was an autobiography written in a borrowed tongue.

After the restaurant closed, I was, naturally, crushed. Not only was I gutted personally, my life upended, but I was gutted emotionally, too. Having so closely entwined my own life with the menu, the rejection of the restaurant felt like a negation of my own self-worth. Nevertheless, when it came time to regroup, I quickly realized that I wanted to tell the story not just of myself but of my people, my kith, my kin. At my second restaurant, I developed a menu made up of what was familiar to me: the seafood gumbo and dirty rice of my mother and maternal grandmother, the buljol and roti from my Trinidadian grandfather Papa Winston, the suya and fufu I remember from Nigeria, the curried goat and brown stew chicken from Jamaican Grandma Gloria, my dad's mom. And, of course, because the food of the Bronx is as much a part of me as all that, I saw a place on the menu too for rice and beans, pollo asado with a side of mojo, tostones and maduros.

As I began to excavate deeper my ancestral kitchen, two things became clear. The first was that I didn't know nearly as much as I thought I did. Just because I had spent my entire life eating my mother's cooking, or my grandmother's, didn't mean I could cook it myself. Thus began an almost weekly call that was like an oral history of my family's kitchen. My mother, reluctantly, imparted the secret ratios of her house spice, the exact proportions of her famous gumbo, and more. I called my cousins on my mom's side in Louisiana to glean precious information about how to fry the crispiest cracklins and asked cousins on my father's side for the precise blend of aromatics for red stew. I revisited the bakeries I had grown up going to, stuffing myself with coco bread and moon-shaped patties. This food, my food, I had always understood from the outside. Now I learned it from the inside out.

The second realization was even more profound. As I began to delve deeper into the food I had grown up eating on street corners and cramped kitchens, food cooked on fire escapes and bayou backyards, I saw how deep their roots ran and how, deep down, they were intertwined. As my knowledge of the genealogy of Carolina Gold rice, or the history of Jamaican jerk seasoning expanded, I began to see just how interconnected these diasporic cuisines are. They are not islands but part of the same river. I saw diasporic cuisine as a writhing, thriving, living thing. I saw jollof and jambalaya as two traditions that fed Africans in vastly different circumstances. I heard the echoes of the one-pot stews of Nigeria in the one-pot stews of the American South. I saw the twined influences of East Indians and West Africans in the Indies. As you'll see in these pages, so much of diasporic cuisine, not just from the American South but from the Caribbean, too, as well as African cuisine itself—has been influenced by the slave trade. Rice, for instance, which West Africans excelled in cultivating, made them particularly attractive to human traffickers who needed skilled workers in the Lowcountry of South Carolina. One reason

collard greens are so important is that they were one of the few ways enslaved Africans could feed themselves. Jerk was originally developed by Maroons—freed African slaves in Jamaica—to preserve meat without being detected and then captured and killed. These recipes represent survival. They represent suffering that has been sanctified at great human cost. Even the sweetest dessert is, therefore, bittersweet.

As I ventured deeper, I began also to enlarge my idea of who my people were and where my place was. I am a Black American, of course, but what does that mean? My people are the millions of Africans—both those who still live in the motherland and those who were scattered by slavery wherever that murderous institution touched. My people are those who have made homes of their own in these lands to which they first came as captives, those who—despite unimaginable cruelty and inhumane treatment—nevertheless created what is, to my mind, the world's wisest food.

As my own sense of who my people are has continued to grow, what it means to be a Black chef in America continues to evolve. It should go without saying that I reserve the right to cook whatever I please. There are, and should be, as many kinds of Black chefs as there are Black chefs. At the same time, for me personally, venerating my ancestors by keeping their recipes alive has become even more meaningful.

This book is an expression of the fact that I too am part of this diaspora. It is the story of the diaspora in its larger sense and of my own travels and circumstances transposed on it. To truly understand where I sit on this land, and what this land is, I traveled to the stops so many of my ancestors made before they settled in America: I return again and again to Nigeria, the Caribbean, and the American South, all areas that have been important in my own life. During the writing of this book, I went back to those places to enrich my memory with new experiences, often traveling with loved ones, and you'll find the stories of those travels interspersed in essays throughout. By necessity, many threads of the diaspora are left unwound. Brazil, for instance, and many parts of South America are left out. In Africa, with the exception of Ethiopia—a community close to my heart after living in Washington, D.C., home to the largest Ethiopian community in the United States—much of East Africa, South Africa, and North Africa didn't make it in. These deserve, and will be and have been afforded, books of their own. *My America* is the story of this specific diaspora, but it isn't the only one. It isn't a historical document or an academic text. It isn't even a re-creation of delicious historic recipes. It's an exploration of the past, of individual lifetimes and societal lifelines, told through recipes. It's ancestral knowledge that I've married with my own unique personal experience and culinary know-how to show how brilliant the kitchens of my people are. I use stocks and some of the French techniques I picked up in my years in fine-dining kitchens. You might not find these in "traditional" recipes, but no one can argue with the flavor-boosting brilliance of a well-made stock or the benefits of carefully julienned vegetables. So much has been taken from us; there's no harm in taking some back. I even improvise across the world in ways none of my ancestors could have imagined. In my pantry, palm oil is only a few inches from Ethiopian berbere or Jamaican jerk powder. They meet, in the pot, as distant cousins and new friends.

This is a book full of proper names—Jewel, Papa Winston, Uncle Rupert, and many more—for *My America* is a love letter to those who made it here, made me here. But it's also full of those whose names I never knew. *My America* is also dedicated to, built on, includes these souls. *My America* is for my mom and her people, my dad and his. It's a land that belongs to you and yours and to me and mine.

PANTRY

*T*he work of cooking is like dancing on an iceberg, the whorl of action in the kitchen, the so-called active time, relies on hours of hidden labor, the slow and steady penetration of flavors, the canny use of the hot sauces, marinades, powders, infusions, pastes, and spices you find in the pantry.

Though many of the world's culinary traditions rely on the pantry to turn relatively simple dishes into flavor bombs—Korea's gochujang, for instance, or Japan's katsuobushi—few kitchens are more invested in it than the diasporic one. From the fiery red stew (obe ate din din) of Nigeria to the mojo of the Caribbean kitchen to the berbere of Ethiopia, the long walk to the dinner table starts hours, if not months, before dinnertime.

I'd always known the pantry to be important, the spices to be key, so much so that when I opened Shaw Bijou, my first restaurant, I spent hours collecting a wall of spices that would both greet the diner and inspire my cooking. But it wasn't until my next project, Kith and Kin, that I dove deeply into the pantries of the African diaspora in particular. And there I found the foundations of my culinary home.

Why has the pantry come to define the food of the African diaspora? One reason is that for many of Africa's children, their lives were not their own, their time not theirs to spend. It was stolen by the institution of slavery in the United States, in the Caribbean, and elsewhere. After emancipation, economic hardship and continued systemic oppression often meant cooking in snatched minutes, reclaimed time, taking advantage of what moments one could. Spice mixtures like House Spice (page 6), bases like Sofrito (page 28) and Recaito (page 30), all maximized the precious moments spent in the kitchen.

In some cases, the spices we celebrate today are a direct result of persecution. The cayenne-flecked hot sauce that my taste buds crave—and the use of chili peppers in general in the United States—has its roots in slavery. Cayenne and later tabasco peppers—and hot sauce in particular, though at the time it was called pepper vinegar—were given to Africans as a tonic to keep them healthy enough to work. The pantry has given us the power to transcend these rotten roots.

The pantry is the soul of the diasporic kitchen, where hardship has been alchemized into, for my money, the richest, deepest, most delicious flavors of the world. It all begins here. The pantry is a cabinet of truth, passed down and discovered anew, that time is your friend in the kitchen. The pantry offers a continuity of flavor, the vascular system of a cuisine, over thousands of years. (You can trace your way from Ethiopia's berbere along the Silk Road trade route to China, or cayenne pepper from South America to West Africa and then to North.) These spices and pantry items form the arteries stretching over the Atlantic Ocean and through the years and tides of my own life. And although I had long understood them each in their own context, bringing them here has been an *Avengers Assemble* moment. To understand that Sofrito (page 28), the Puerto Rican mixture of achiote-tinged red pepper, tomato, and onions, is not that dissimilar to the Holy Trinity of southern cuisine: onions, bell peppers, and celery. Or to note how Shado Beni Chutney (page 27), Trini Green Seasoning (page 29), and Recaito (page 30) are echoes of each other, riffs on the same melody.

And finally, I'm happy to say it, the pantry is my secret weapon. Almost all of the recipes that follow utilize some element of the pantry. The work happens in the next few pages. Then it's largely smooth sailing. Know these recipes and you'll know my cooking from the inside out. As you'll see, there are two pantry elements that make their way into almost every one of my recipes. The first is traditional, the second isn't. House Spice (page 6), a blend of cayenne, Worcestershire powder, salt, garlic, and paprika, is what my mom kept in her pantry. If there's a bit of Kwame, and by extension my mother, Jewel, and her mother, Cassie, and so on and so forth, in my cooking, it's found here. The second is an expression of my culinary peregrination, Ginger-Garlic Purée (page 5), or GGP, which I picked up from a friend in India. Because not all journeys are made by our ancestors.

GINGER-GARLIC PURÉE (GGP)

Together with Peppa Sauce (page 25), GGP—ginger-garlic purée—is a key ingredient in the majority of dishes that come out of my kitchen. The combination of the wake-up-your-mouth zing of ginger and the slightly softer garlic is common throughout the Caribbean, but I owe this particular preparation to my friend Alex Sanchez. Alex and I worked together at Eleven Madison Park. At the time, I thought he was just some bright, friendly kid from San Francisco. But at one point, we had a culinary student from India come in, who told me, eyes wide, "I just never thought I'd be working next to Alex Sanchez. *The* Alex Sanchez." I looked over at Alex, and he looked a little embarrassed. Turns out he was, even then, a celebrity chef in India, where he ran the Table, one of the country's best fine-dining restaurants. He had never mentioned that to me. Over the years, I've visited him a few times in Mumbai to do pop-ups. On one visit, I wanted to make a curry, and his cooks reached for the GGP. They told me it's in everything they make, and, once I started using it as a base flavor, I understood why.

Combine all the ingredients in a high-powered blender or food processor and process until smooth.

ORIGIN: India
YIELD: 1 pint

2 large stems ginger, peeled and thinly sliced
1½ cups garlic cloves
¾ cup grapeseed oil

Ginger-garlic purée will keep in an airtight container in the refrigerator for up to 1 week, or in the freezer for up to 6 months.

HOUSE SPICE

Nearly every kitchen I've been to in that stretch of Louisiana and Texas known as the Creole Coast has, somewhere in it, a jar of house spice. This mixture, made with varying degrees of heat, goes on everything: into the flour with which you fry chicken, onto a steak before it's seared, into the eggs in the morning. Growing up in the Bronx, we had it too, made from scratch by my mom, whose roots are in the marshes of southern Louisiana. These flavors are the underpainting for my palette. House spice is as elemental in the kitchens I love as salt. This version is based on my mom's but kicked up a notch with Worcestershire powder for a touch of acidity and umami.

Combine all the ingredients in a large bowl and whisk well to combine.

ORIGIN: American South
YIELD: 3 cups

½ cup + 2 tablespoons kosher salt

¾ cup + 1 tablespoon freshly ground black pepper

½ cup + 1 tablespoon + 2 teaspoons granulated garlic

¼ cup + 3 tablespoons + 1½ teaspoons granulated onion

½ cup Worcestershire powder

5 tablespoons + 2 teaspoons cayenne

5 tablespoons + 2 teaspoons sweet paprika

House spice keeps in an airtight container in a cool dark place for up to 4 months.

OPPOSITE: *from top to bottom,* House Spice, Curry Powder, Jerk Powder, Suya, Berbere

SUYA SPICE

The first time I came across suya sellers was when I was sent to live with my grandfather, an obi, or chief, in Nigeria. From over the walls of his compound drifted intoxicating smells of spice-touched smoked meat called Suya (page 198), meat I later learned was marinated in suya spice, also called yaji spice. But due to tradition, which stated that no one from the house of an obi could eat outside the home, my grandfather forbade us from eating from these mai suya, as the vendors are called. It wasn't until later that I came to fully appreciate the magic this spice mixture, developed by the northern Hausa tribe of Nigeria, works on meat. It is the grandfather of American barbecue. Built around the native ingredients of West Africa—chili pepper, onion, and ground nuts—and layered with the char of an open flame, Nigerian suya is often made with beef or goat. But it turns everything, from duck and chicken to shrimp and even brussels sprouts, into a deeply flavorful, almost irresistible meal.

Blitz the grains of paradise in a high-powered blender or spice grinder until finely powdered, then set aside in a medium bowl. Blitz Maggi cubes until finely ground, then add to the bowl with the grains of paradise. Add all the other ingredients to the bowl and whisk well to combine.

ORIGIN: Nigeria
YIELD: 1 pint

---

2 tablespoons + 1½ teaspoons grains of paradise
(or alligator pepper)
5 Maggi Seasoning cubes
(vegetable flavor)
6 tablespoons + 1½ teaspoons cayenne
½ cup peanut butter powder
2 tablespoons + 1½ teaspoons sweet paprika
2 tablespoons + 1½ teaspoons onion powder
2 tablespoons + 1½ teaspoons garlic powder
2 tablespoons ground ginger

Suya spice will keep in an airtight container in a cool dark place for up to 4 months.

BERBERE

Berbere means "hot" in Amharic, the language of Ethiopia, and this berbere spice blend contains a kick for sure, but a lot of other flavorful spices too, such as fenugreek, chili, paprika, cumin, and black pepper. These spices of the Silk Road made their way to Ethiopian kitchens in the second century, when the Axumite empire controlled the Red Sea. Berbere is to Ethiopian cuisine what House Spice (page 6) is to Creole: a backbone, a signature. At this point, the unique flavors of berbere have become synonymous with Ethiopian food. It is what gives Doro Wat—stewed chicken, Ethiopia's most famous dish (page 170)—its brick-red color and lends Misir Wat (a lentil dish, page 116) its signature eye-watering heat.

In a medium skillet set over medium heat, lightly toast the chipotle peppers and the whole spices (coriander seeds through allspice berry), stirring or swirling the pan frequently so they toast evenly, until very fragrant, 2 to 3 minutes.

Let cool slightly, then transfer to a spice grinder or high-powered blender. Process until finely ground, then stir in the paprika, granulated garlic, granulated onion, salt, ginger, turmeric, and nutmeg.

ORIGIN: Ethiopia
YIELD: ½ cup

2 whole dried chipotle peppers
1 tablespoon coriander seeds
2 teaspoons black peppercorns
½ teaspoon cumin seeds
½ teaspoon fenugreek seeds
½ teaspoon black cardamom seeds (about 2 pods)
One 1-inch piece cinnamon stick
1 allspice berry
2 tablespoons sweet paprika
1 teaspoon granulated garlic
1 teaspoon granulated onion
1 teaspoon kosher salt
½ teaspoon ground ginger
½ teaspoon ground turmeric
½ teaspoon freshly grated nutmeg

Berbere will keep in an airtight container at room temperature for up to 6 months.

CURRY POWDER

What we call curry is at the heart of Caribbean cuisine. And, at the heart of curry is, naturally, curry powder. Brought to the Caribbean not by indentured Indian laborers themselves but by their colonial employers (curry powder, though obviously not curry, is a British, not Indian, creation), over time Caribbean curry has developed an identity of its own. In contrast to Madras curry powder, which was the most popular variation in the eighteenth century, this one features the distinctive flavor of anise seeds. It's used to do everything from marinating Braised Oxtails (page 221) to adding spice to Curried Goat (page 223) and Curried Chicken (page 177) to giving Jollof Rice (page 57) its distinctive scent.

Heat the oven to 400°F. Spread all spices except turmeric on a sheet tray and toast for 5 minutes, until deeply toasted and fragrant. Immediately transfer to a bowl to keep the spices from burning and let cool slightly.

Transfer toasted spices to a spice grinder or blender. Blitz into a fine powder and combine with the turmeric.

ORIGIN: Trinidad and Tobago
YIELD: 1 pint

1¼ cup + 1 tablespoon whole coriander seeds

5 tablespoons whole cumin seeds

5 tablespoons anise seeds

¼ cup whole allspice berries

1 tablespoon + 1 teaspoon yellow mustard seeds

1 tablespoon whole fenugreek seeds

¾ cup + 1½ teaspoons ground turmeric

Curry powder keeps in an airtight container in a cool dark place for up to 4 months.

ROASTED GARLIC PURÉE (RGP)

Roasting garlic unleashes its natural sweetness. In traditional French kitchens, from which this technique comes, the garlic is confited—a confit just means the thing being cooked is submerged in fat but not fried in it—in a neutral oil like canola. Here, I use the warming spices of Ethiopian Nitter Kibbeh Oil (NKO) to deepen the flavors. I use the resulting purée for everything from simply smearing on a piece of toast for a delicious snack to serving as a base for aioli.

Heat the oven to 250°F.

Place the garlic in a baking dish and pour the NKO over the top; the oil should cover the garlic completely; if it doesn't, add a little more. Fold a piece of parchment paper and set evenly on the surface of the oil, pushing down gently to eliminate any air bubbles. Cover the dish very tightly with foil and bake for 2 hours. The garlic should be extremely fragrant, golden, and completely tender.

Cool to room temperature, then strain the mixture through a fine-mesh sieve. Set the roasted garlic oil aside. Transfer the garlic to a blender or food processor and purée until totally smooth.

ORIGIN: Various places
YIELD: 1 cup roasted garlic–infused NKO and 1 cup Roasted Garlic Purée

---

1½ cups garlic cloves (from ½ pound garlic, about 5 heads)
2 cups NKO (page 21)

Roasted garlic purée will keep in an airtight container in the refrigerator for up to 2 weeks or 6 months in the freezer. Garlic-infused NKO will keep in an airtight container in the refrigerator for up to 1 week.

TAMARIND GLAZE

The tamarind tree is tall and beautiful with heavy fruit pods, and it grows throughout the Caribbean, Southeast Asia, Africa, and North and South America. Thanks to the influence of the Indian laborers who arrived in the mid-nineteenth century, it is widespread in Caribbean cuisine, from sweet sugar-dusted tamarind balls in Trinidad, to Jamaican Jerk Paste (page 17), to agua frescas in Puerto Rico. I make mine with seedless tamarind paste, also called pulp, which saves the extra step of sieving out the seeds. It's also easily available online and at most Latin American or Southeast Asian grocery stores.

ORIGIN: Caribbean
YIELD: 2 cups

⅔ cup seedless **tamarind paste**
1¾ cups **palm sugar**
1 **garlic clove**, crushed
½ teaspoon **Peppa Sauce** (page 25)
1½ cup + 4 tablespoons **water**
1 tablespoon **honey**
Kosher salt, to taste

Tamarind glaze will keep in an airtight container in the refrigerator for up to 1 month.

Combine all the ingredients but honey and salt in a medium pot with and bring to a simmer over medium heat. Simmer gently, stirring often, for 15 minutes, until thick, glossy, and darkened in color. Reduce heat as needed to avoid spattering.

Remove from the heat and let cool slightly. Transfer the mixture to a blender and purée until smooth. You may need to add a bit of water, up to ¼ cup, to get the glaze to the right consistency—it should be almost like mayonnaise. Strain through a fine-mesh sieve.

Finish the glaze by stirring in the honey, then season with salt to taste.

BROWNING

Used primarily as a coloring agent—hence the name—Browning nonetheless imparts a sweet caramel flavor to whatever it is added to. It is literally the secret sauce in many Caribbean dishes from Rice and Peas (page 49) to Braised Oxtails (page 221) and Brown Stew Chicken (page 168). I grew up with a bottle of commercially-made Grace Browning in my mother's kitchen but it's so easy to make at home, I started making my own a few years ago.

In a small pot or pan, heat the oil over high heat. When it shimmers, add the sugar and cook to a dark caramel, about 3 minutes, swirling the pan occasionally to cook the sugar evenly—it should be very dark and almost smoking. Remove the pan from the heat and carefully stir in ¼ cup water 1 tablespoon at a time, being careful of hot sugar splatter.

ORIGIN: Caribbean

YIELD: Scant ½ cup

¼ cup vegetable oil, such as canola

3 tablespoons white granulated sugar

Browning will keep in an airtight container at room temperature for up to 1 month. Stir well before using.

JERK POWDER

Once you discover the heat of jerk, you want it on everything. Jerk is like an Instagram filter: it makes reality better. I made this powder—using ingredients found online—to more easily apply jerk seasoning to everything from popcorn to bacon to French fries. I have yet to find a snack not improved by a generous sprinkling.

In a high-powered bender or spice grinder, combine the all-spice berries, thyme, bay leaves, cinnamon stick, and cloves; blend until finely powdered. Stir together with the remaining ingredients.

ORIGIN: Caribbean
YIELD: 1 pint

---

1 tablespoon + 2 teaspoons whole **allspice berries**

1 tablespoon + 1½ teaspoons dried **thyme**

¾ loosely packed cup dried **bay leaves**

One 2-inch (approximately) whole **cinnamon stick**

1½ teaspoons whole **cloves**

1 teaspoon dried ground **habanero pepper**

¾ cup + 1½ teaspoons **green onion powder**

¾ cup + 3 tablespoons dried **parsley**

4¼ teaspoons **soy sauce powder**

2 tablespoons + 1¼ teaspoons **Worcestershire powder**

1½ teaspoons **garlic powder**

2 teaspoons **ginger powder**

Jerk powder will keep in an airtight container in a cool dark place for up to 4 months.

JERK PASTE

Jerk is a dish of survival. In the seventeenth century, when the British overtook the Spanish as the colonial occupiers of Jamaica, the Spaniards set free many of their African slaves. Rather than submit to the British, these men, women, and children took to the Blue Mountains and became known as Maroons. There they lived a hardscrabble existence, eking out a life from subsistence farming and occasional raids on the British occupiers. Fortunately for them, Jamaican pepper, what we call allspice or pimento, as well as Thai bird chili, wild thyme, and a bunch of other herbs, grew wild, as did a breed of wild hog first brought over by the ancestors of the Taino people from South America. Jerk was born, and it lives still two hundred years later, in the stalls that line Boston Beach in Jamaica, and in the shops of Flatbush and the North Bronx in New York and Croydon, Lambeth, and Brixton in London, and wherever else the Jamaican diaspora has reached.

Combine all the ingredients in a blender and blend on high until they form a smooth paste.

ORIGIN: Caribbean
YIELD: 1 pint

¼ cup + 2 tablespoons + 1 teaspoon **soy sauce**

4 **green onions**, root ends trimmed, roughly chopped

⅔ cup **Peppa Sauce** (page 25)

¼ cup **Tamarind Glaze** (page 12)

½ cup roughly chopped fresh **thyme sprigs**, woody stems removed

1 tablespoon + 1 teaspoon **Worcestershire sauce**

¼ cup **GGP** (page 5)

1¾ teaspoons **light brown sugar**

2 teaspoons **kosher salt**

1 tablespoon whole **allspice berries**

Half of one 2-inch **cinnamon stick** (smashed with a knife to split)

1 fresh **bay leaf**

5 whole **cloves**

Jerk paste will keep in an airtight container in the refrigerator for up to 1 month, or in the freezer for up to 6 months.

JERK BBQ SAUCE

Mixing barbecue sauce and jerk sauce isn't authentic—or it is. It all depends on whether you think food is something that evolves or something that sits still. It is true that historically jerk, which comes from the Caribbean, and barbecue sauce, which comes from the American South, rarely met in the bottle. But in the Bronx, where I first had jerk BBQ sauce, everything is subject to change. Me? I'm a fan. The sweetness of the barbecue sauce cuts the heat of the jerk paste in a perfect marriage between southern BBQ and Caribbean grilling. Once you taste it, questions of authenticity quickly dissolve. The proof is the sauce.

Heat the oil in a medium pot over medium heat. When it shimmers, add the GGP and onions. Sauté until the onions start to become translucent, about 5 minutes. Add the remaining ingredients and bring to a simmer over medium heat; simmer gently, uncovered, for 1 hour, stirring frequently to prevent sticking and burning. The sauce should be thick, glossy, and deep red. Remove from the heat and let cool slightly.

Transfer the mixture to a blender and blend on high until completely smooth. Strain through a fine-mesh sieve.

ORIGIN: American South and Caribbean
YIELD: 1 pint

¼ cup grapeseed oil
2 tablespoons GGP (page 5)
2 cups diced yellow onion (about 1 large onion)
½ cup light brown sugar
1¾ cups ketchup
¼ cup + 2 tablespoons Jerk Paste (page 17)

Jerk BBQ sauce will keep in an airtight container in the refrigerator for up to 3 weeks.

REMOULADE

Remoulade may have been invented in France, where it still lives as an accompaniment most often to celery root, as celeri remoulade, but by the time I was growing up in the Bronx and my mother kept a jar of homemade remoulade in the fridge, the cold mustard-mayonnaise condiment had been transformed by the cauldron of Creole cuisine into a spice-laden sauce that I used as a dip for just about everything. Fish sticks? Remoulade. Fried shrimp? Remoulade. Crab cakes? Remoulade. In a New Orleans remoulade, the demure Dijon and mayo are coursed through with house spice, Worcestershire sauce, and, at least in my kitchen, a touch of ginger-garlic purée. My mom used it as a base for the Salmon Cakes (page 130) we had on Sunday mornings and that I looked forward to all week. Today, I use this delicious sauce as a base for lobster salad and smoked whitefish—and, of course, I still dip everything I possibly can into it.

In a large bowl, whisk together the GGP, house spice, parsley, mustard, Worcestershire sauce, and aioli. Season with lemon juice and salt to taste.

ORIGIN: American South
YIELD: 1½ cups

---

1 tablespoon + 1 teaspoon GGP (page 5)

3 tablespoons House Spice (page 6)

½ tightly packed cup fresh parsley leaves, chiffonade

1 tablespoon + 2 teaspoons whole-grain mustard

1 tablespoon + 2 teaspoons Worcestershire sauce

1 cup Garlic Aioli (page 20)

Freshly squeezed lemon juice, to taste

Kosher salt, to taste

Remoulade keeps in an airtight container in the refrigerator for up to 1 week.

GARLIC AIOLI

Combine the egg yolks and the GGP in the bowl of a food processor and pulse to combine. With the motor running, slowly drizzle in the oil until emulsified and thickened, about 1 minute—it should be thicker than heavy cream but not as thick as mayonnaise. Add the lemon juice and salt to taste, pulsing a few times to combine.

ORIGIN: Spain
YIELD: 2 cups

10 **egg yolks**

2 tablespoons **GGP** (page 5)

¾ cup + 2 tablespoons + 2 teaspoons **grapeseed oil**

3 tablespoons freshly squeezed **lemon juice** (about 1 lemon)

Kosher salt, to taste

Garlic aioli will keep in an airtight container in the refrigerator for up to 1 week.

NITTER KIBBEH OIL (NKO)

Just after the demise of my first restaurant, the Shaw Bijou, I found my way back into the kitchen with Gorsha, a fast-casual Ethiopian concept I opened with my friend Hiyaw Gebreyohannes in Washington, D.C.'s Union Market. We served injera—a silken Ethiopian bread made with teff—pockets and rice bowls with proteins like berbere chicken and lamb shoulder. The venture was deeply nourishing. It felt good to get back into the groove of cooking, this time with no expectations beyond making great-tasting food. And it felt good to get better acquainted with Ethiopian cuisine, which, like most East African cuisine, I'd had little contact with growing up but which, in D.C.—a city with one of the largest Ethiopian populations in the United States—is plentiful. One of my favorite new discoveries was nitter kibbeh oil, shortened to NKO, which is at the base of much Ethiopian and Eritrean cooking. Traditionally made with drawn butter, almost like ghee, NKO is flavored with an array of warm spices from cumin and allspice to cinnamon and coriander. NKO finds its way into many of my savory preparations, from lentils to escovitch and curries. Here I've substituted the butter with grapeseed oil to render the preparation vegan. Technically this is called ye'qimem zeyet, but at Gorsha we always called it NKO, and it serves the same purpose.

ORIGIN: Ethiopia
YIELD: 1 quart

---

1 quart **grapeseed oil**

1 tablespoon whole **cumin seeds**

1 tablespoon + 1 teaspoon whole **allspice berries**

Two 2-inch **cinnamon sticks**

2 tablespoons whole **coriander seeds**

6 pods **black cardamom**

¼ cup + 1 tablespoon dried **koseret** or **oregano**

NKO will keep in an airtight container in a cool dark place for up to 1 month.

Combine all the ingredients in a large, heavy-bottomed pot set over medium-low heat. Heat the oil gently, to infuse it without ever bringing it to a simmer, for 90 minutes, then remove from the heat and let cool slightly. Transfer to a high-powered blender. Blend on high until the spices are completely broken up, then strain through a fine-mesh sieve.

OBE ATA DIN DIN (RED STEW)

The secret ingredient for many Nigerian dishes is a small cube of compressed flavor invented in Switzerland in the early twentieth century: Maggi Seasoning. A combination typically of salt, MSG, onion powder, sugar, turmeric, wheat flour, and palm oil pressed into the shape of a die, the Maggi cube made its way to Africa in the 1940s, after the company was acquired by Nestlé. Immediately, the magic Maggi cube added depths of flavor while cutting out hours of time from the stew- and soup-heavy canon of the Naija home kitchen. In this spiced tomato sauce—called obe ate din din, or red stew—Maggi is part of a versatile ensemble cast that supports and adds depth to classic Nigerian dishes, like Chicken in Red Stew (page 167), as well as those calling for a burst of spicy flavor, like Calamari Veracruz (page 150).

Combine all the ingredients except the grapeseed oil in a food processor or blender and blend until you have a smooth purée.

Set a large pot or pan over medium heat and add the oil. When it shimmers, add the purée. Bring to a simmer and cook, stirring frequently, until it has reduced to 2½ cups, 45 minutes to an hour. Taste and adjust seasonings, then set aside.

ORIGIN: Nigeria

YIELD: 2½ cups

---

1 large **red bell pepper**, roughly chopped

3 **Roma tomatoes**, roughly chopped

4 tablespoons **tomato paste**

1 medium **red onion**, roughly chopped

2 tablespoons **GGP** (page 5)

6 **Maggi Seasoning cubes**

1 teaspoon **Peppa Sauce** (page 25)

1 teaspoon **Curry Powder** (page 10)

4 teaspoons **kosher salt**

¼ cup **grapeseed oil**

Obe ata din din will keep in an airtight container in the refrigerator for up to 4 days, or in the freezer for up to 6 months.

LOUISIANA-STYLE HOT SAUCE

When it comes to hot sauce, the question isn't what I put it on but what I *don't*. Of course, it's more complicated than that. Not all hot sauces are right for every dish. I would turn to a fiercely spicy Scotch bonnet pepper to cut curried goat, or a strong culantro-based hot sauce for salt cod fritters, or calypso sauce for beef patties. But when it comes to fried chicken when it's 11 p.m. on a street corner and I'm starving, nothing can beat Louisiana-style hot sauce. More vegetal and less hot than its Caribbean cousins, this one features red long chilies and red bell peppers and won't burn your mouth, while still waking up your taste buds. The vinegar of the spice pickling liquid adds an edge that cuts but doesn't overpower.

Heat the oil in a medium pot over medium heat; when it shimmers, add the onions and sweat for 5 minutes, until they begin to turn translucent. Add GGP and cook for another 3 minutes, stirring constantly. Add the bell peppers, chilies, paprika, and cayenne and cook, stirring often, until soft, about 7 to 10 minutes.

Add the spice pickling liquid and salt and bring to a boil over medium-high heat, scraping the bottom of the pot. Once it comes to a boil, remove from the heat and let cool slightly.

Transfer the mixture to a blender and purée until smooth. Then strain through a fine mesh strainer.

ORIGIN: American South
YIELD: 1 pint

---

2 tablespoons grapeseed oil

⅓ cup diced yellow onion (about ½ small onion)

1½ teaspoons GGP (page 5)

1 cup diced red bell pepper (about ½ large pepper)

½ cup stemmed and thinly sliced red long chilies (or another fruity red hot pepper, like Fresno) (keep the seeds)

1 teaspoon sweet paprika

1 teaspoon cayenne

1⅓ cups Spice Pickling Liquid (page 32)

¼ teaspoon kosher salt

Hot sauce keeps in an airtight container in the refrigerator for up to 2 months.

CALYPSO SAUCE

In its narrow-necked red bottle, easily mistaken for Heinz ketchup, Matouk's Calypso Sauce was omnipresent on the tables of the Jamaican takeout joints I grew up going to in the Bronx. Within the family of hot sauces, Calypso sauce, which is also found in Trinidad and Tobago, stands out for the delicate balance of sweetness and notes from the yellow bell pepper. (In this recipe, that sweetness is highlighted by the addition of carrot juice.) It isn't the hottest of hot sauces, but it is one of my favorites.

In a large pot or skillet, heat the oil over medium heat until shimmering. Add the onions and sauté until they start to become translucent, about 5 minutes, then add the peppers, GGP, and peppa sauce. Sauté, stirring frequently to prevent sticking, until the peppers are soft, about 7 minutes.

Add the mustard and carrot juice and bring to a simmer over medium heat. Simmer, stirring occasionally, until reduced to a syrupy consistency, about 7 minutes. Let cool slightly, then transfer to a blender. Purée until completely smooth.

Pass through a fine-mesh sieve and transfer to an airtight container to cool completely in the refrigerator. When cool, season with vinegar, lime juice, and salt.

ORIGIN: Jamaica

YIELD: 1 cup

---

2 tablespoons grapeseed oil

½ medium yellow onion, thinly sliced

1 medium yellow bell pepper, thinly sliced

1 tablespoon + ¾ teaspoon GGP (page 5)

2½ teaspoons Peppa Sauce (page 25)

½ teaspoon yellow mustard

⅔ cup carrot juice

2 tablespoons cane vinegar

2 tablespoons freshly squeezed lime juice

Kosher salt, to taste

Calypso sauce will keep in an airtight container in the refrigerator for up to 1 week.

PEPPA SAUCE

The Scotch bonnet pepper is the star in this fiery but fruity hot sauce. The Scotch bonnet, a member of the *Capsicum chinense* family, which also includes habaneros, is neither Scottish nor Chinese in origin. It is indigenous to the Caribbean, where it is prized for its combination of intense heat—it's about forty times hotter than a jalapeño—and its touch of tropical fruitiness.

Like most hot sauces, this one relies on the alchemy between vinegar and heat. To bump up the flavor, I use spice pickling liquid, an infused vinegar touched with ginger, thyme, and coriander. This recipe makes a quart, which is a lot, but trust me, this stuff goes fast. The French have their five mother sauces; I have my peppa sauce. I use it all the time, from jerk paste to curried chicken; I use it as a marinade and as a finishing sauce. It is always on my kitchen table and always in my pantry. And the best part is, like so many vinegar-based infused sauces, it gets better with age.

Combine all the ingredients in a food processor. Process until smooth, then transfer to a jar. Place a sheet of wax paper on top and then screw on the lid. (The paper prevents the vinegar from reacting with the lid.) Let sit in a cool, dark place for a day, then move the jar to the refrigerator.

ORIGIN: Trinidad and Tobago
YIELD: 1 quart

---

50 red Scotch bonnet peppers, stemmed and roughly chopped

2 cups **Spice Pickling Liquid** (page 32)

¾ cup **garlic cloves** (2 to 3 heads)

Peppa sauce will keep in an airtight container in the refrigerator for at least 6 months.

PIQUE

A clear bottle of pique, bright peppers visible in the vinegar, is part of almost every Puerto Rican restaurant's tablescape in the Bronx. Piqué, also called Piqué Boriqua or sometimes Pike Boriqua, is a mild hot sauce, though it can get quite spicy. Since pique is an infused vinegar—unlike Calypso or Louisiana-style hot sauce, it isn't blended—the longer it sits, the more the vinegar is infused and the spicier it becomes. So there's the thrill of the unknown when applying it. Every cuchifritos place, not to mention the vast majority of Puerto Rican homes, has its own twist and preferred timing, and really, you can and should experiment with both when making it yourself. Pineapple adds a nice tropical flavor, for instance.

Combine all the ingredients in a large clean jar with a tight-fitting lid. Place a sheet of wax paper on top and then screw on the lid. (The paper prevents the vinegar from reacting with the lid.) Store at room temperature for 2 days, then transfer to the refrigerator.

ORIGIN: Puerto Rico
YIELD: 1 pint

1½ cups apple cider vinegar
½ cup freshly squeezed lime juice (about 3 limes)
1 jalapeño, stemmed, seeded, and thinly sliced into rounds
2 garlic cloves, crushed
5 whole black peppercorns
5 fresh cilantro stems
¾ teaspoon kosher salt
1 small sprig fresh oregano
1 small sprig fresh thyme

Pique will keep in an airtight container in the refrigerator for at least 6 months.

SHADO BENI CHUTNEY

In 1807, the British outlawed the slave trade. A few decades later, however, they began a program of indentured servitude, scattering millions of Indians—mostly from Northeast and Central India—throughout the British empire. Between 1834, when the British government began the program, and 1917, when it was abolished, about 1.5 million Indians were dispersed throughout the empire, including 144,000 to Trinidad and Tobago. As all peoples do, they brought with them flavors from their now-distant home. Among these were a taste for rice, ghee, dal, curries, and chutney. Obviously substitutions were made, including swapping the strong-tasting culantro—called shado beni or shadow beni or chadon beni or, from the Hindi, bhandhania—for fresh cilantro, which doesn't grow in the Caribbean. (Where culantro *isn't* available, feel free to substitute with cilantro.) Many Trini dishes contain at least a hint of shado beni. But to me, this sauce, which accompanies doubles, roti, and poularie, is the signal flavor of Trinidad, a combination of sweetness and heat.

Place all the ingredients but the lime juice in a blender and purée for 5 minutes, or until the sauce begins to change to a bright green color.

Season only the amount you are using with a squeeze of lime right before use.

ORIGIN: Trinidad and Tobago
YIELD: 1 cup

3 cups roughly chopped fresh culantro or cilantro, leaves and tender stems only

1½ tablespoons GGP (page 5)

2 teaspoons Peppa Sauce (page 25)

½ cup Vegetable Stock (page 36) or water

¾ teaspoon kosher salt

Freshly squeezed lime juice, to taste

Shado beni chutney keeps in an airtight container in the refrigerator for up to 1 week.

SOFRITO

When Spanish colonists arrived in the Caribbean in the 1400s, they brought with them the Catalan sofregit, a mixture of onions or leeks slowly cooked in pork fat that they used as a base for much of their cooking. In the intervening years and with the intermix of culture, sofrito has evolved to include tomatoes, peppers (of both the spicy and mild variety), and the all-important culantro that is found in so much Latin cuisine. Like its cousin Recaito (page 30), sofrito is one of the foundations on which nearly the entire palace of Latin Caribbean deliciousness rests. It gives instant depth to rices and marinades. It's what makes Pollo Guisado (page 176) so addictive. Like so much of the food I love, the genius of sofrito is that it's made ahead, usually in batches, by people with little time to cook, which means you have intense flavor instantly when you want it. There are many variations of sofrito, as there tend to be with such a highly utilized ingredient. This is mine.

In a large pot over medium heat, heat the olive oil. When it shimmers, add the onions and cook until they begin to turn translucent, about 5 minutes, stirring occasionally. Add the Sazón, GGP, tomato paste, and aji amarillo paste, and cook, stirring often, until the mixture has darkened somewhat in color and the oil has separated, another 5 minutes. Add the tomatoes and cook for 5 minutes, then add the red bell pepper. Cook for another 5 minutes, then add the jalapeño. Cook for 5 minutes more, then stir in the culantro and cook again for 5 minutes, constantly stirring. Simmer, stirring often, for 1 hour on medium-low heat until thick, glossy, and deep red; the oil should rise to the surface. Taste and adjust salt if desired.

ORIGIN: Puerto Rico
YIELD: 3 cups

½ cup **extra-virgin olive oil**

3 cups diced **yellow onions** (about 2 medium onions)

2 teaspoon **sazón con culantro y achiote**

5 tablespoons **GGP** (page 5)

3½ teaspoons **tomato paste**

1 tablespoon **aji amarillo paste**

3½ cups diced ripe **plum tomatoes** (about 5 tomatoes)

½ medium **red bell pepper**, diced

1 **jalapeño**, stemmed, seeded, and thinly sliced into rings

¼ packed cup roughly chopped fresh **culantro**, or **cilantro**, if necessary, leaves and tender stems only

Kosher salt, to taste

Sofrito will keep in an airtight container in the refrigerator for up to 1 week, or in the freezer for up to 6 months.

GREEN SEASONING

Green seasoning—also called marination or blend up in Jamaica—is a bright, vibrant, and versatile ingredient. I use it in my aioli, as a base for my curries, and to marinate everything from cucumbers to meat. For me, the mix of culantro (or shado beni, as it is also called), celery, and herbs, together with the kick of heat from the peppa sauce, define the pith flavors of Caribbean cooking.

Roughly chop the celery, onion, green onions, culantro, and thyme. Add all the ingredients to a blender, then purée on high speed until smooth.

ORIGIN: Trinidad and Tobago
YIELD: 1½ cups

---

1 stalk celery

⅓ small yellow onion

2 green onions

¾ cup culantro (or cilantro, if necessary)

2 tablespoons roughly chopped fresh thyme leaves

2½ tablespoons GGP (page 5)

2 tablespoons + 1 teaspoon Peppa Sauce (page 25)

½ cup grapeseed oil

Green seasoning will keep in an airtight container in the refrigerator up to 1 week, or in the freezer for up to 2 months.

RECAITO

Recaito is a remarkably useful green seasoning from Puerto Rico. Its name comes from recao, the Spanish word for culantro (or, as it is called in Trinidad and Tobago, shado beni). With the addition of tomatoes and red pepper, recaito is often used as a base for Sofrito (page 28) and, like sofrito, has countless applications in the kitchen. It adds a kick of vegetal flavor to your Pique (page 26) or your Mojo Sauce (page 31), and I also like to use it on its own to season rice, beans, and stews.

Place all of the ingredients in a blender. Blend on low speed, gradually increasing speed to high until smooth, about 1 minute.

ORIGIN: Puerto Rico

YIELD: 2 cups

---

1 medium **green bell pepper**, roughly chopped

1 medium **yellow onion**, roughly chopped

½ head **garlic** (about 6 large cloves)

½ packed cup roughly chopped fresh **culantro**, or **cilantro**, if necessary, leaves and tender stems only

---

Recaito will keep in an airtight container in the refrigerator for up to 1 week, or in the freezer for up to 6 months.

MOJO SAUCE

Mojo, which comes from the Portuguese word for sauce, molho, originated in the Canary Islands but has since spread throughout the Caribbean. Caribbean mojo is heavy on the pimenton and comes in red or green shades. It is primarily used as a dipping sauce. By the time it made its way to Cuba and Puerto Rico (and the Bronx), the peppers were out and citrus juice was in. This Cuban or Boricuan mojo is more a marinade than a sauce. Tingling with garlic, coriander, and cumin, it supercharges proteins from pork to cassava to chicken. It's an automatic flavor enhancer. Up on Burnside Avenue in the Bronx, $5 gets you half a mojo-marinated chicken with a side of rice and beans that stretches into two full meals. Two full *delicious* meals.

In a high-powered blender, combine all the ingredients except the olive oil. Blend on high until combined. With the blender still running, slowly drizzle in the oil until the sauce is somewhat emulsified.

ORIGIN: Caribbean

YIELD: ¾ cup

---

3 tablespoons freshly squeezed tangerine juice (about half of 1 tangerine)

2 tablespoons freshly squeezed lemon juice (about half of 1 lemon)

1½ tablespoons freshly squeezed lime juice (about half of 1 lime)

1 tablespoon freshly squeezed grapefruit juice

1 tablespoon freshly squeezed orange juice

1 garlic clove, crushed

1½ teaspoons coriander seeds

¾ teaspoon cumin seeds

½ packed teaspoon fresh oregano leaves

½ teaspoon kosher salt

2 tablespoons extra-virgin olive oil

Mojo sauce will keep in an airtight container in the refrigerator for up to 1 week.

SPICE PICKLING LIQUID

Pickling is an act of food preservation and also, thankfully for us, adds an entire dimension of bright angular flavors. This pickling liquid includes a touch of spice but is largely neutral, allowing the flavors of the pickled vegetables to emerge. I like the balance between the thyme and coriander on the softer herbal side with the habanero and ginger more biting, but play around as you like. Garlic goes well, ditto allspice, cloves, and bay leaf. Here's your chance to go freeform and experiment with what aromatics you use in the pickling liquid and what you pickle. Among my favorite vegetables to pickle are onions, mushrooms, and pig's feet—which aren't a vegetable at all, of course, but are delicious.

Place all the ingredients into a medium pot and bring to a boil over high heat. As soon as it comes to a boil, remove it from the heat. Let cool completely, then strain through a fine-mesh sieve and transfer to a clean jar with a tight-fitting lid.

ORIGIN: American South
YIELD: 3 cups

1¾ cups white wine vinegar

¼ cup granulated white sugar

3 tablespoons + 1 teaspoon kosher salt

12 fresh thyme sprigs

4 teaspoons whole coriander seeds

½ habanero pepper, stemmed, seeded, and roughly chopped

2 thin slices ginger, about 2–3 inches long

2 cups water

Spice pickling liquid will keep in an airtight container in the refrigerator for up to 6 months.

CHICKEN STOCK

Stock is a building block of flavor, the foundation on which it rests. It takes time to make, but that time is well spent, in my opinion. Cooking with stock instead of water creates a unique depth of flavor. Most traditional diasporic stews and curries do not use stock, exactly. Instead, chefs utilize the entire chicken at once. So the stock is there—and the resulting depth of flavor—but not as a separate element. The use of stock itself comes from the French culinary traditions of the famous chefs Auguste Escoffier and Marie-Antoine Carême. It is something that I feel happy to add to the diasporic kitchen—a kitchen that has always evolved and always will.

I perfected my stock-making technique in the kitchen at Per Se in New York City, where Thomas Keller's mastery of and devotion to French cuisine is legendary. The stock there is a pure chicken stock, skimmed and clarified until it's crystalline. But I first learned how to make stock in my mother's kitchen as a child. Her roast chicken stock, the recipe below, relies on the gelatin present in the chicken feet to add a beautiful sheen. The roasted chickens provide a depth of flavor. I use this stock for everything from blanching vegetables to making curries.

ORIGIN: Various places
YIELD: 10 cups

---

3 pounds chicken bones

2 chicken legs (about 1½ pounds)

1 pound chicken feet

1 pound yellow onions (about 2 large), quartered

½ pound carrots (about 2 large), peeled and cut into 1-inch chunks

½ pound celery (about 6 stalks), trimmed and cut into 1-inch chunks

2 heads garlic, halved crosswise

10 fresh thyme sprigs

5 fresh parsley stems

10 whole black peppercorns

Chicken stock keeps in an airtight container in the refrigerator for up to 1 week, or in the freezer for up to 6 months.

Heat the oven to 450°F. Place the chicken bones and legs on a sheet tray and roast for 40 minutes, rotating the pan halfway through cooking or until browned.

In a large pot (at least 7 quarts), add the roasted chicken bones, legs, and feet, plus any roasting fat and juices, then all the remaining ingredients. Add water to cover, approximately 4 quarts, and bring to a simmer over medium-high heat. Lower the heat as necessary to keep the pot simmering gently, uncovered, for 6 hours.

Strain the finished stock through a fine-mesh sieve.

VEGETABLE STOCK

Due to the large Indian population in Trinidad, there are a fair number of vegetarians, none of whom, I imagine, feel like they're missing out on any flavor in the least. And they aren't. This stock—which I make using a meat grinder to grind the vegetables (a food processor will work just fine)—adds a ton of flavor and serves as the base for dishes like chickpeas and red bean sofrito. But you can also substitute it, where you'd like, for chicken or shrimp stock.

Roughly chop the onion, leek, carrot, and celery into 1-inch pieces. Add to a food processor, working in batches as necessary, and pulse into uniformly small, coarse pieces.

Transfer the vegetables, garlic, thyme, parsley, peppercorns, and minced ginger to a large pot and add water, 2 quarts, plus more if needed to cover. Set over medium heat and bring to a simmer; simmer uncovered for 1½ hours. Strain through a fine-mesh sieve.

ORIGIN: Various places
YIELD: 2 pints

---

1 large **yellow onion** (½ pound)
½ medium **leek** (¼ pound), well cleaned
1 medium **carrot** (¼ pound), peeled
3 stalks **celery** (¼ pound)
½ head **garlic**, halved crosswise
3 fresh **thyme sprigs**
2 fresh **parsley stems**
5 whole **black peppercorns**
1 teaspoon minced **ginger**

Vegetable stock will keep in an airtight container in the refrigerator for up to 2 weeks, or in the freezer for up to 6 months.

SHRIMP STOCK

When I'm dead and gone and they cut open my body, they'll find shrimp stock running through my veins. Though less widely used than chicken or veal stock in traditional French cuisine—where shrimp didn't hold pride of place as they do on the shorelines of Louisiana— shrimp stock is at the base of so much of the food I love, from Shrimp Étouffée (page 133) to Seafood Gumbo (page 138) and Jambalaya (page 59). I grew up saving the shells of the shrimp we ate in order to make this stock, ziplock bags of which lined our freezer shelves, ready and willing to add its deep crustacean flavor when called upon to do so.

In a large pot over high heat, heat 2 tablespoons of oil. When it shimmers, add the shrimp shells and sauté until deeply browned and fragrant, 7 to 10 minutes.

Add the remaining 2 tablespoons of oil and the tomato paste and cook, stirring often, until caramelized, 1 to 2 minutes. Add the onions, carrots, and celery and sauté until the onions are translucent and softened, about 5 minutes. Add the remaining ingredients along with 4 quarts of water, and bring to a boil, scraping the bottom of the pot to loosen any browned bits, then reduce to a simmer. Simmer, uncovered, for 2 hours.

Strain through a fine-mesh sieve before using.

ORIGIN: American South

YIELD: 3 quarts

¼ cup **grapeseed oil**, divided

1 pound **shrimp shells** (and heads, if available)

1½ tablespoons **tomato paste**

1 medium **yellow onion**, roughly chopped

1 medium **carrot**, peeled and roughly chopped

2 stalks **celery**, roughly chopped

6 **garlic cloves**, halved

3 fresh **thyme sprigs**

2 fresh **parsley stems**

4 whole **black peppercorns**

Shrimp stock will keep in an airtight container in the refrigerator for up to 3 days, or in the freezer for up to 6 months.

LOUISIANA

I don't remember my first words, but I do remember the first entries into my dictionary of flavor. I was still a toddler, and it was in the kitchen of my apartment in the Bronx, that small sacred space where my mother always seemed to be. It was just past Christmas, and the tree was still up. My Grandma Cassie had just left, back to her home on Long Island. Shrimp stock simmered in a well-worn soup pot on the stove, full of shrimp shells and the Holy Trinity: a mirepoix of onions, bell peppers, and celery. When that stock made it into the shrimp étouffée, alongside crawfish tails packed in crawfish fat and even more shrimp, and my mom served it to me and my sister later for dinner—that's the moment I remember best. I hadn't yet been to the sea, but I could taste the sea in it. I didn't know what the trinity was, the mixture that forms the base of so much Creole food—but I could taste the trinity in it. I didn't know how, and hardly do now, to find the words to describe the dish—buttery, silky, rich, deep, multileveled—but those words, those flavors, were set into me like scrawls on wet cement. Whatever words I later found to describe them, these flavors meant one thing to me: home.

Children think their first memories are the start of their story. In a way, for children, that's true. As adults we learn that it isn't so. Though the knowledge of our past isn't always easy to take on, for Black Americans it's especially uneasy. For many of us, our ancestors have often been overlooked, either actively erased or simply deemed not important enough to be taught to us in schools. Meanwhile, at home, the past can seem a story too painful to tell or to hear. But in the kitchen, the past speaks volumes. Even when I was a toddler, my mom didn't claim sole credit for her étouffée recipe. I always knew it came from Grandma Cassie, a woman bursting with warmth, and with a syrupy southern accent, who visited us around Christmas, driving to New York City from Texas with a suitcase full of boudin and frozen crawfish tails. But it wasn't until I was in my thirties on a trip down to Louisiana with my grandmother that I fully understood that I was born into the story in media res.

I met Grandma Cassie at the Lafayette Regional Airport for a journey through the kitchens and foodways of the South, *her* South. She, like I, makes sense of the world through food, and she, like I, was eager to start eating. I was wearing my Malcolm X hat, given to me by her husband, Winston, with whom I had recently traveled to his home in Trinidad and Tobago, and I noticed she wore hers, too. The *X* was in a lovely floral pattern. Our route would start in a small town called Mamou in Louisiana where my grandmother was born,

and end in Beaumont, Texas, where she grew up. She was excited to be going back home with me, her only grandson, and we had planned to meet up with family along the way.

So much is made, rightly, of the city of New Orleans that it is easy to forget that far from the Lower Ninth and the Treme, the state is made up of small towns and vast stretches of bayou and forest. Driving north from Lafayette to Mamou, the wetlands stretch on either side of us. Swallows and kites zip through the air. Hardwood forests fuzz the horizon line. There are few old buildings in these parts and little of the showy architecture of the French Quarter. Houses are ranches, modest and set back from the road. Most businesses are gas stations and farm repair shops. It isn't an unfriendly place, necessarily, but it's not one overly concerned with what you think of it. This is a Louisiana you have to work to know. A place where the best food isn't in restaurants but in homes you need an invitation to. Thankfully, I had Grandma Cassie.

Mamou is a small town of eight thousand residents in the Evangeline Parish. Though my great-grandmother Momo, a French-speaking restaurateur, lived in Ville Platte, when my grandma was born Momo had to travel to Mamou, the only town for miles with a maternity ward for Black women. Our family roots run deep here, or as deep as they can in an area that is half water. I had visited a few times, first as a toddler, which I hardly remember, and then later as a surly teenager, which I hardly want to remember. We—the

Lartigue clan, my grandmother's people—would gather at the small house in Beaumont for family reunions.

Grandma Cassie and I got to Mamou, which bills itself as the birthplace of Mardi Gras, just in time for the Courir du Mardi Gras, a procession to kick off the Mardi Gras season. It was early on a Sunday and the shops on the tiny Main Street were mostly closed. Grandma and I headed toward a group of revelers, asking a passerby where the start of the parade was. "Oh," said the man, older, white, and friendly, "you're looking for the other Mardi Gras." He directed us to a parallel parade, starting a few blocks away, and nearly all Black. We joined at the start of the procession, bartering a spot on the No Limit Southern Riders float. This was a far cry from the glitz and glamour of New Orleans. The floats were simple flatbed trucks with a few streamers and plywood barriers on the side and a porta potty on the back. But you don't need much for a celebration. I helped Grandma onto the float and then joined her. With a jump, we began. The route moved leisurely through the small town, slow and gentle enough that onlookers sauntered from their porches to the roadside. Many were holding plates of boudain, sausage made of rice, pork, and spices, steaming in the cold morning. As we made our way past them, they approached with a link or two. We gave them beads; they gave us boudain—and I think we got the

better part of that deal. Each bite burst with flavor, an alchemy of the rice soaking up the pork juices, made even more flavorful with the addition of liver, house spice, and, of course, the most sacred of all Creole seasoning: the Holy Trinity. House spice—that blend of paprika, garlic, onion, pepper, and more—is as varied as it is omnipresent. So as we passed each house, tasting the proffered boudain, we could taste the subtle variations that came from each kitchen. We got off that float an hour or so later stuffed and sated and headed to a chicken run, which is exactly as it sounds: chicken and children squawking in equal volume as they try to catch each other. We adults watched, eating—because who could resist—plates of cracklings, red beans and rice, and fried shrimp.

But soon Grandma Cassie and I had to move on. We had a date in Beaumont, two hours to the west off I-10, which runs straight along the southern coast. As we drove on the highway, crawfish ponds and rice paddies blurred by. My grandmother told me about her mother, Momo, real name Emily Philips, a woman who with her preacher husband ran a small restaurant out of their home in Beaumont. That's where hospitality entered our bloodstream. Grandma told me about her own life, too, most of which I knew, some of which I didn't, about the journey out of the South to Chicago, when she worried about where she—a single Black mother with three young children—might be able to stop to spend the night and how often that was just pulled over at the side of the road. We stopped on the way for sustenance at the Sausage Link, a high temple of boudin, in Sulfur, Louisiana, near Lake Charles. Through the small ordering window, I could see a man stuffing boudin into casing in the back. Ours burst with flavor, an indelible connection to the past. An hour or so later we visited Momo's grave in a Black cemetery on a hill in Beaumont. As we walked the lanes between gravestones, Grandma Cassie told me how proud she was that I was interested in listening to these stories of our family. "Of course I am, Grandma," I said, "they're the ones who made me who I am."

By the time we pulled up to the small house in Beaumont where my grandmother grew up and my cousin still lives, it was dusk. Uncle Herm and Cousin LG were standing in the driveway. LG, a high-energy guy, approached and enveloped me in a hug so big my feet lifted from the pavement. "My brother! My brother!" he shouted. Inside the kitchen, Aunt Yolanda was putting the finishing touches on her banana pudding, in its large aluminum tin. Uncle Herm, Grandma Cassie's brother, was tending to a shrimp and okra stew. White rice was steaming from the cooker, and red beans studded with ham hock were on the stove. And next to those beans was a soup pot full of shrimp stock, the makings of an étouffée, which I immediately recognized from the earliest pages of my life.

These flavors of home had been stewing in Beaumont well before I tasted them as a toddler in the Bronx and, before Beaumont, in homes I don't know stretching back through time.

RICE

White and steamed; yellow and run through with peppers and achiote; tomato-kissed and seafood-studded—rice holds a place of honor in the pantheon of diasporic cuisine. Rice has walked with me through the streets of the Bronx via the Caribbean, where it's gotten with hot sauce and red beans; in the coastal bayous of Louisiana, where it is eaten as jambalaya or under meaty red beans; on visits to South Carolina, the heart of the rice coast, in pilau and Hoppin' John; all the way to courtyard kitchens of Nigeria, home of jambalaya's ancestor, jollof. Rice is everywhere.

But I can't help but think of rice as both a blessing and a curse. A blessing because it sustained my ancestors both in the Americas and in Africa and continues to do so. A blessing because all of my favorite foods have rice in their name. A blessing because it was the smell of garlic goldening that I woke up too, overjoyed because it meant rice and eggs. A blessing because rice is a perfect wingman for flavor when needed, serves as a structural support for soups and stews when wanted, yet is capable of great performance when called upon as a lead actor. Rice is everywhere, a blessing.

Rice is also a curse. A curse because it was rice—and the knowledge of how to grow it—that brought my West African ancestors in bondage from Africa to the American South in the seventeenth century. For those who hailed from the western coast from Gambia down to Liberia, it is rice that kept most of them alive during the unendurable middle passage. Once in America, it was rice farming, among the most cruel of all slaving crops, that killed so many of them in and around Charleston, South Carolina, and all along the Lowcountry coast. Rice is the bridge built across the Atlantic. Rice was the engine for so much of the southern economy, which before the Civil War relied largely on rice sold to points north, to the Caribbean, and back to Europe. The ingenuity, skill, and life experience of Africans were perversely used to ensure their continued exploitation. Today, when I visit my family in coastal Louisiana, the blur of rice paddies off the interstate reminds me how important rice continues to be. The fact that at nearly every meal rice is on the table in some form just shows that no matter how I think about its legacy, it continues to be sustenance, continues to deserve its place of honor.

PERFECTLY STEAMED RICE

Rice is the ideal sideman. Goes with anything. Goes with everything. Isn't obtrusive but retains its character. The secret to perfectly steamed rice lies in toasting the grains before they go into the water. This gives them a wonderful nutty flavor that carries through and is augmented by stock and aromatics. It isn't strictly necessary, of course, but once you start toasting, you'll never go back to straight steaming again.

Heat the oven to 350°F. Rinse the rice until water runs clear, then set aside.

In a small saucepan with a tight-fitting lid, heat the oil over medium-high heat. When it shimmers, add the rice and toast, stirring frequently, for 8 minutes.

Add the stock, thyme, bay leaf, and salt. Bring to a boil, stirring frequently, then remove from the heat and cover with the lid. Place the pot in the oven for 18 minutes.

Remove the pot from the oven and let it sit, covered, for 5 minutes. Uncover, fluff the rice gently with a fork, and let it steam out for another 5 minutes. Taste, add more salt if desired, remove the thyme and bay leaf, and serve.

ORIGIN: Africa/South America/ Latin America/North America/ The Caribbean

YIELD: 2 to 3 servings

---

1 cup jasmine rice

2 tablespoons grapeseed oil

1½ cups Chicken Stock (page 33)

3 fresh thyme sprigs

1 fresh bay leaf

1½ teaspoons kosher salt, plus more to taste

Steamed rice will keep in an airtight container in the refrigerator for up to 4 days.

CAROLINA GOLD RICE WITH ROASTED GARLIC AND BAY LEAF

Carolina Gold is an heirloom-variety rice (not to be confused with the Carolina brand). The original long-grain rice in America and, for a time in the eighteenth century, the most popular, Carolina Gold grew in the Lowcountry of North Carolina, South Carolina, and Georgia. The grains were carried by West Africans, who were brought to the United States precisely because they knew how best to grow it. In fact, not just in America but in the Dutch Indies too, African women braided kernels of the rice into their hair, swallowed them, or otherwise spirited them to this continent as a means, no matter how meager, to try to provide for themselves in a foreign land. Carolina Gold can be a difficult rice to cook. Like the arborio rice found in risotto, it can turn to a sticky mush if handled roughly or cooked aggressively. Once you master the process—the key is to add the stock gradually—you'll be rewarded with a rice with character, fluffy, with a slight hazelnut element, and extremely tasty.

ORIGIN: American South
YIELD: 4 servings

4 tablespoons unsalted butter, divided
1 tablespoon RGP (page 11)
1 cup Carolina Gold rice
1 fresh bay leaf
4 cups hot Vegetable Stock (page 36)
Kosher salt, to taste

Carolina Gold rice will keep in an airtight container in the refrigerator for up to 4 days.

In a medium-sized pot over medium heat, melt 1 tablespoon of butter. Add RGP and rice and sauté for 5 minutes, stirring often. Add the bay leaf and just enough of the hot stock to cover the rice. Bring to a simmer, stirring frequently. Once the rice has absorbed the stock, add another ½ cup. Continue to simmer and stir frequently, adding more stock ½ cup at a time once the rice has absorbed the liquid, until the rice is completely tender, 30 to 35 minutes total.

Remove from the heat and discard the bay leaf. Stir in the remaining 3 tablespoons of butter, and season to taste with salt. Serve immediately.

RICE AND PEAS

Every island in the Caribbean has a variation on rice and peas. Most commonly used is the pigeon pea, a protein-rich pulse that was brought to the New World by Africans. (It is also common in South Asia.) This version comes from Jamaica, where pigeon peas go by the name gungo peas. It's a version I grew up eating at my Auntie Pauline's house in Mt. Vernon, just north of the Bronx. I'd eat bowls and bowls of it. Why? Simple. The Browning forms a sort of caramelized canvas to which the Scotch bonnet pepper adds some fruit (but little heat), while the coconut milk gives a touch of sweetness and the aromatics add touches of flavor. To this traditional mix, I've added some GGP to bump up the treble notes and bouillon to boost the bass. It's a beautiful pot of rice that goes particularly well with stews like Braised Oxtails (page 221) and Jerk Chicken (page 174).

Cover the peas with a few inches of water and soak overnight in the refrigerator. Drain and rinse well.

Place the soaked peas in a medium pot with 4 cups of water. Bring to a boil over high heat, then reduce heat to a brisk simmer and cook until completely tender, about 20 minutes. Drain the peas, being sure to reserve the liquid, and spread in an even layer on a sheet tray to cool while you make the rice. (Add water to the pigeon pea liquid if necessary to get 2 cups.)

In a medium pot over medium heat, melt 2 tablespoons of butter. Add the onion and sauté until tender, about 10 minutes, then add the GGP and cook for 5 minutes more, stirring often.

While the GGP cooks, rinse the rice in a fine-mesh strainer until the water is clear. Add the rice to the pot and cook, stirring often, until toasted, about 5 minutes.

Add the remaining ingredients and 1 tablespoon butter. Bring the mixture to a boil over high heat, stirring occasionally to prevent sticking, then reduce heat to low and cover. Cook until the liquid has been absorbed, 18 minutes. →

ORIGIN: Jamaica
YIELD: 4 to 6 servings

¼ cup dried pigeon peas

3 tablespoons unsalted butter, divided

1 medium yellow onion, diced

2 tablespoons GGP (page 5)

1½ cups jasmine rice

½ cup coconut milk

2 tablespoons Browning (page 13)

2 fresh thyme sprigs

One 1-inch stem ginger, peeled

1 fresh bay leaf

1 red Scotch bonnet pepper

1½ tablespoons palm sugar

2½ teaspoons kosher salt

1 packet powdered chicken boulllon, such as Knorr (.35 oz), or 2 bouillon cubes

Rice and peas will keep in an airtight container in the refrigerator for up to 4 days.

Remove the pot from heat and let rest, covered, for 5 minutes, then uncover. Remove and discard the thyme, ginger, bay leaf, and Scotch bonnet (being careful not to puncture it). Fluff with a fork and let sit uncovered, 5 minutes more.

Fold in the remaining tablespoon of butter and season to taste with salt.

YELLOW RICE

When I was growing up in a heavily Puerto Rican section of the Bronx, yellow rice was a given. The base of many boriqua meals, yellow rice gets its color and name from annatto, a derivative from the achiote tree, and its supercharged flavor from the combination of sofrito, bouillon, aromatics, and little silver packets of achiote and coriander seasoning. They're like steroids for flavor.

Heat the oven to 350°F. Rinse the rice until water runs clear, then set aside.

Heat the oil in a medium pot over medium heat. When it shimmers, add garlic and sauté until fragrant, 2 to 3 minutes, then add the onions and sauté until translucent, 7 to 10 minutes more. Increase the heat to medium-high, then add the sofrito and cook for 8 minutes, stirring and scraping often, until very fragrant and somewhat caramelized. Add the rice and cook, stirring constantly, until lightly toasted, about 5 minutes.

Add the remaining ingredients and bring to a boil, stirring frequently. Remove from the heat, cover the pot with a tight-fitting lid, and place in the oven for 18 minutes.

Remove from the oven and let sit, covered, for 5 minutes. Remove the lid, fluff the rice with a fork, and let it steam out for 5 minutes more. Remove and discard thyme and bay leaf. Taste, adjust seasoning, and serve.

ORIGIN: Puerto Rico
YIELD: 4 servings

2 cups **jasmine rice**
(such as Mahatma Extra Long Grain Enriched Rice)

2 tablespoons **grapeseed oil**

5 **garlic cloves**, minced

1 medium **yellow onion**, diced

1 cup **Sofrito** (page 28)

Two 5-gram packets
(or 2½ teaspoons) **sazón con culantro y achiote**

One 6-gram cube **powdered chicken bouillon**, such as Knorr, crushed (or 1½ teaspoons powdered)

3 cups **Chicken Stock** (page 33)
(or salt-free store-bought)

3 fresh **thyme sprigs**

1 fresh **bay leaf**

Kosher salt, to taste

Yellow rice will keep in the refrigerator for up to 3 days.

RED BEANS AND RICE

Everyone with roots in southern Louisiana, where red beans and rice is a staple, thinks that their mom makes the best version. But I'm the only one who's right. Growing up, my mom used this recipe as a base, sometimes adding in smoked turkey necks or smoked, spiced, and cured tasso ham, in addition to the ham hocks and andouille sausage that impart their smoke, fat, and spice to the Holy Trinity (celery, bell peppers, and onions) and, of course, the sturdy red kidney beans. The beans were brought to New Orleans by Haitians fleeing the Haitian Revolution in the early nineteenth century and quickly became part of the Creole canon. Red beans and rice takes time. The dish was traditionally made in Creole kitchens on Mondays, which were laundry days and therefore gave ample time for home cooks to allow their beans to simmer as they did the wash — while also providing an outlet for leftovers from Sunday suppers. Even today in New Orleans, this dish is often only available at restaurants on Mondays, but why make RB&R a once-a-week dinner? I'd make it every day if I could — I mean, not everyone's mom has the world's best recipe.

Place the beans in a medium pot or bowl and add water to cover by 2 inches. Cover and refrigerate overnight.

When ready to cook, heat a Dutch oven over medium-high heat. Add the oil. When it shimmers, add the andouille and brown on both sides. Remove the sausage to a plate and set aside. Add the garlic to the pot and cook, stirring often, for 3 minutes, then add the onions, celery, and bell peppers. Sauté until tender, about 10 minutes, then stir in the house spice and cook for another 3 minutes. Add the beans, stock, thyme, bay leaves, and ham hocks.

Bring to a simmer over medium-high heat, then reduce the heat to low, cover, and cook very gently until beans are completely tender. Start checking for doneness after about 1 hour (the beans could take up to 3 hours, depending on how old they are).

ORIGIN: American South

YIELD: 6 to 8 servings

---

2 cups dried **red kidney beans**

2 tablespoons **grapeseed oil**

2 **andouille sausages,** sliced crosswise into 1½-inch-thick pieces

8 **garlic cloves,** minced

2 medium **yellow onions,** diced

2 stalks **celery,** diced

2 **green bell peppers,** diced

2 tablespoons **House Spice** (page 6)

2 quarts **Vegetable Stock** (page 36)

6 fresh **thyme sprigs**

3 fresh **bay leaves**

3 **ham hocks**

Kosher salt, to taste

Perfectly Steamed Rice (page 46), to serve

Red beans and rice will keep in an airtight container in the refrigerator for up to 4 days, or in the freezer for up to 3 months.

When the beans are completely tender, remove from the heat. Remove thyme sprigs and bay leaves and discard. Remove the hocks and, in a small bowl, shred any meat and reserve (discard the bones). Measure out 2 cups of beans and transfer to a blender; blend on high until velvety smooth, adding bean broth as needed to achieve a purée, then stir them back into the pot, along with the shredded ham and the andouille. Taste and season with salt, then serve with Perfectly Steamed Rice.

DIRTY RICE

Dirty rice, a southern Louisiana staple, traditionally made with chicken gizzards, livers, and hearts—the least desirable, and therefore cheapest, parts of a bird—is a testament to the transformative power of house spice and the Holy Trinity of onions, bell peppers, and celery. Growing up, it was the only way my mom could get me to eat chicken liver, which gives the dish both its protein and its flavor. (Feel free to use pork liver, too, a common practice.) For this version, I've added veal to the liver mix for a more tender texture and a beefier taste. Note: Do not skip soaking the liver in milk, which helps to remove any metallic flavors and impurities.

Place the livers in a small bowl and cover with the whole milk. Cover with plastic wrap and refrigerate overnight. The next day, drain and rinse the livers, pat them dry, then freeze them for 15 minutes. (This will firm them up so pulsing them in the food processor grinds rather than purées them.) Transfer to a food processor and pulse until coarsely ground.

Heat the oil in a large cast-iron skillet over medium heat. When it shimmers, add the garlic and sauté until fragrant, 2 to 3 minutes. Add the ground chicken livers and the veal and increase heat to medium-high. Cook, stirring occasionally, until the meat is a crispy deep golden brown, 10 to 15 minutes. When browned, stop stirring and allow a crust to form—just be careful not to let it burn.

Add the onions, bell pepper, celery, and house spice and scrape the pan to break up the crust. Stir in the stock and 1 teaspoon salt, then cover tightly. Simmer over low heat for 20 minutes.

Remove the lid and stir in the parsley, green onions, hot sauce, Worcestershire sauce, and butter, then fold in the rice. Add more salt to taste, then serve.

ORIGIN: American South
YIELD: 4 servings

½ pound **chicken** or **pork livers**

1 cup **whole milk**

2 tablespoons **grapeseed oil**

4 **garlic cloves**, minced

¾ pound ground **veal**

2 medium **yellow onions**, finely diced

1 **green bell pepper**, finely diced

1 stalk **celery**, minced

1½ tablespoons **House Spice** (page 6)

½ cup **Chicken Stock** (page 33)

1 teaspoon **kosher salt**, plus more to taste

2 tablespoons chopped fresh **parsley**

1 **green onion**, thinly sliced

1 tablespoon **Louisiana-Style Hot Sauce** (page 23)

2 teaspoons **Worcestershire sauce**

4 tablespoons **unsalted butter**

2 cups **Perfectly Steamed Rice** (page 46)

Dirty rice will keep in an airtight container in the refrigerator for up to 3 days.

RICE AND EGGS

I have no idea where this fits into the diaspora except in my own kitchen, and I'm thankful for that. It's a perfect way to turn the leftovers of last night's dinner into a tempting breakfast. On mornings after my mom made rice pilau or dirty rice or yellow rice or rice and beans—that is to say, on many mornings—I would wake up to the wonderful smell of garlic and onions softening in a pan. It was the world's best alarm clock. I knew we'd be having rice and eggs. Rice is easy to make a lot of, more than you can consume in one meal, so a way to use up the leftovers is key. (This is the same logic behind Cantonese stir-fry.) It was especially in a house like mine, where we had to stretch every dollar. This dish, which we just called rice and eggs, was so good that sometimes I purposefully went easy at dinner the night before.

In a large pan over medium heat, melt the butter. Add the garlic and sauté until fragrant, 2 to 3 minutes, then add the onions and cook until translucent, 5 to 7 minutes. Stir in the house spice and salt.

Raise the heat to medium-high and add the rice, breaking up any clumps. Stirring occasionally, let the rice become browned and crispy. Meanwhile, in a medium bowl, beat the eggs and season with salt to taste.

Once the rice is toasted, push it to the corner of the pan and reduce the heat to medium. If the pan seems dry, add another tablespoon of butter. Pour in the beaten eggs and scramble. After between 30 seconds and 1 minute, when the eggs are 80 percent cooked or have reached your preferred consistency, fold in the rice to finish cooking.

Taste and adjust seasoning with salt and house spice, then garnish with sliced green onions and serve with Louisiana-Style Hot Sauce (page 23).

ORIGIN: American South
YIELD: 2 servings

---

2 tablespoons **unsalted butter**, plus more as needed

2 **garlic cloves**, minced

½ medium **yellow onion**, diced

2 teaspoons **House Spice** (page 6), plus more to taste

¼ teaspoon **kosher salt**, plus more to taste

1 cup cold **leftover rice** from Perfectly Steamed Rice (page 46), Jollof Rice (page 57), Dirty Rice (page 54), or any other rice dish

4 **eggs**

1 tablespoon sliced **green onion**

Rice and eggs is best served immediately.

JOLLOF RICE

On Sundays in my grandfather's compound in Ibusa in northern Nigeria, his second wife—a young pretty woman we called Auntie Mi—would call us into the kitchen for the midday meal. Invariably, what she was stirring was a pot of fragrant jollof rice. The lush smell of tomato and the steam from the rice filled that small kitchen so appetizingly that, even in the heat, we rushed in. Jollof rice unites nearly all of West Africa, with perhaps Nigeria and Ghana being the two countries best known for it. It is to West Africa what jambalaya is to Louisiana: a dish that is not just food but a cultural emblem. The comparison isn't random, either. Jollof rice is the precursor to jambalaya, the source code, brought to the New World by kidnapped West Africans.

There are a few theories of how and why it became so widespread all along western Africa in the first place. Many scholars say that jollof rice originated with the Wolof or Jolof empire in the Senegambia region, which encompasses modern-day Senegal and the Gambia, in the fourteenth to sixteenth century. It was the marriage of tomatoes, brought by Portuguese traders, and rice, already abundant, that became the basis of jollof. Others believe that the path of jollof rice instead followed the trade-loving Djula people, who carried both their foodways and Islam through the African coast during the Kong dynasty (1710–1898). Regardless of how it got there, today Senegal, Gambia, Nigeria, and even Cameroon and Liberia, all have versions of the dish about which each feels passionately. How passionately? Just search the hashtag #jollofwars on Twitter. Senegalese jollof, called thieboudienne, is touched by tamarind and usually features seafood. Ghanaian jollof uses short-grain rice and is warmed by clove and cinnamon. Cameroonian jollof is studded with green beans and carrots. Perhaps because it calls to mind those Sundays in Nigeria—or perhaps because if I didn't say so I'd never be allowed back in the country—I've always preferred the bold tomato-heavy Nigerian version, which uses obe ata din din and jasmine rice. →

ORIGIN: Nigeria
YIELD: 4 servings

---

2 tablespoons grapeseed oil

1½ cups jasmine rice

1¼ cups Obe Ata Din Din (page 22)

4 teaspoons kosher salt

2 teaspoons Peppa Sauce (page 25)

2¼ cups water

Jollof rice will keep in an airtight container in the refrigerator for 4 days.

Heat the oil in a medium pot over medium-high heat. When the oil shimmers, add the rice and stir frequently until it is toasted, 3 to 4 minutes. Stir in the obe ata din din, salt, peppa sauce, and water, bring to a simmer, then reduce heat to low. Cover tightly and cook until the rice has absorbed the liquid, about 18 minutes.

For the last 5 minutes of cooking, place on high heat. This will burn the pan, giving the rice a smoky taste.

Remove the rice from the heat and let rest, covered, for 5 minutes. Uncover, fluff with a fork, and let it sit another 5 minutes before serving with Sweet Plantains (page 79).

When fluffing, make sure not to scrape the bottom of the pan, so you don't mix in the burned grains.

JAMBALAYA

I grew up eating Nigerian Jollof Rice (page 57), a recipe from my father's side of the family, and Creole jambalaya, one from my mother's. So for me the two were always interconnected. Both are one-pot rice-based dishes, colored and flavored by the addition of tomatoes and brought to life with a similar spice profile. Jambalaya, however, hails from Louisiana, where many Africans worked the rice fields the two continents shared. They brought with them not just the knowledge of how to grow but also how to prepare rice. Once in Louisiana, proto-jollof incorporated whatever proteins were available: andouille sausage, abundant shrimp from coastal waters, and chicken, another economical choice. Also added were influences from the Spanish settlers who yearned for the paella of their home; and the French, the masters of roux. Now jambalaya sits at the heart of Creole cuisine. Like gumbo, every family has its own variation. Some use roux, some don't. Some add andouille; others stick to seafood and chicken. Some families use short-grain rice, in a nod to paella; others use long. I prefer long-grain rice, which both gives texture to the jambalaya and is a callback to the rice used in Nigerian jollof. And as far as protein goes, I'm more "yes and" than "either or." Meaty, filling, comforting, jambalaya reminds me of both my childhood and my ancestral home.

Rinse the rice in cool water until the water runs clear, then set aside.

In a large Dutch oven, heat 2 tablespoons oil over medium-high heat until shimmering. Add the sausage and brown on all sides, 2 minutes per side, then remove to a plate and reserve for later.

While the sausage browns, season the chicken on all sides with salt and house spice. Once you've removed the sausage, add the chicken to the pot and sear until deep golden brown on both sides, 4 minutes per side. Remove to a plate and reserve for later. →

ORIGIN: American South

YIELD: 6 to 8 servings

1½ cups **jasmine rice**

2 tablespoons **grapeseed oil**, plus more as needed

¾ pound **andouille sausage**, sliced into ¼-inch-thick coins

1 pound boneless, skinless **chicken thighs**, cut into 1-inch cubes

1½ teaspoons **kosher salt**, plus more to taste

2 tablespoons **House Spice** (page 6), plus more to taste

1 pound large (16–20 size) **shrimp**, tail on, peeled, and deveined

5 **garlic cloves**, minced

1 medium **yellow onion**, diced

1 **red bell pepper**, diced

2 stalks **celery**, diced

One 14-ounce can **crushed tomatoes**

4 fresh **thyme sprigs**

2 teaspoons dried **oregano**

3 fresh **bay leaves**

2 tablespoons **Louisiana-Style Hot Sauce** (page 23)

2 teaspoons **Worcestershire sauce**

1¼ cups **Chicken Stock** (page 33)

1¼ cups **Shrimp Stock** (page 37)

2 tablespoons roughly chopped fresh **parsley**

4 tablespoons sliced **green onion**

While the chicken browns, season the shrimp all over with salt and house spice. Once you've removed the chicken, add another tablespoon of oil if the pot seems dry, then add the shrimp. Sear the shrimp until deep golden brown on both sides, 1 to 2 minutes per side. Remove to a plate and reserve for later.

Heat the oven to 350°F. Decrease the heat on the stove to medium. Add another tablespoon of oil if the pot seems dry, then add the garlic. Sauté until fragrant, 2 to 3 minutes, then add the onions, bell peppers, and celery. Sauté until tender, 8 to 10 minutes, then add the crushed tomatoes, oregano, bay leaves, thyme, hot sauce, Worcestershire sauce, and 2 tablespoons house spice. Return the andouille and chicken to the pot and simmer gently, stirring occasionally, for 20 minutes.

Add the rice and stir frequently for 5 minutes, until toasty. Add the chicken and shrimp stocks and 1 teaspoon salt, then increase heat to high and bring the mixture to a boil, stirring frequently. Once boiling, remove from the heat, cover tightly, and place in the oven for 18 minutes.

Remove the jambalaya from the oven and let rest, covered, for 5 minutes, then uncover and fluff gently with a fork and fold in the shrimp. Let it sit uncovered for 5 minutes more before folding in the parsley and green onions. Taste and adjust seasoning with salt, house spice, and hot sauce.

Jambalaya will keep in an airtight container in the refrigerator for up to 2 days.

LOWCOUNTRY RICE

Like its cousin Jambalaya (page 59), Lowcountry rice is the child of West African Jollof Rice (page 57). But whereas jambalaya hails from the Cajun and Creole country of Louisiana, Lowcountry rice is the product of South Carolina's southern coastal provinces—the Lowcountry. This area, in and around Charleston, a major port in the slave trade, was good for growing crops and also offered slave owners easy access to so-called saltwater slaves, newly arrived from West Africa. Such a readily replenished workforce meant slave owners often treated the enslaved Africans with even more callous disregard. Eventually, though, large communities of African Americans took root, and their unique culture—called Gullah Geechee—continues to flourish. This rice dish, even closer to jollof than jambalaya, is perhaps the most well known of all Gullah Geechee specialties, and one of the tastiest, too.

Heat the oven to 350°F. Rinse the rice until water runs clear, then set aside.

To a large Dutch oven over medium heat, add the oil and bacon. Cook, stirring often, until the bacon has rendered its fat, about 5 minutes. Increase the heat to medium-high and add the sausage. Transfer 3 tablespoons fat from the pot to a second large pot (supplement with neutral oil if needed to reach 3 tablespoons). Cook for 5 minutes more, then add the garlic, onions, bell peppers, and celery. Sauté until the celery is tender and the onions are translucent, 7 to 10 minutes. By this time, the bacon should be crispy. Add the tomato paste and cook, stirring often, 10 to 12 minutes, until deeply caramelized and brick red. Remove from the heat and set aside.

While the vegetables cook, heat the second pot over medium heat until the oil shimmers. Add the diced tomatoes (including the liquid), thyme, bay leaves, hot sauce, 1 tablespoon house spice, and 1 teaspoon salt. Bring to a boil, then reduce to a brisk simmer and cook, stirring frequently, until thickened and almost

ORIGIN: American South
YIELD: 4 to 6 servings

1½ cups **jasmine rice**

2 tablespoons **grapeseed oil**

4 slices thick-cut **bacon**, sliced crosswise into ¼-inch lardons

2 smoked **pork sausages**, such as andouille, sliced into ¼-inch-thick coins

3 **garlic cloves**, minced

1 medium **yellow onion**, diced

1 **green bell pepper**, diced

1 **red bell pepper**, diced

2 stalks **celery**, diced

One 6-ounce can **tomato paste**

One 14-ounce can **diced tomatoes**

4 fresh **thyme sprigs**

3 fresh **bay leaves**

2 tablespoons **Louisiana-Style Hot Sauce** (page 23)

1 tablespoon **House Spice** (page 6), plus more to taste

1½ teaspoons **kosher salt**, plus more to taste

2¼ cups **Chicken Stock** (page 33)

2 tablespoons roughly chopped fresh **parsley**

¼ cup sliced **green onion**

Lowcountry rice will keep in an airtight container in the refrigerator for up to 3 days.

pasty, 15 to 20 minutes. Add the rice and cook, stirring often to keep from burning, 5 minutes, then add the stock. Bring to a boil, then remove from the heat, cover, and place in the oven for 18 minutes.

Remove from the oven and let rest, covered, for 5 minutes. Uncover and fluff gently with a fork. Let stand for 5 minutes, then fold in the tomato-vegetable mixture. Finally, fold in parsley and green onions. Taste and adjust seasoning with salt, house spice, and hot sauce.

NIGERIA

I left New York on a frigid February day. Ten hours later, I emerged into the heat and noise and unmistakable bustle of Murtala Muhammed International Airport in Lagos, Nigeria. The first thing that hit me, more than the bulldozer of heat that turned the night air almost solid, was the smell: a mixture of gasoline, suya spice, notes of red clay, and the not-unpleasant scent of a distant fire. As a chef, and as a human, smell is an immediate transporter. Arriving here, for a five-day residency at one of Lagos's most well-known restaurants, I was momentarily slingshotted to that moment when, as a ten-year-old from the Bronx, I arrived here beside my grandfather for the first time. My mother had sent me for what I thought was the summer. It turned out to be a two-year stay. But this trip, as an adult, was my first time staying in this shimmering chaotic metropolis. When I was with Granddad, we traveled straight to Ibusa, the northern Nigerian town where he lived. This time around I'd be staying in Lagos proper, exploring the restaurants, the markets, and the hawkers and, finally, cooking for Nigeria's urban glitterati.

My guide on this trip was Michael Elégbèdé, a longtime friend and fellow chef, who had helped arrange the stay and who met me at the airport. I first met Michael on the line at Eleven Madison Park in New York City years ago. Two sons of Nigeria in that sterile, not-very-friendly kitchen, we immediately became close. In some ways, Michael and I have had inverse paths. Michael, who moved to Chicago from Nigeria at age thirteen, had recently returned to live in Lagos, where he had opened up a restaurant called Itan and become a leader in the city's restaurant scene. I, on the other hand, was born in and grew up in the Bronx, lived briefly in Nigeria, and had built my career in Washington, D.C., where I had just closed my restaurant the Shaw Bijou. Though Michael had his own restaurant, he was also helping out at the first African Heritage Week at R.S.V.P. Lagos, a high-end "New American" restaurant run by a Lebanese couple in one of Lagos's fanciest neighborhoods, Victoria Island. There were layers upon layers of history to unpack over these five days, some of it at the table, some not. The trip, my first true trip to Africa as an adult, seemed to embody the cross-currents of my life, the relationship between America and Nigeria, a relationship felt in every interaction between my twinned identity as both an African American and a Nigerian American. In some ways, it was a homecoming. In others, an exploration.

But first, there was food to be had. I threw my bags in the back of a taxi and headed to Grover's Court in Ikoyi, the center of Lagos's suya scene. The Lagos that I remembered as blurred images from the back of a car as a young boy came into focus as a city of endless energy, a thrilling chaos of human life. Nowhere is this more evident than with the street vendors and their delicious offerings, from suya to chin chin. As a boy, I was never allowed to partake in the offerings of the mai suya, or suya hawkers, since custom dictated—or at least my grandfather insisted—that as a son of a chief, eating outside his compound was forbidden. But now, nothing was off-limits. Through the cloud of spice-laden smoke I saw the faces of the hawkers, mostly men from the Hausa tribe in northern Nigeria, from where suya comes. They were blurs of constant motion. Over the open flames, they grilled beef. The yaji spice, with which suya is made, released its oniony, paprika-y, garlicky scents into the air. These were hints of memories from my childhood, augmented, through the years, by my own stateside exploration of West African cooking. But it was an entirely different beast here. I ordered way too much, not only because I was hungry, not only because I was curious, but because here I was able to finally enjoy these flavors that had kept me company my entire life in their true context. A skewer is not simply a skewer. Meat is not just meat. Food is not just the proteins and fats that form it. It is a continuation of culture, the expression of a society, an embodiment of the tastes and customs of a people. In this hot dark night, that is what I was savoring: suya, at home.

The next morning Michael and I made our way to the Epe Fish Market, one of the country's largest fish markets, on the northern shore of the Lekki Lagoon just outside Lagos. The sun was beginning its ascent, turning the calm water, covered with water lilies, pink. Hundreds of fish vendors, almost all of whom were women, began retrieving thousands of fish, either from wicker baskets kept in the shallows or from cold storage. There were fish here with which I was familiar: shimmering prawns, tilapia, catfish, northern pike, and others I had never seen before, like the electric African knifefish, a long creature, called eja osan in Yoruban. As fishermen arrived on the shore in their narrow skiffs, nets neatly arranged and fish still glistening, Lagosian shoppers came too, haggling over piles of fresh prawns and still-swimming fish. I bought a few pounds of prawns and headed back to familiar territory, the kitchen.

Victoria Island is a world of shimmering skyscrapers and upscale boutiques, of nightclubs and cocktail bars, restaurants and hotels. It is a side of Lagos I had never experienced before. It reminded me in so many ways of back home in New York City or Washington, D.C. The rhythms of the professional kitchen were also an embassy of home. My plan was to present a five-course meal that touched on Nigerian traditions but were infused with my own culinary point of view. Though I had made a name for myself in the United States by suffusing African, mostly Nigerian, flavors and techniques into fine dining, this was the first time I was cooking in Africa. And that meant, for instance, that in the marinated cucumber salad I was planning, the red stew marmalade—based on Nigeria's red stew, or obe ate din din—would be immediately recognizable to the diners, and that the suya spice with which I was roasting the brussels sprouts would be familiar to the audience, and it was likely that many of them had had it the night before, just as I had.

Five days of cooking passed by in what felt like an instant. Long days in the fluorescent lights of the kitchen were interrupted by joyful dinner services. But I also managed to squeeze in trips to the farmer's markets in the mornings, restaurants for plates of jollof and ofado rice during a break in prep, and to the clubs after service, often so late I'd go straight to the market from there. Predictably, Lagos was a blur, but an unforgettable one. During the afternoons, I led the Nigerian kitchen staff through meal prep. The menu was ambitious: marinated cucumber with whipped homemade ricotta and red stew marmalade; brussels sprouts with suya spice, chili honey, and roasted tomato soubise; salmon with escovitch sauce, plantain, smoked carrot, and yogurt; a few kernels of torched corn with toasted gari and corn velouté; lamb, both chop and shoulder, served with confit potato, braised celery and curry jus; and a soursop and mango granita. These recipes—many of which you'll find in this book—represented my own diasporic experience. They celebrated both African heritage and my own personal story. The chefs and cooks were attentive and easily picked up the novel preparations, later additions to diasporic cuisine. After expediting the first few courses, during dinner service I left the line in the capable hands of the kitchen crew and, as is my custom, ventured into the dining room. As I walked through the well-appointed space, I saw on the faces of the guests that mixture of recognition and discovery that I, too, felt coming back to this place. As I neared the tables, the guests, happily chatting in Yoruba and Igbo, seamlessly switched to English for my benefit. "I've never had gari like this," said one woman, as she bit into the gari-spiced kernels of corn I served as the third course. I knew what she meant. I, like so many children of the African diaspora, felt both my connection and how far my own path had diverged from this country, from this continent, which was a place both new and known. And I realized that these plates, the plates I sent out tonight, the plates I've been sending out my whole career, the plates I make for myself, are one of the ways in which I have kept close to my history and carried it with me—reinventing or reimaging a way to make the history of my people my own story, too. Bringing the flavors of my life—touching, as it does, so many points along the diasporic journey, through my grandparents in the American South and the Caribbean, and my parents in Jamaica and the Northeast—back to Nigeria was a way to harmonize and add my own voice to the chorus of history and the call of home.

GREENS AND OTHER VEGETABLES

*L*ong before kale became a bourgeois obsession, it counted
among the brassicas that sustained generations of Black
Americans. During the years of our bondage, the small
gardens of Africans provided not just a bit of sovereignty
and independence but also the kale, callaloo, collards, and mustard
greens that, slowly boiled in water with as much meat as could be
spared—a hock here, a knuckle there, a turkey neck or a trotter—
simmered until the liquid, the famous potlikker, became enriched
with precious nutrients. These were techniques born in West
Africa and brought to the United States: greens for the adults and
potlikker for the kids, nothing was wasted or could afford to be
wasted. Gardens, tolerated and envied by owners, symbolized that
these men and women could bring forth life and beauty themselves, that no one could deny them that divinity. Greens were,
and are, a form of resistance.

Today's collard greens are the most direct descendants of that
tradition. But even though "soul food"—a complicated term coined
in the 1960s to refer to the recipes many southern Black émigrés
enjoyed at home and brought north with them—has an unfair
reputation for being unhealthy, vegetables have long played a part
in the cuisine of African Americans. The fact that, after the Great
Migration, so many Black Americans were again denied access to

fresh food—thanks to redlining and systemic disinvestment, many Black Americans still live in urban food deserts—has made urban gardening another act of resistance. Through sweat and labor, some empty city plots are starting to overflow with ears of corn, orbs of cabbage, eager tomatoes, and loose-leaf bunches of collards.

Elsewhere, and particularly in the West Indies, where much of the population is vegetarian thanks to the large East Indian influence, vegetables have traditionally been given the full respect they deserve. Whether this is eggplant or green beans, carrots or peas, dasheen or green banana, vegetables are not kept away from the array of spices. This chapter is devoted to recipes in which vegetables serve as the main stars, but, of course, they also play a key supporting role in most diasporic cuisine. After all, the divinity of the Holy Trinity, on which much Creole and Cajun cuisine is built, rests on the power of onions, bell peppers, and celery.

JAMAICAN CALLALOO

What to call callaloo is a problem that has bedeviled Caribbean cooks forever. In Jamaica, the name refers both to the leafy greens of amaranth and the dish made from braising those leaves down in stock with aromatics. The protein-rich leaves are cooked until tender, and given spice and fulsome flavor with the addition of peppers and tomatoes. Callaloo is best eaten as part of a traditional Jamaican breakfast, alongside Ackee and Saltfish (page 149). Confusingly, callaloo also can refer to water spinach, which is a completely different plant and not suitable for this recipe. To further confuse matters, in Trinidad and Tobago, callaloo is made with dasheen, or taro, leaves. (A recipe for Trinidadian callaloo is found following this one.)

In a large pot, heat the oil over medium heat. When it shimmers, add the garlic and sauté until fragrant, about 3 minutes. Add the onions, bell peppers, and peppa sauce, and cook for another 10 minutes, then add the callaloo, tomatoes, house spice, and vegetable stock. Cook, stirring occasionally, for 5 minutes, then bring to a simmer over medium-high heat. Cover and cook for 1 hour, until the callaloo is tender, then remove the lid and simmer until just enough liquid remains to coat the greens. Season with salt to taste and serve.

ORIGIN: Jamaica
YIELD: 4 servings

2 tablespoons grapeseed oil

5 garlic cloves, minced

1 medium yellow onion, diced

1 red bell pepper, diced

1 teaspoon Peppa Sauce (page 25)

1 pound callaloo, leaves and tender stems only, cleaned and roughly chopped (about 7 packed cups of leaves)

2 ripe Roma tomatoes, diced

2 teaspoons House Spice (page 6)

2 cups Vegetable Stock (page 36)

Kosher salt, to taste

Callaloo will keep in an airtight container in the refrigerator for up to 4 days.

TRINIDADIAN CALLALOO

Trini callaloo is made with the leaves of dasheen, or taro, not amaranth, as it is in Jamaica (see the previous recipe). It's an altogether creamier dish, more akin to creamed spinach than the heat-tinged Jamaican version. Taro was likely brought over from South India in the mid-nineteenth century, along with coconut milk, which is traditionally used in callaloo. For this creamier version, I use heavy cream along with unsweetened coconut cream—which is, it's important to know, not the same as the much sweeter cream of coconut.

Heat the oil in a large pot over medium heat. When it shimmers, add the garlic and sauté until fragrant, 2 to 3 minutes. Add the onions, bell peppers, and peppa sauce and cook, stirring often, until the onions are translucent, about 10 minutes. Stir in the taro and house spice and cook for 5 minutes, then add the coconut cream, heavy cream, and vegetable stock. Bring to a simmer, then reduce heat to low and cover. Simmer gently for 1 hour, then remove the lid and continue to cook until thick and creamy—the callaloo should resemble creamed spinach. Add salt to taste and serve.

ORIGIN: Trinidad and Tobago
YIELD: 4 servings

2 tablespoons grapeseed oil

5 garlic cloves, minced

1 medium yellow onion, diced

1 red bell pepper, diced

1 teaspoon Peppa Sauce (page 25)

1 pound taro, leaves and tender stems only, cleaned and roughly chopped (about 7 packed cups of leaves)

2 teaspoons House Spice (page 6)

2 cups unsweetened coconut cream

2 cups heavy cream

2 cups Vegetable Stock (page 36)

Kosher salt, to taste

Callaloo will keep in an airtight container in the refrigerator for up to 4 days.

COLLARD GREENS

Of all the greens in the southern pantheon, collards are my favorite. It might be because the leaves turn to silk in the low simmer, or the way the ham hocks release their deep smokiness, or that the potlikker becomes so rich and flavorful it could be the star of the show on its own. It's all of this, of course, plus the fact that collard greens, though originally from the Mediterranean, were one of the few crops Africans were permitted to grow on their own and thus these leaves have been cooked down, and added to, and served shimmering in the homes of my ancestors for centuries before they arrived at my table.

Sauté the aromatics: Heat the oil in a large pot over medium heat. When it shimmers, add the garlic and sauté for 3 minutes, until fragrant. Add the onions and sauté until translucent, 10 minutes. Fold in the collards, sautéing until bright green and beginning to soften, about 5 minutes, then add the vinegar, brown sugar, house spice, ham hocks, and vegetable stock.

Cook the greens: Bring to a simmer, then reduce the heat to low and cover. Cook for 2 hours, stirring occasionally, until the greens are completely tender and you can shred any meat from the ham hocks. (Add that shredded meat to the pot and discard the bones.) Add salt to taste, then serve.

ORIGIN: American South
YIELD: 4 servings

---

2 tablespoons **grapeseed oil**

8 **garlic cloves**, minced

2 medium **yellow onions**, diced

1 pound **collard greens**, stems removed, roughly chopped

3 tablespoons **white vinegar**

1½ teaspoons **light brown sugar**

1 tablespoon **House Spice** (page 6)

4 **ham hocks**

2 cups **Vegetable Stock** (page 36)

Kosher salt, to taste

Collard greens will keep in an airtight container in the refrigerator for up to 4 days.

STEWED OKRA AND SHRIMP

Okra is slimy. It just is, and the quicker you embrace the slime the sooner you fall in love with this small flowering mallow. That sliminess is what endeared okra to the West African cooks from Nigeria and Ghana, who have used it as a thickener for stews for centuries. When they brought okra to the New World, that same sliminess gave gumbo its silky thick texture. In fact, the word gumbo comes from the Angolan word for okra, ki-ngombo.

But that sliminess can take some getting used to, I know. When I lived in Nigeria, it took me nearly a year to fall in love with the okra stew with goat meat my grandmother made. It took me less time to fall in love with this Creole stewed okra and shrimp, which utilizes okra's thickening properties yet tastes of the sea and of the Holy Trinity of onions, bell peppers, and celery.

Heat a large cast-iron skillet over medium-high heat. When hot, add the okra and char on all sides, about 10 minutes. Remove from the pan and set aside.

Reduce the heat to medium and add the oil to the pan. When it shimmers, add the garlic and cook, stirring often, until fragrant, about 2 minutes. Add the onions, celery, and bell peppers, and sauté until the celery is tender and the onions are translucent, about 5 minutes. Add the tomato paste and cook, stirring often, until brick red and fragrant, 3 to 5 minutes, then add the charred okra, crushed tomatoes, thyme, bay leaf, and house spice. Increase the heat to medium-high and cook until thick and jam-like, 3 to 5 minutes more. Add the shrimp stock and simmer until saucy, about 5 minutes, then fold in the shrimp.

Simmer, stirring occasionally, until somewhat reduced—the sauce should coat the shrimp and okra. Remove and discard the thyme and bay leaf, season to taste with salt and house spice, then serve with Perfectly Steamed Rice (page 46).

ORIGIN: American South
YIELD: 2 servings

½ pound okra, stemmed and cut into 1-inch pieces
2 tablespoons grapeseed oil
3 garlic cloves, minced
½ medium yellow onion, diced
1 stalk celery, diced
½ green bell pepper, diced
1 tablespoon tomato paste
2 cups canned crushed tomatoes
3 fresh thyme sprigs
1 fresh bay leaf
2 tablespoons House Spice (page 6), plus more to taste
1 cup Shrimp Stock (page 37)
½ pound medium (26–30 size) shrimp, peeled and deveined
Kosher salt, to taste

Stewed okra and shrimp is best served immediately, but will keep in the refrigerator for up to 2 days.

FOSSOLIA

Green beans and carrots have a bad reputation. Order it at a restaurant here in America, and you're likely to get a mixture defined more by texture than flavor. There is, no doubt, something pleasing about the crunch of carrots against the fresh snap of green beans. But fossolia, or ፎሶሊያ in Amharic, isn't that. In this dish, one I discovered while researching sides for my fast-casual Ethiopian concept restaurant Gorsha, the string beans and carrots are just part of a chorus of flavors that includes the warming spices of NKO, the sweetness of sautéed onions, and the bracing heat of berbere. I immediately fell in love with it, as a complement to spicier, heartier Ethiopian fare like Doro Wat (page 170).

Sauté the aromatics: In a medium saucepan, heat the NKO over medium heat. Add the onions and sauté for 10 minutes, then add the GGP and cook, stirring frequently, until fragrant, 3 minutes. Add the tomato paste and berbere and continue to stir until the mixture has turned brick red, 7 to 10 minutes.

Cook the vegetables: Stir in the carrots and sauté until just beginning to cook, 6 minutes, then add the green beans and a pinch of salt. Cook, stirring often, until the carrots are al dente, 2 to 3 minutes more. Add more salt to taste and serve.

ORIGIN: Ethiopia
YIELD: 2 to 4 servings

---

2 tablespoons NKO (page 21)

1 medium yellow onion, thinly sliced into half-moons

1½ tablespoons GGP (page 5)

2½ tablespoons tomato paste

1 teaspoon Berbere (page 9)

2 large carrots, peeled and cut into pieces, 2 inches x ¼ inch x ¼ inches, batonnet

¼ pound green beans, trimmed, cut into 2-inch pieces, batonnet

Kosher salt, to taste

Fossolia will keep in an airtight container in the refrigerator for up to 4 days.

TOSTONES

The crispier, more savory cousin of Sweet Plantains (page 79), tostones are twice-fried plantains. The first fry softens them, the second crisps. The result is something between a chip and a chewy wafer. Salty, sweet, and crisp, tostones are everywhere in Puerto Rico and the DR and everywhere in the Bronx. Not everyone goes through the extra step of tossing with a spice blend, and it's true that plain tostones are delicious, but I think the extra kick of flavor is worth it, especially if you already have a jar of house spice in your pantry.

In a heavy-bottomed pot or skillet, add enough oil to come 1 inch up the sides of the pot. Heat over medium to 300°F.

While the oil heats, peel the plantains, cut them into 1-inch pieces, and set aside. In a medium bowl, stir together the garlic, lime juice, 2 teaspoons salt, and the hot water until the salt dissolves.

In another bowl, combine the house spice, curry powder, cumin, powdered sugar, and remaining 1 teaspoon salt.

Fry the plantains until they begin to turn light brown, working in batches as necessary to avoid crowding the pan and turning once, about 4 minutes in total. Remove from the oil and drain on a paper towel–lined plate. After 2 minutes, use a wooden spoon to flatten the plantains, then transfer to the bowl with the garlic-lime water. Drain well and pat dry.

After all the plantains have been flattened and soaked, raise the temperature of the oil to 350°F. Fry the plantains again for 3 to 4 minutes per side, until they are deep golden brown. Transfer to a fresh paper towel–lined plate to drain, then toss with the spice mixture. Enjoy with Louisiana-Style Hot Sauce (page 23).

ORIGIN: Caribbean
YIELD: 2 to 4 servings

Vegetable oil, such as canola, for frying

2 green plantains

2 tablespoons minced garlic

Juice from 1 lime

3 teaspoons kosher salt, divided

4 cups hot water

2 teaspoons House Spice (page 6)

2 teaspoons Curry Powder (page 10)

½ teaspoon ground cumin

1½ tablespoons powdered sugar

Tostones are best served immediately.

SWEET PLANTAINS

Plantains are among the most widely grown and important crops in the world. Starchier and more robust than their cousin, the banana, you'll find them everywhere from India to the West Coast of Africa, Latin and South America, the Caribbean, and up to Louisiana and Florida, often as a cash crop and as a staple starch. Hardy and plentiful, the plantain is a versatile ingredient not unlike a potato or cassava. Depending on their level of ripeness, plantains can be savory or sweet. They can be ground into flour; they can be mashed into fritters and fried; they can be baked; they can be roasted. Growing up in the Bronx, I was exposed mostly to plantains at Dominican or Puerto Rican restaurants, where they generally came either alongside oxtail stew as Tostones (page 77), twice-fried and savory, or after the meal, as these maduros, softer, sweeter, and made from riper fruit. The avocado crema, my own addition, adds a touch of acidity that complements the sweetness of the plantain.

ORIGIN: Caribbean

YIELD: 4 to 6 servings

For the avocado crema
1 ripe **avocado**
1 clove **garlic**
¾ cup **sour cream**
3 tablespoons **mayonnaise**
Juice of 1 **lime**
Kosher salt, to taste

For the plantains
Vegetable oil, such as canola, for frying
2 very ripe (mostly black) **plantains**, sliced ¾ inch thick on the bias
Kosher salt, to taste

Serve fried plantains immediately, with avocado crema alongside for dipping. Any leftover crema will keep in an airtight container in the refrigerator for up to 2 days.

For the avocado crema

Peel and pit the avocado and scoop the flesh into the bowl of a food processor. Add the remaining ingredients, seasoning to taste with salt, and purée until smooth. Set aside while you fry the plantains.

For the plantains

In a large pan over medium-high heat, heat ⅛ inch oil to 350°F. Add the plantains and cook, flipping every 3 minutes or so, until deeply golden brown, soft, and juicy, about 12 minutes total. Remove the fried plantains to a plate lined with paper towel, and sprinkle with salt.

BAIGAN CHOKA

Charring vegetables, a technique called choka, is an easy and quick way to add flavor. It is common in Trinidad and Tobago as well as in parts of India like Bihari, where the technique originated. The Trini version comes with bursts of pepper heat as well as the softening addition of butter at the very end. There are as many chokas as there are vegetables (though ones with softer skins work best). Eggplant, or baigan in Hindi, holds up especially well, but tomato choka is also one of my favorites. I wrap a scoop in fresh roti for a healthy and deeply flavored snack.

Note: To make this recipe without a grill, cook the vegetables directly over a gas stove burner. (Line the drip plate with foil first to make cleanup easier.) If you don't have a gas stove, cook on a foil-lined sheet pan under a broiler set to high.

Prepare a grill for high heat. Rub the eggplant and tomato lightly with oil and season with salt and pepper.

When the grill is hot, reduce heat to medium-high and set the eggplant and tomato directly on the grates. Char the vegetables, using tongs to turn them often, until the skin is totally charred and the flesh is soft, 10 minutes for the tomato and 30 to 45 minutes for the eggplant. Set aside in a bowl to cool slightly. Trim away the eggplant's stem, then roughly chop the eggplant and the tomato, leaving the charred skin on.

In a large pan over medium heat, heat the 2 tablespoons of oil. When it shimmers, add the onions and sauté until translucent, about 5 minutes. Add the GGP and cook until fragrant, about 1 minute, then add peppa sauce, RGP, thyme, chopped eggplant and tomato, and any juices from the eggplant and tomato. Bring to a simmer over medium heat and cook, stirring often, until most of the liquid has evaporated, about 5 to 7 minutes.

Add the butter a few cubes at a time, stirring to melt completely before adding more, then remove from the heat. Season with lime juice and salt then garnish with parsley and serve warm.

ORIGIN: Trinidad and Tobago
YIELD: 1 quart (4 to 6 servings)

---

1 eggplant

1 Roma tomato

2 tablespoons grapeseed oil, plus more as needed for oiling vegetables

Kosher salt, to taste

Freshly ground black pepper, to taste

2 large yellow onions, thinly sliced

2 teaspoons GGP (page 5)

1 teaspoon Peppa Sauce (page 25)

2 teaspoons RGP (page 11)

8 fresh thyme sprigs, leaves picked and stems discarded

2 tablespoons unsalted butter, cubed

Freshly squeezed lime juice, to taste

8 parsley leaves, chiffonade

Baigan choka will keep in an airtight container in the refrigerator for up 1 week.

TOMATO CHOKA

Prepare a grill for high heat (or set a large cast-iron skillet over high heat). In a large bowl, toss together 2 tablespoons grapeseed oil and the tomatoes, and add salt and pepper to taste. Once the grill or skillet is hot, reduce the heat to medium-high and add the tomatoes atop the grates. Cook, turning often, until the tomatoes are charred on all sides, about 15 minutes. Set the tomatoes aside to cool slightly before roughly chopping.

In a large pan over medium heat, heat the remaining 2 tablespoons of oil until shimmering. Add the onions and cook, stirring often, until they are soft and translucent, 10 minutes. Add the GGP and cook until fragrant, 2 to 3 minutes.

Add the chopped tomatoes, peppa sauce, RGP, thyme, palm sugar, and cumin and simmer over medium heat, stirring often, until most of the liquid has evaporated, about 10 minutes. Remove from the heat and add the butter a few cubes at a time, stirring to melt between additions. Season with freshly squeezed lime juice and additional salt to taste, then serve.

ORIGIN: Trinidad and Tobago
YIELD: 4 to 6 servings

¼ cup **grapeseed oil**, divided

8 **Roma tomatoes**

Kosher salt and freshly ground **black pepper**, to taste

4 medium **yellow onions**, diced

2 teaspoons **GGP** (page 5)

1 teaspoon **Peppa Sauce** (page 25)

2 teaspoons **RGP** (page 11)

8 fresh **thyme sprigs**, leaves only

1 tablespoon **palm sugar**

½ teaspoon ground **cumin**

2 tablespoons **unsalted butter**, cubed

Juice of 2 limes

Tomato choka will keep in an airtight container in the refrigerator for up to 1 week.

CORN MAQUE CHOUX

When French colonists established Le Nouvelle Orleans in 1718, they quickly found that the wheat they were used to did not grow in the bayou, at the mouth of the Mississippi. Thankfully—at least for them—they were introduced to corn by the local Native American tribe, the Muskogee, on whose land New Orleans sits, which they quickly combined with the other gift to Cajun cuisine, the Holy Trinity of onions, bell peppers, and celery. Thus was born this Creole sauté. As in so much of New Orleanian cuisine, the dish—whose name is a French transliteration of a Native American term—was tumbled through the French idiom in which cream trumps all. By the time I learned this recipe from my mother, whose roots run deep in Louisiana, maque choux had become a staple of the Cajun table, whose creaminess I cut through with the twinned heat of house spice and hot sauce.

In a large pan over medium heat, melt the butter. Sauté the bell peppers, onions, celery, and garlic until tender but not browned, 10 minutes. Add the corn and cook for 5 minutes more.

Stir in the RGP, hot sauce, house spice, cream, thyme, and bay leaves, then bring to a simmer over medium heat. Cook, stirring occasionally, until the liquid is reduced and thick, about 5 minutes.

Remove from the heat and remove the thyme sprigs and bay leaves. Fold in the parsley and basil, season with salt and lemon juice, and serve warm.

ORIGIN: American South
YIELD: 3½ cups (4 servings)

1 tablespoon unsalted butter

½ red bell pepper, finely diced

½ green bell pepper, finely diced

1 medium yellow onion, finely diced

1 stalk celery, diced

10 garlic cloves, minced

Kernels from 2 ears sweet corn

1 tablespoon RGP (page 11)

½ tablespoon Louisiana-Style Hot Sauce (page 23)

1 teaspoon House Spice (page 6)

½ cup heavy cream

3 fresh thyme sprigs

2 bay leaves

1 tablespoon finely chopped parsley leaves

1 tablespoon finely chopped basil leaves

Kosher salt, to taste

Freshly squeezed lemon juice, to taste

Corn maque choux will keep in an airtight container in the refrigerator for up to 5 days.

BUTTERED GRITS

Like corn maque choux, grits are another debt owed to the Muskogee people. Grits began as a sort of ground maize called rockhomine, made by grinding kernels of corn that had been soaked in an alkaline solution to remove the hull. (This process is called nixtamalization.) This became hominy grits, which, with the addition of milk, cheese, and ungodly amounts of butter, are what thousands of very lucky people now eat for breakfast every day. After a long dry spell, when grits were wrongly overlooked, we're now in the middle of a grits revival. They now come in both hominy and non-nixtamalized corn varieties, in both yellow and white, and with special attention paid to heirloom varieties. All work, but it's important that the grits be stone-ground, which better preserves the proteins and flavors. Though the so-called Grits Belt runs from D.C. to South Carolina, where grits is the official state food, to Texas, the reach of grits extends well beyond. (It's a regular Bahamian breakfast, where it arrived with slavery in the eighteenth century, and where it's often served with corned beef, tuna, and sardines.)

ORIGIN: American South
YIELD: 4 servings

4 cups **whole milk**

1 cup stone-ground **white grits**

4 tablespoons **unsalted butter,** cubed

4 slices (about 2.5 ounces total) **yellow American cheese,** roughly chopped

Kosher salt and freshly ground **black pepper,** or **white granulated sugar,** to taste (optional)

Buttered grits are best served immediately, but will keep in an airtight container in the refrigerator for up to 5 days.

In a medium pot over medium-high heat, bring the milk to a simmer. Meanwhile, stir together grits and 1 cup water in a small bowl.

Gradually add the grits-water mixture to the simmering milk, whisking constantly to avoid clumping. Simmer gently, whisking frequently, for 15 to 20 minutes, until the grits are tender and thick. Adjust the heat as needed to avoid scorching or sputtering. If the grits become thick before they're tender, add a bit more water and continue to simmer.

Whisk in the butter and cheese. Season to taste with salt, pepper, and/or sugar, then serve—and watch fights ensue.

BRAISED CABBAGE AND CARROTS

Cabbage is often steamed in Jamaica and served alongside oxtail, jerk chicken, or rice and peas. It functions much like Yekik Alicha (page 109), as a counterbalancing cooling element to spicier food. But I personally have always found steamed cabbage to be bland. So to give it some flavor, I braise it in coconut milk, add the acidity of citrus and a punch of GGP, then mount the vegetables with a good amount of butter, a trick lifted from French culinary kitchens. The result is a soothing, creamy-but-light accompaniment that can stand its own against the aggressive flavors of jerk and not be overshadowed.

Heat the oven to 300°F and grease an oven-safe pot or 9-x-13-inch baking pan with oil.

In a large bowl, combine the cabbage, carrots, GGP, onions, coconut milk, and salt. Transfer to the prepared pot or pan and cover tightly with foil (if using a pot, you can just use the pot lid). Transfer to the oven and cook for 1 hour 40 minutes.

Carefully uncover the pan. The cabbage should be translucent and very tender. Drop a few pieces of butter into the hot vegetables and stir constantly to melt the butter and emulsify the mixture. Repeat until you've added all the butter. Season with lemon juice and salt to taste and serve.

ORIGIN: Jamaica
YIELD: 6 to 8 servings

Grapeseed oil, for greasing pan

1 medium head green cabbage (about 2½ pounds), julienned

4 medium carrots (about ½ pound), peeled and shredded

6 tablespoons GGP (page 5)

2 yellow onions, diced

12 ounces coconut milk

1 tablespoon kosher salt, plus more to taste

12 tablespoons unsalted butter, cubed

Freshly squeezed lemon juice, to taste

Braised cabbage and carrots will keep in an airtight container in the refrigerator for up to 4 days.

CUCUMBER AND AVOCADO SALAD

When I first began this project of delving deeply into diasporic cooking, I kept my streams separate. I deconstructed curried goat from Trinidad or stew peas from Jamaica or Nigerian moi moi or Ethiopian wots until I understood each individual part, and then I reassembled them. But as I began to fully grasp each element, I constructed my own sentences using words that had never been combined before. Such is the nature of this cucumber and avocado salad. Fresh salads like this aren't very common in the diaspora. And though cucumber is found often, avocado isn't. Never mind the gooseberry, a small tart relative of the currant. Nevertheless, the way I treat the cucumber is akin to how meat is often used in Trinidadian cooking: marinated in a mixture of acid and green seasoning. Other than the presence of the gooseberry, the piri piri is a classic of the South African pantry. And the avocado, whose creaminess softens the otherwise acidic salad—well, who doesn't love an avocado?

ORIGIN: Everywhere
YIELD: 4 to 6 Servings

For the marinated cucumbers
2 Persian cucumbers, peeled
½ cup **Green Seasoning** (page 29)
3 tablespoons **white balsamic vinegar**
2½ teaspoons **white granulated sugar**
¼ teaspoon **kosher salt**

For the gooseberry piri piri
½ **yellow bell pepper**, roughly chopped
Freshly squeezed **juice of 1 lemon**
Freshly squeezed **juice of 1½ limes**
3 **Sungold tomatoes**
5 **gooseberries** (or goldenberries)
2½ teaspoons **white granulated sugar**
2½ teaspoons **white balsamic vinegar**
2 teaspoons minced **red onion**
1 **clove garlic**
¼ teaspoon **Peppa Sauce** (page 25)
¼ teaspoon dried **oregano**
1 teaspoon **kosher salt** →

For the marinated cucumbers

Trim the ends from the cucumber on a bias, then halve lengthwise. Holding your knife at a 45-degree angle, cut the cucumber into 4 to 5 pieces, turning the cucumber a quarter-turn with each cut. (You're looking for triangle-shaped pieces.)

Combine the remaining ingredients in a medium bowl, then add the cucumbers and stir well to combine. Transfer to a ziplock bag and seal, pushing out as much air as possible. Place in bowl and let marinate in the refrigerator for at least 1 hour and up to 3 hours.

For the gooseberry piri piri

Combine all the ingredients in a blender and purée until completely smooth. Pour through a fine-mesh sieve and refrigerate until ready to serve. →

Cucumber and Avocado Salad (continued)

To assemble

Halve the avocado, remove the pit, and carefully peel the fruit. Dice each avocado half into 9 pieces.

In a shallow bowl, randomly arrange the pieces of avocado, then the cucumber, followed by the gooseberries and tomatoes. Garnish with torn mint, season with salt, then pour piri piri into the bowl and serve.

To assemble

1 ripe but firm Hass avocado

Marinated cucumbers (above)

8 gooseberries (or goldenberries), halved

8 Sungold tomatoes, halved

5 mint leaves, torn

Kosher salt, to taste

½ cup gooseberry piri piri (above)

• 88 • GREENS AND OTHER VEGETABLES

VEGETARIAN DULET

Though the presentation is anything but traditional, the soul of this dish is Ethiopian. It is a spin on dulet, a mixture of raw organ meat flavored with a cardamom-rich spice blend called mitmita. When I was opening my second restaurant, I knew it would be a hard sell for a crowd unaccustomed to its delicious but offal-y flavor and, looking for a vegetarian item, figured mushrooms would be a great substitute. The duxelles, a finely chopped mixture of mushrooms, traditionally made with onions and shallots but here with NKO, GGP, and peppa sauce, was the starting point for what I listed on the menu as "Mushroom Forest." Then I began to play, adding the smokiness of baigan choka to the flavors of NKO and GGP. The labneh, a later addition we call Aubrey sauce—named after the line cook Aubrey Graham, who whipped it up—adds not just soothing dairy but a bracing dose of Trini green seasoning. M'semen, a North African flatbread, is the perfect sop.

ORIGIN: Ethiopia
YIELD: 4 servings

For the herbed labneh
¼ cup whole-milk Greek yogurt
1 tablespoon Green Seasoning (page 29)
Freshly squeezed juice of 1 lemon
½ teaspoon kosher salt, plus more to taste

For the pickled Fresno chilies
1 Fresno chili, stemmed and thinly sliced into ⅛-inch rounds
½ cup Spice Pickling Liquid (page 32)

For the duxelles
2 teaspoons NKO (page 21)
2 tablespoons GGP (page 5)
1 tablespoon Berbere (page 9)
½ cup Green Seasoning (page 29)
1 pound white button mushrooms, stems trimmed, finely chopped
1 teaspoon Peppa Sauce (page 25)
1 teaspoon kosher salt, plus more to taste

For the toasted garlic purée
1 cup water
20 garlic cloves
2 tablespoons RGP (page 11)
Freshly squeezed juice of 1 lemon
½ teaspoon kosher salt, plus more to taste →

Two days ahead

Make the herbed labneh: Place the Greek yogurt in a strainer lined with cheesecloth. Set over a bowl and refrigerate for 2 days (or at least overnight). Before serving, fold in the remaining ingredients, then taste and adjust the seasoning. Transfer to a squeeze bottle if you have one, then set aside.

Make the pickled Fresno chilies: Place the sliced chilies in a jar (or other nonreactive container) and cover completely with spice pickling liquid. Refrigerate for 2 days.

One day ahead

Make the duxelles: Heat a large pan over medium heat with 2 teaspoons NKO. Add the GGP, Berbere, and green seasoning and cook until fragrant and toasted, 10 minutes, stirring constantly. Add the mushrooms, peppa sauce, and 1 teaspoon salt. Cook, stirring and scraping the pan occasionally as the mushrooms release their liquid, until all of the liquid has evaporated, 5 to 7 minutes. Taste and adjust seasoning. You should have about 1½ cups. Set aside until cool, then refrigerate until ready to assemble. →

Make the toasted garlic purée: Combine water and garlic in a small pot. Bring to a boil over high heat, then strain, reserving the garlic. Repeat this 4 more times, using fresh water each time. Add the garlic to a blender along with the RGP, lemon juice, and ½ teaspoon salt. Blend until velvety smooth, then taste and adjust seasoning. You should have about ½ cup. Refrigerate until ready to assemble.

Make the pickled mushrooms: Trim the mushroom stems so they're only ¼ inch long. Place in a jar (or other nonreactive container) and cover completely with spice pickling liquid. Refrigerate overnight.

Make the pickled red pearl onions: Trim off the onion stems, then cut the onions in half lengthwise. Gently peel onions, then separate the petals, being careful not to tear them. Heat a medium nonreactive pan over high heat, then add the onions and beet to the pan. Sauté for 30 seconds, then add the spice pickling liquid. Bring to a simmer, then remove from the heat. Transfer to a jar (or other nonreactive container) to cool, then refrigerate until ready to assemble.

Day of

To assemble: Heat a large pan over medium-high heat with the oil. Add the maitake, oyster, and hon shimeji mushrooms, plus ½ teaspoon salt. Cook until golden brown, stirring occasionally, about 6 to 8 minutes. Add the butter and continue to cook and stir until deeply golden brown, 2 to 3 minutes more. Taste and adjust seasoning.

Meanwhile, warm choka and duxelles in small pans over low heat.

To serve, spread the toasted garlic purée in a circle on a large plate or platter. Top with the duxelles, spreading to the edges of the garlic purée, then drape the seared mushrooms over the duxelles. Spoon in the choka. Finally, dot with the herb labneh and garnish with the pickled mushrooms, Fresno chilies, and pearl onions. Scatter with parsley leaves and serve immediately with m'semen.

For the pickled mushrooms
4 ounces **white beech mushrooms**

½ cup **Spice Pickling Liquid** (page 32)

For the pickled red pearl onion
4 **red pearl onions**

½ small **red beet**, peeled and cut into ½-inch dice

1 cup **Spice Pickling Liquid** (page 32)

To assemble
1 tablespoon **grapeseed oil**

4 ounces **maitake mushrooms**, cleaned, stems trimmed, and torn into 1-inch pieces

4 ounces **oyster mushrooms**, cleaned, stems trimmed, torn into 1-inch pieces

4 ounces **hon shimeji mushrooms**, cleaned, stems trimmed, and separated into individual stems

½ teaspoon **kosher salt**, plus more to taste

2 tablespoons **unsalted butter**

2 tablespoons + 2 teaspoons **Baigan Choka** (page 80)

1 cup **duxelles** (above)

¼ cup toasted **garlic purée**

2 tablespoons + 2 teaspoons **herb labneh** (above)

9 **pickled mushrooms** (above)

9 slices **pickled Fresno chili** (above)

9 pickled **red pearl onion** petals (above)

7 **parsley leaves**

8 **M'semen** (page 242), to serve

Vegetarian dulet is best served immediately.

TRINIDAD AND TOBAGO

The rub of time is that when you meet your ancestors, they're already old. I remember my grandfather not as a young man, clean cut with unlined skin and a skinny tie, but as Papa Winston, a cloud of a white beard ringing his chin and laugh lines like rivers creasing his eyes. But I have to admit, when I saw him in Miami a few months ago on our way to Trinidad and Tobago together, he had all the joy of a young man embarking on a new adventure. So did I. That's what we were. Or at least a journey was what we were on.

My grandfather was born on the Caribbean island on Christmas Day in 1941 and moved to the United States at the age of twenty-five. He carried with him, in no specific order: determination, Scotch bonnet peppers, a college degree, and dreams. He met my Grandma Cassie in 1977 and settled first in Long Island and then in Yorktown, Virginia. Time flew, he grew, became a father, then a grandfather ten times over, then a great-grandfather. He didn't make it back to Trinidad often, but he carried his home in his West Indian accent, and in the flavors of his cooking, and in his memory. Since he retired, Papa has been back a few times, mostly for funerals, as his siblings have been whittled down from a dozen to now just eight. But I had never gone back with him to visit. This was our chance.

We arrived in the Port of Spain and stepped directly into history. Trinidad and Tobago, the twinned island states, have been deeply imprinted by centuries of colonialism. The legacy of British, French, and Spanish occupation, the importation of Indian labor and African slaves, not to mention the exploitation of indigenous Carib and Taino cultures, have, nevertheless, resulted in an astonishing vibrant mix of cultures. Nowhere is this felt more than in the kitchen. You can trace a straight line from the fluffy plates of cou-cou, a polenta made of cornmeal and sometimes studded with okra, and ground provisions, which include pretty much every tuber and root vegetable and accompany nearly every meal, back to the first African slaves who arrived in the eighteenth century. There are French riffs on dishes like buljol, a salt cod, pepper, and tomato salad, which are chopped-and-screwed through the Trini patois and come out a thousand times better and spicier. Thanks to the large Indian population— first brought as indentured servants in the eighteenth and nineteenth centuries—spicy poulari, an evolution of pakora, and golden

fried mashed potato pockets called aloo pie are hawked on every street corner. Roti, another Indian flatbread, is available fresh everywhere and irresistible when filled with a thin layer of ground dhal or yellow split peas and wrapped around curried goat, spiny lobster, and even conch. Cumin, a staple in the Indian pantry, is here called jeera and used in my favorite Trini dish ever: chunks of flavorful pork geerah.

Fresh from the plane, Papa and I were hungry and made a beeline for the parking lot. There a man sold doubles—two pieces of bara, a flatbread, with curried chickpea (channa), tamarind, and shado beni—as well as a Scotch bonnet hot sauce that burned my face off. But it was delicious. A man, a cooler for drinks, and a shopping cart for ingredients, selling lunch in the blazing sun. It was feeding people at its most elemental. Papa and I ate, checked into our hotel, and waited for the sun to set and the air to cool.

In the morning, Papa said he wanted to show me something. We took a car to St. James, a sprawling neighborhood in the north of the city where my grandfather grew up. Through the narrow streets we drove, past greengrocers selling fruit from the back of their trucks and halal butcher shops. Papa led me to where his house was. *Was.* The corrugated-tin walls had been replaced by something *slightly* more permanent. We walked by the concrete slab where his outhouse had been. That was paved over, but the stream behind the house, which cut through St. James and served as a shortcut from one friend's house to another, still flowed. He walked me by the church where he'd roll into 6 a.m. mass from staying out all night long and to the Catholic school where he won the scholarship that eventually got him to America and therefore led to this story.

Then back into the car we went, to drive north toward Maracas Bay, along a winding road riddled with landslides—it being rainy season—from the green cliffs on one side and the ocean stretching blue on the other. We stopped for lunch at Richard's Bake and Shark, a Trinidadian institution. Back home, Papa often made me many of the offerings on the menu—buljol, sardines, curried goat and beef—but here, the dogfish and the bake, a puff of fried bread, was so fresh it felt completely new. We sat together quietly by the side of the road, eating our lunch together. Neither of us knew that within in a year's time, my grandfather would be gone. Well, perhaps he did, but I didn't. I think back to that afternoon, to this trip that was a discovery for me and a homecoming for him, to that moment in the sun by the side of the road, when the clouds parted and the sun lit up Papa Winston's white beard and frizzy white hair like a halo. I hear the waves lapping the shores of the island, rustling the leaves of the trees, and I allow all his love to fill my heart once again.

LEGUMES AND TUBERS

Beans are the sustainer of great swaths of Latin America, the Caribbean, and southern and eastern Africa. I can't think of the Bronx, where I grew up, and which is home to nearly 300,000 Puerto Ricans and as many Dominicans, without immediately picturing a pot of garlic-studded beans simmering. Those beans were so good I'd often rip open the to-go container, taking a second to mix the yellow rice and red beans, and then devour the thing before I made it home. Beans, called peas by Jamaicans, are a staple: black, red, white, brown, dimpled, dappled, and speckled. Beans sustain. Black-eyed peas (actually black-eyed beans) are known to be particularly auspicious, perhaps a holdover from their role in the Yoruba culture of Nigeria, where they were used to feed the orishas, or god protectors. Brought over from Africa by the same ships that carried kidnapped Africans, beans, like rice, grew along the Gulf Coast, providing cheap rations. Along the way, through time, we took what was a ration and turned it into something that is ours. We reclaimed something that is, that always was, ours to grow, to eat, and to enjoy.

Beyond beans, tubers, such as the yam in West Africa, the potato in the Americas, and cassava and taro in the Caribbean, are perhaps the closest, most direct connection that binds one Black kitchen to another, across space and time. The yam itself—a proper yam—is grown and consumed in astonishing quantities in Nigeria. Those and other tubers became ground provisions of the West Indies. (What we call yams in the United States are actually sweet potatoes—something that has caused confusion for the past 400 years.) Growing up, my experience of tubers, like many Americans, was limited to the potato and most often in French fry form from McDonald's. Nevertheless, I was graced with a mother who could turn a sack of potatoes into something special for a Sunday morning, and I wouldn't be a good son if I didn't include that here.

CREOLE HASHBROWNS

I fought a lot with my mom growing up. And my sister. And my stepdad, too. We were four big personalities in a small apartment, so small I slept in the closet for a while. But we always could—and always did—come together around the Sunday breakfast table, summoned by Salmon Cakes (page 130) and Rice and Eggs (page 55) and glued there by these Creole hashbrowns.

These aren't the shredded, molded hashbrowns you'll see at an average diner, but rather the rich stewed hashbrowns of heaven. My mom's secret was to get up earlier than the rest of us, letting the hashbrowns reduce and reduce, getting richer in flavor and darker in color. The result was deeply caramelized, buttery, soft hashbrowns, so delicious there could be no argument.

In a large nonstick or cast-iron pan, melt the butter over medium-high heat. Add the garlic and sauté until fragrant, 2 to 3 minutes, then add the onions. Sauté for 5 minutes, then add the bell pepper and 1 tablespoon house spice. Sauté for another 5 minutes, then add the potatoes, thyme, bay leaf, 1 cup chicken stock, and a big pinch of salt. Bring to a simmer, stirring frequently, then reduce heat to low and cook for 1 hour, adding stock ½ cup at a time as the liquid evaporates. (You may not need all the stock.) As the potatoes become tender, stir gently and less frequently—you want to keep most of the potatoes from breaking up, though some will and that's okay. Don't stir at all in the last 15 minutes of cooking. The sauce should be thick and stew-like, and the potatoes should form a deep golden crust on the bottom. Taste and adjust the seasoning with salt and house spice, then serve.

ORIGIN: American South
YIELD: 4 servings

---

4 tablespoons unsalted butter

6 garlic cloves, minced

1 medium yellow onion, thinly sliced

1 red bell pepper, thinly sliced lengthwise

1 tablespoon House Spice (page 6), plus more to taste

4 large Yukon Gold potatoes (about 2 pounds total), peeled and sliced ¼ inch thick

10 fresh thyme sprigs

1 fresh bay leaf

1 quart Chicken Stock (page 33), or as needed

Kosher salt, to taste

Creole hashbrowns are best served immediately, but leftovers will keep in an airtight container in the refrigerator for up to 3 days.

RED BEAN SOFRITO

Red bean sofrito doesn't look like much more than a simple mash of unassuming beans. But this dish, eaten all throughout the Latin Caribbean region, is powerfully flavored and deceptively deep. The secret is the sofrito, that fragrant flavorful backbone of Puerto Rican and Dominican cuisine. Here the tomatoes, onions, and garlic of sofrito work their magic on another long-lasting pantry staple: the red bean. Red beans soak up all that flavor, softening during a long simmer. A touch of acidic pique at the end adds a bit of structure and kick. Often served with yellow rice—the Barack to its Michelle—red bean sofrito can stand as a side to pollo guisado or pollo asado on its own, too.

Place the beans in a bowl and cover with a few inches of water. Soak overnight, then drain well.

In a medium pot over medium heat, add the lard or olive oil. When it shimmers, add the sofrito and cook, stirring often, for 5 minutes.

Meanwhile, make a bouquet garni: Tie the cilantro, thyme, and bay leaves into a bundle with kitchen twine. Add to the pot with the sofrito, then add the beans and water to cover.

Bring the beans to a boil, then reduce the heat so the pot simmers very gently. Cover the pot and cook until the beans are tender all the way through, 1 to 3 hours, depending on how old your beans are.

Remove the bouquet garni. Season to taste with pique, lime juice, and salt, and serve immediately, or cool in the liquid until ready to use.

ORIGIN: Caribbean

YIELD: 6 cups

½ pound (2 cups) dried red kidney beans

2 tablespoons lard or olive oil

2 cups Sofrito (page 28)

6 fresh cilantro sprigs

4 fresh thyme sprigs

2 fresh bay leaves

Pique (page 26), to taste

Freshly squeezed lime juice, to taste

Kosher salt, to taste

Red bean sofrito will keep in an airtight container in the refrigerator for up to 4 days, or in the freezer for up to 2 months.

STEW PEAS

The salty, slightly tropical, totally comforting taste of stew peas, as these meat-studded kidney beans are called, will make every Jamaican think of home. They make me think of Little Jamaica in the Bronx, where my father—Nigerian on his father's side, Jamaican on his mother's—took me for Jerk Chicken (page 174), Brown Stew Chicken (page 168), oxtail, and, of course, stew peas. Similar to a Brazilian feijoada, stew peas are a classic one-pot stew, where the flavors of the salt pork, the texture of the beans, and the nuttiness of the coconut milk commingle into a flavorful meal that stretches for days.

ORIGIN: Jamaica
YIELD: 4 to 6 servings

For the stew peas
2 cups dried **kidney beans**
2 tablespoons **grapeseed oil**
3 tablespoons **GGP** (page 5)
1 medium **yellow onion**, diced
1 bunch **scallions**, white and light green parts only, thinly sliced
1½ teaspoons **House Spice** (page 6)
2 smoked **ham hocks**
½ pound **salted pig tails**
3 quarts **Chicken Stock** (page 33)
One 14-ounce can **unsweetened coconut cream**
6 fresh **thyme sprigs**
2 fresh **bay leaves**
1 **red Scotch bonnet pepper**
Kosher salt, to taste

For the dumplings
1 cup **all-purpose flour**
1 teaspoon **kosher salt**
½ cup **warm water**

Stew peas will keep in an airtight container in the refrigerator for up to 4 days, or in the freezer for up to 2 months.

For the stew peas

Place the beans in a large bowl and cover with 2 inches cold water. Soak overnight.

When ready to cook, heat the oil in a Dutch oven over medium heat. When it shimmers, add the GGP and sauté until fragrant and beginning to toast, 5 to 8 minutes. Add the onions and cook for 5 minutes more, then add the scallions. Sauté for another 5 minutes, then add all remaining ingredients except the salt. Bring to a boil, then reduce the heat to a gentle simmer. Cook for 1 hour, until the beans are almost completely tender.

For the dumplings

Stir together the flour, salt, and water in a medium bowl. Dump and knead and until elastic, 15 minutes. Then cover with plastic wrap and let rest for 20 minutes, then divide into 8 portions. Roll each into a finger-length cylinder, cover loosely with plastic wrap, and set aside.

After the beans have cooked for 1 hour, add the dumplings to the pot. Cook for another 20 minutes, or until the beans, ham hocks, and pig tails are tender and the broth has reduced to just cover the beans and meat. Shred any meat from the ham hocks and discard the bones.

Season to taste with salt and serve.

BRAISED WHITE BEANS

You can—and probably should—eat beans seven days a week in New Orleans. Hopscotch from restaurant to restaurant, from the red beans and rice at Joey K's uptown to butter beans and shrimp at Dooky Chase's, and, of course, to the braised white beans at Willie Mae's. Those buttery, garlicky beans are a classic for a reason. They're comforting, stomach filling, nutritious, and easy to make, and they are the inspiration behind this recipe. I just found out that Willie Mae's version is vegan, which impressed the hell out of me, but in my version I've gone to the old southern ace in a hole, bacon and ham hock, to add even more flavor. The key here, as in any braise, is to keep the heat low and slow. Most of the time it takes to make these is passive, except for the brief flurry of activity as you eat them in all of seven minutes flat.

Heat the oil in a large pot over medium heat. When it shimmers, add the bacon and cook, stirring frequently, until just starting to brown, about 3 minutes. Add the onions, garlic, bell peppers, and celery. Cook, stirring, until beginning to soften, about 5 minutes.

Stir in the beans, ham hock, thyme, and bay leaves, then add enough stock to just cover the bean mixture. Bring to a simmer over medium heat. Simmer gently, adjusting the heat as necessary, until the beans are completely tender and the stock is reduced, as little as 1 hour and up to 3 hours, depending on how old your beans are. If the liquid seems to be reducing too quickly, top off with a little vegetable stock or water.

Remove from the heat and discard the thyme sprigs and bay leaves. Remove the ham hock and use a fork to shred any meat into the pot and discard the bone. Season with house spice and salt to taste, then serve over hot rice.

ORIGIN: American South
YIELD: 6 cups (4 to 6 servings)

2 tablespoons grapeseed oil

2 slices bacon, diced

1 medium yellow onion, diced

10 garlic cloves, minced

1 green bell pepper, diced

1 stalk celery, diced

2 cups dried navy beans, soaked overnight and drained

1 smoked ham hock

3 fresh thyme sprigs

2 bay leaves

1 quart Vegetable Stock (page 36), plus more as needed

House Spice (page 6), to taste

Kosher salt, to taste

Braised white beans will keep in an airtight container in the refrigerator for up to 4 days, or in the freezer for up to 2 months.

CHANNA (CHICKPEA CURRY)

Chickpeas, or channa, are another Indian influence felt in Trini cooking. They are the star filling of Trini sandwiches made with Dhal Puri Roti (page 239) and often paired with potatoes, or aloo. Here it's the addition of the green seasoning, with its culantro kick, that gives the curry its uniquely West Indian profile. I could eat bowls of channa curry on its own, but I love it best when sandwiched between two crisp pieces of curry-scented bara to form a double.

In a medium pot over medium heat, heat the oil. When it shimmers, add the onions and sauté until translucent, 5 to 7 minutes.

Add the GGP and green seasoning and cook, stirring often, until the color deepens and the flavor mellows, about 10 minutes. Add the curry powder and cook for 2 minutes more, then stir in the chickpeas and the vegetable stock.

Bring to a simmer over medium heat and simmer gently until the sauce thickens, 15 to 20 minutes. Season with salt to taste.

ORIGIN: Trinidad and Tobago
YIELD: 1 quart (4 servings)

2 tablespoons **grapeseed oil**

2 small **yellow onions**, diced

¼ cup **GGP** (page 5)

½ cup **Green Seasoning** (page 29)

2 teaspoons **Curry Powder** (page 10)

Two 15-ounce cans **chickpeas**, drained and rinsed

2 cups **Vegetable Stock** (page 36)

Kosher salt, to taste

Channa will keep in an airtight container in the refrigerator for up to 4 days, or in the freezer for up to 2 months.

MOI MOI

Black-eyed peas made their way from West Africa to the Caribbean and to the American South—and then to Fergie and from Fergie to your ears forever—thanks to their nutritiousness and versatility. (Yes, they're beans, not peas, but both are legumes.) What we call black-eyed peas are descendants of cowpeas and still called that in much of Africa. In Nigeria, they're made into this dense yet tender pudding and sold on street corners. Steamed bean purée might sound bland, but moi moi—also spelled moin moin—is really a vehicle for flavor. Some people—many people, actually—add everything from hard-boiled eggs to sardines in the center, but I prefer the trifecta of GGP, Maggi, and peppa sauce. Moi moi should be firm, and springy but not rubbery, and it's a lot of labor to get it just right, but, once you do, you won't regret it. I've included here both the more traditional method of wrapping the moi moi in banana leaf and the somewhat easier method of simply steaming it in ramekins.

ORIGIN: Nigeria

YIELD: 6 servings

---

2 cups (½ pound) dried **black-eyed peas**

1 small **red bell pepper**, roughly chopped

½ small **red onion**, roughly chopped

1½ tablespoons **GGP** (page 5)

7 **Maggi Seasoning cubes**

1½ teaspoons **Peppa Sauce** (page 25)

½ cup **palm oil**

Kosher salt, to taste

½ pound **banana leaves** (optional), wiped clean

Moi moi will keep tightly covered or in an airtight container in the refrigerator for up to 4 days.

Soak the black-eyed peas overnight in a quart of water. The next day, drain the peas and rinse vigorously, then transfer to a blender. Add enough water that there is twice as much water as there are peas, then pulse 8 to 10 times, until the skins begin to slip off. Transfer the peas to a large bowl, cover with fresh water by a few inches, and stir vigorously with your hands to loosen the skins further; they should float to the surface. Carefully pour out the water over a strainer, making sure the peas stay in the bowl while the skins drain away. Repeat this rinsing and stirring process 3 to 4 times, or until the skins have all been removed.

Return the peeled peas to the blender along with ¼ cup + 1 tablespoon water, the bell peppers, onions, GGP, Maggi, and peppa sauce. Purée until completely smooth. With moi moi, texture is key, so if it's not totally smooth, keep blending. With the blender running, slowly stream in the oil until combined. Season to taste with salt.

To cook, divide the mixture between six 6-ounce heatproof rame-kins and cover each tightly with foil. Set in a pot large enough to hold the ramekins in an even layer and carefully pour in enough water to come halfway up the sides of the ramekins.

Alternately, cook the moi moi in banana leaves: If the leaves are very large, trim them into 15-x-20-inch sheets. Hold a leaf so there is a corner pointing straight up. Fold the left corner toward the leaf's center, rolling the leaf into a cone shape that is →

mostly closed at the bottom and open at the top; the seam of the cone should be along the back. Fold the bottom point of the cone backward over the seam to seal it. (If your cone has any holes, patch it with a small piece of another leaf.) Fill the cone with about ¾ cup batter, then fold the top over to seal: Fold one side of the opening over the filling, then the other side, then fold the leaf back so the package is sealed and the folded top and bottom "flaps" are on the same side (which should be the seam side). Set the rolled banana leaves seam side down in a single layer in a steamer basket. →

Bring the water to a simmer over medium heat, then reduce the heat to medium-low, cover tightly with the pot's lid, and steam until fully set, 35 to 45 minutes. A knife inserted into the center of the moi moi should come out clean. If you've cooked the moi moi in banana leaves, the packages should be firm enough to lift out of the pot without falling apart while still soft enough to have some give; they'll continue to firm up as they cool.

Carefully remove the foil from the ramekins (or unwrap the banana leaves) and serve immediately with Obe Ata Din Din (page 22) and/or Peppa Sauce (page 25).

YEKIK ALICHA

Washington, D.C., has the largest Ethiopian population in the United States. That's one of the reasons I opened Gorsha, an Ethiopian fast-casual concept in Union Market, with my friend Hiyaw Gebreyo-hannes. One of the first things I discovered as Hiyaw and I ate our way through Little Ethiopia is how the pleasure of an Ethiopian meal is based on searingly spicy food. On one side are the hearty meat stews or wats, bursting with berbere. Counterbalancing these are injera, the soft sourdough bread and perhaps the best extinguisher of heat, as well as the bright yellow split peas of yekik alicha. It is the turmeric, an import from India in the ninth century, that gives the split peas their neon brightness. (Ethiopia is the largest exporter of turmeric in Africa.)

In a medium pot over medium heat, heat the NKO. Add the onions and sauté until translucent, about 5 minutes. Add the GGP and sauté for 5 minutes more, stirring constantly. Add the turmeric and cook for 2 minutes. Note: Make sure to stir constantly when the turmeric is added, as it can burn easily and become bitter.

Add the split peas and sauté for 5 minutes, then stir in 2 cups water and the salt. Bring to a simmer and cook until split peas are fully tender, 30 to 45 minutes, adding more water as needed if the pot seems dry. Season with salt to taste.

ORIGIN: Ethiopia
YIELD: 4 servings

2 tablespoons **NKO** (page 21)
½ medium **yellow onion**, diced
¼ cup **GGP** (page 5)
1 teaspoon ground **turmeric**
½ pound (¾ cup + 2 tablespoons) **yellow split peas**
1 teaspoon **kosher salt**, plus more to taste

Yekik alicha will keep in an airtight container in the refrigerator for up to 4 days, or in the freezer for up to 2 months.

FUFU

Cassava came to Nigeria, where it is perhaps the most important staple crop, via Portuguese settlers who had discovered the tuberous root in Brazil in the sixteenth century. Later on, in the early nineteenth century, formerly enslaved Nigerians from Brazil returned home, and popularized cassava in the kitchen. Today Nigeria is the world's largest producer of cassava, a crop so embedded in Nigerian life it finds itself in everything from glue to pharmaceuticals and, of course, in the kitchen, as flour, paste, and, here, a swallow. A swallow is a genre of Nigerian food that helps you, well, swallow. It soaks up stews and pads out meals and keeps those who might need to be full for a long time full. There are many swallows, made of starchy foods like plantains, sorghum, rice hulls, yams, and, of course, cassava. Though it looks like a bao—smooth, white, perfectly round—fufu is much heavier, with a consistency of very firm mashed potatoes. No bowl of Egusi Stew with Goat (page 227) or Groundnut Stew (page 112) is complete without fufu.

ORIGIN: Nigeria
YIELD: 4 servings

2 cups of **fufu flour**
4 cups **water**
1 teaspoon of **kosher salt**

Fufu is best served immediately.

In a small saucepan whisk the flour into the water in increments until smooth. Heat over medium heat, add salt, and then stir constantly with a wooden spoon, making sure to scrape the bottom of the pot. Cook for 15 minutes or until the dough starts to grow firm. Remove from heat. Wet your hands with room-temperature water and then form the fufu into a small ball, about 4–6 inches in diameter, and place on a plate. Continue until all the dough is used up. (You should have about 8–9 4-inch balls or 2–3 6-inch ones.) Serve immediately or wrap tightly in plastic wrap and reserve for later use. If using later, microwave for about 60 seconds, until warmed through, before serving.

GROUNDNUT STEW

Like cassava, groundnuts, a family of legumes that includes peanuts, originally arrived on the Gold Coast of Africa sometime in the 1500s, aboard Portuguese ships from Brazil, where they are endemic. They quickly became a massive international export in French-controlled West Africa. Much of the processing of peanuts into, for instance, oil, was discouraged by tariffs, so the wealth was extracted from Africa in the form of raw material and sent abroad for more lucrative processing. The peanut made its return trip across the Atlantic to the American South, aboard slave ships carrying Africans. It grew plentifully, and some, like the great agricultural scientist George Washington Carver, saw it as a form of economic liberation from the tyranny of cotton.

But peanuts never made their way into my family's cooking. My first real experience, and still my most precious memories, of groundnut stew was from trips with my mom down to Le Petit Senegal on 116th between Lenox and Frederick Douglass Avenue in Harlem. There restaurants serve intensely flavorful red stews thickened with peanut butter, called groundnut stew, or sometimes peanut stew. Hopping from one to the other, we found places that added beef, or chicken, or lamb, and others that served vegetarian versions. But at them all, the thick rich nuttiness of the peanuts shone through brilliantly.

ORIGIN: Nigeria/Ghana/Senegal

YIELD: 4 servings

---

4 cross-cut **beef shanks**

Kosher salt, to taste

Freshly ground **black pepper**, to taste

2 tablespoons **grapeseed oil**

½ cup **GGP** (page 5)

2 **red onions**, thinly sliced

4 **Roma tomatoes**, cut into ½-inch dice

1½ cups **smooth unsalted natural peanut butter**, well stirred

1½ cups **Oba Ata Din Din** (page 22)

6 cups **Chicken Stock** (page 33)

5 **Maggi Seasoning cubes**, crushed

2 teaspoons **Peppa Sauce** (page 25)

2 teaspoons **crayfish powder**

Groundnut stew will keep in an airtight container in the refrigerator for up to 4 days, or in the freezer for up to 2 months.

Heat the oven to 300°F.

Season the beef shanks generously with salt and black pepper and let sit at room temperature for 20 minutes.

Heat the oil in a Dutch oven over medium-high heat. When it shimmers, add the beef shanks and sear on all sides until deeply browned, about 4 minutes per side. Remove to a bowl and set aside.

Reduce the heat to medium-low and add GGP. Cook, stirring constantly, until fragrant and just starting to toast, 5 minutes. Add the red onions and tomatoes and cook for 10 minutes more, then stir in the peanut butter, oba ata din din, stock, Maggi, peppa sauce, and crayfish powder. Return the beef shanks to the pot and bring to a boil.

Cover the pot and place in the oven for 2 hours, then remove and return to the stove over medium heat. Simmer for another hour, partially covered, stirring occasionally until the sauce thickens.

Season to taste with salt, then serve with Fufu (page 111).

SWEET POTATO VELOUTÉ WITH CRAB SALAD

Comb through the archives of recipes from Africa or the American South and you won't find velouté, a French "mother sauce," made light with cream and milk. Practically speaking, both were expensive in the American South and rare in Africa. But to me this velouté perfectly represents diasporic cooking. Why? Back before I got anywhere close to appearing on television, I had the opportunity to cook for a television producer, a white woman. I was excited and pulled out all the stops, trying to show her my prowess as a chef—and, I think, I succeeded. A velouté was one of the dishes I prepared, along with port-glazed quail and a brussels sprout petal salad. Her response was that though she enjoyed her meal enormously, America wasn't yet ready, in her opinion, for a Black chef who didn't cook "Black food." Though this book is largely dedicated to recipes many Black Americans will recognize from their own homes, either in their finished form or as the descendants of an older dish (as Jambalaya, page 59, is to Jollof Rice, page 57), this recipe is a reminder that there should be no limits to what so-called Black food can be, certainly none erected by out-group gatekeepers. Plus, for what it's worth, the luxurious creaminess of this autumnal velouté, spiced with a bit of Creole crab salad, is one of the recipes I'm most proud of developing. It's easy to make, yet contains so many levels of flavor.

ORIGIN: France

YIELD: 4 servings

For the velouté

2 tablespoons grapeseed oil

3 medium yellow onions, thinly sliced

15 garlic cloves, minced

15 fresh sage sprigs

30 fresh thyme sprigs

3 cups heavy cream

3 cups whole milk

2 pounds sweet potatoes, peeled and diced

Kosher salt, to taste

For the crab salad

2 tablespoons unsalted butter

1 cup (8 ounces) jumbo lump crab, well drained and picked through

2 tablespoons Remoulade (page 19)

Sweet potato velouté (without the crab) will keep in an airtight container in the refrigerator for up to 5 days, or in the freezer for up to 2 months. Crab salad is best served immediately.

For the velouté

Heat the oil in a large pot over medium-low heat. When it shimmers, add the onions and cook gently, stirring often, until very soft, dark, and sweet, 25 to 30 minutes. Reduce the heat to low as needed to keep from burning.

Add the garlic and cook for another 7 to 10 minutes, stirring often, until fragrant. Using kitchen twine, tie the sage and thyme into a bouquet garni. Add them to the pot along with the cream, milk, and sweet potatoes.

Bring to a simmer over medium heat, then reduce to medium-low and cook until the sweet potatoes are completely tender, 5 to 10 minutes. Remove from the heat, then remove the herb bundle, squeezing out any liquid, and discard.

Let the velouté mixture cool slightly, then transfer to a blender and purée on high until velvety smooth. Strain through a fine-mesh sieve, then season to taste with salt. Return to the pot and heat gently until hot.

For the crab salad

While the velouté mixture warms, make the crab salad: Melt the butter in a medium pan over medium heat. Add the crab and cook, stirring occasionally, for 5 minutes, until warm and browned in places. Remove from the heat and stir in the remoulade.

To serve, divide the crab salad between 4 shallow bowls, piling it in the center of each bowl. Pour the hot velouté around the crab and enjoy immediately.

MISIR WAT

Flavor is layered at every step of this hearty lentil stew. It starts with sautéing the onions in NKO, continues with the addition of GGP, then bursts into Technicolor with a mix of spices and spice blends including berbere, the fiery Ethiopian mixture; paprika; cardamom; and my own addition: House Spice. This all forms the backdrop against which the lentils are gently simmered. The process is straightforward, but the result is a complex suite of flavors that build in heat and intensity with each delicious bite.

In a medium pot, heat NKO over medium heat. When it shimmers, add the onions and sauté until translucent, 5 to 7 minutes. Add the GGP and cook, stirring constantly, another 5 minutes.

Stir in the tomato paste, paprika, berbere, house spice, and cardamom and cook, stirring frequently, until the mixture is very aromatic and the tomato paste has darkened, 5 to 7 minutes.

Add the lentils and 5 cups water and bring to a boil. Reduce heat to low to maintain a gentle simmer. Cook for 20 minutes, until the lentils are completely tender and thickened, then remove from the heat and season with salt to taste.

ORIGIN: Ethiopia
YIELD: 6 cups (4 to 6 servings)

¼ cup NKO (page 21)
1 cup diced yellow onions (about 1 small onion)
5 tablespoons GGP (page 5)
2 tablespoons tomato paste
3 teaspoons sweet paprika
3 teaspoons Berbere (page 9)
2 teaspoons House Spice (page 6)
½ teaspoon ground cardamom
1 cup dried red lentils
Kosher salt, to taste

Misir wat will keep in an airtight container in the refrigerator for up to 4 days, or in the freezer for up to 2 months.

SEAFOOD
AND
SHELLFISH

Fish, shrimp, crawfish, lobsters, and crabs are the kings and queens of the kitchens of my ancestors, especially those from the American South. Seafood Gumbo (page 138), the crown jewel of southern stews and the most joyful chord of my childhood, rests on the mantle of shellfish. In fact, all permutations of shrimp, from peel-and-eat to smothered in roux, are present and accounted for in the cooking of my mother and her family, who hail from along the southern Louisiana coast. The same is true of the Geechee Gullah cooking of the eastern coast of South Carolina, up to North Carolina and down to northern Florida. Shrimp and grits, the Lowcountry staple, combines the shrimp from the marshes and the corn from the low-lying fields.

Their importance is a direct result of the fact that shrimp (and fish) were plentiful in the waterways that course through the South, waterways that my ancestors could in their rare "free" time draw from for precious food to supplement their rations. For those who made fishing their livelihoods, during the years of enslavement, federally issued Seamen's Protection Certificates, originally meant to prevent American sailors from being gang-pressed into British service, served as a back door to freedom—since the papers designated black fishermen as citizens before the Constitution did. After nominal freedom came, many turned toward the ocean to make a living.

There's a long and storied history of Black fishermen, oyster-men, and shrimpers on the Gulf Coast, pursuits that didn't require an immense amount of capital and could be done on a small scale. (Sadly, they were replaced in the twentieth century by mechanized, well-funded operations.)

As with so many foodways, the love of crustaceans traveled north in the Great Migration. Fish fries spread everywhere Black families settled. Today gumbo can be gotten—although in vary-ing quality—nearly everywhere. But to me, New Orleans, Baton Rouge, and Beaumont, Texas, still embody seafood in its highest form: the tumble of a Crawfish Boil (page 127) on newspaper, the still-steaming crimson bodies, the almost fluorescent yellow ears of corn, the overwhelming smell of Creole seasoning mixed with the smell of the sea. As in many Cajun and Creole homes—not to mention New England or Chesapeake homes, where crawfish are replaced by crabs or lobster—all this is followed by the chaos of grabbing as many as you can as quickly as you can before my cousins, aunties, and uncles do. We're a tight family, but all bets are off around a boil. In my mom's kitchen, the smell of shrimp bodies simmering into stock will always bring me back to Baton Rouge, just as crisp Fried Catfish (page 132) returns me to Sunday fish fries, which have deep roots in the Black church, and immedi-ately bring memories of folding chairs and neighborhood gossip.

Catfish, in turn, is a bridge back to West Africa, where the fish is prized, smoked or fresh, in Gambian tradition. In my own Nigeria, although small-scale fishermen do stock the bustling fish markets on the coast, fish never played a huge role in the national cuisine. Still today, Nigerians, despite their coastal territory, consume little fish per capita. Much of what they do consume is dried, as in dried sardines and stockfish, also called saltfish or salt cod. Across the Atlantic, in the Caribbean, where seafood is widely available, saltfish makes its presence felt in Ackee and Saltfish (page 149), Jamaica's national dish, and buljol, a Trini saltfish salad. That the fish, dried Atlantic cod from Norway, originally made its way from Europe to the Caribbean largely as provisions for Africans in no way affects how beloved it has become. Mornings in Jamaica belong to ackee and saltfish. Lunches in Trinidad to buljol. Family gatherings in Baton Rouge to gumbo. And my soul to shrimp, crawfish, lobster, and crab.

LOBSTER REMOULADE SLIDERS

Remoulade, a spicy mustard-mayonnaise mixture with French origins and a Creole heart, is both a sauce and a base. In this preparation, it's the latter, binding what is, in my opinion, the best lobster salad in the world. These sliders are basically southern lobster rolls, but amped up with house spice. In the summer, I often make the remoulade the night before, letting the flavors deepen overnight in the refrigerator, then toast the coco bread and let my friends build their own sandwiches.

ORIGIN: American South
YIELD: 8 servings

For the lobster remoulade
Two 1¼-pound live lobsters
1 cup (8 ounces) jumbo lump crab
⅔ cup Remoulade (page 19)
Freshly squeezed lemon juice, to taste
House Spice (page 6), to taste
Kosher salt, to taste

For the house sauce
¼ cup Hellmann's mayonnaise
2 teaspoons ketchup
2 teaspoons RGP (page 11)
½ teaspoon House Spice (page 6)
¼ teaspoon kosher salt

To assemble
¼ cup parsley leaves
Zest of 2 lemons
8 pieces Coco Bread (page 236), halved lengthwise
8 teaspoons unsalted butter, softened
1 cup shredded romaine lettuce
½ cup house sauce

Lobster remoulade (unassembled) will keep in an airtight container in the refrigerator for up to 1 day.

For the lobster remoulade

Fill a large pot all but 4 inches full with generously salted water and bring to a boil over high heat. When it boils, add the lobsters one by one, then cover. Boil for 9 minutes, flipping the lobster halfway through. Immediately transfer the lobsters to a bowl of ice water to stop the cooking.

When cool enough to handle, remove the claws and set aside. Cut the body in half lengthwise. Being careful to leave the halved lobster body intact (you'll serve the salad in it later), pick out the meat from the body and claws and finely chop. You should have 1 cup finely chopped lobster meat (about ½ pound).

In a large bowl, gently fold together the lobster meat, crab, and remoulade. Adjust the seasoning with lemon juice, house spice, and salt, then cover and reserve in the refrigerator until ready to serve (up to a day).

To assemble

Garnish the lobster with parsley leaves and lemon zest. Spread each piece of coco bread with a teaspoon of softened butter, then lightly toast in a large pan set over medium heat (butter side down). Serve the lobster remoulade with the bread, shredded lettuce, and house sauce for building sliders.

CURRIED CRAB RUN DOWN

The street vendors around Heroes Circle in Kingston, Jamaica, hawk their wares with shouts and cries, but the real advertising is done by sight and smell. The claws of crabs caught in the waters that surround the island, mixed with the sweetness of coconut milk, are impossible to resist. I felt that the first time I visited Jamaica, as a child with my father, eating curried crab run down in the passenger seat of a car, and recently, when I returned for a culinary exploration (page 158). The combination of coconut milk, curry, and crab is a tradition handed down by the Indian laborers who arrived in Jamaica in the nineteenth century and have stayed ever since, adding their curries and spices. Often just called curried crab, the run down, or rondón (the name refers to the coconut milk, which reduces to a creamy consistency), can also be made with snapper, mackerel, cod, or other seafood. But crab remains my favorite, best served with some sort of sopping carb, be it rice, coco bread, or tostones.

ORIGIN: Jamaica
YIELD: 4 servings

4 live blue crabs

2 tablespoons grapeseed oil

1 medium **yellow onion,** halved and thinly sliced

1 medium **green bell pepper,** thinly sliced lengthwise

¾ cup **Green Seasoning** (page 29)

3 tablespoons palm sugar

2 tablespoons **Curry Powder** (page 10)

1½ tablespoons **House Spice** (page 6)

1 cup **Shrimp Stock** (page 37)

One 13.5-ounce can **coconut milk**

1 tablespoon **Peppa Sauce** (page 25)

1 tablespoon **kosher salt,** plus more to taste

2 limes

Curried crab is best served immediately.

Place the live crabs in the freezer for 30 minutes—this will knock them out so that they won't move around (or feel much) when it's time to kill them. Working one at a time, remove a cold crab from the freezer and place it on its back on a cutting board. Break off the flap (aka the apron) at the back of the shell. This will leave a hole; place your thumb in the hole and lift up firmly, which should make the carapace break away. Use a spoon to scrape out the guts, then rinse thoroughly. Use a large sharp knife (or a cleaver if you have one) to cut right down the middle of the crab. Repeat with the remaining crabs.

In a Dutch oven, heat the oil over medium-high heat. Add the onions and bell peppers and sauté until the onions are beginning to turn translucent, about 7 minutes. Stir in the green seasoning and sauté for 5 minutes, then add the palm sugar, curry powder, and house spice and cook for 5 minutes more.

Stir in the shrimp stock, coconut milk, peppa sauce, and 1 table-spoon salt. Bring the mixture to a boil, then reduce to a simmer and add the crabs. Cook for 12 minutes, stirring frequently, until the crabs are bright red and fully cooked. Squeeze in the juice of one lime, then taste. Add more lime juice and salt as needed.

Serve immediately, with Perfectly Steamed Rice (page 46), Coco Bread (page 236), Tostones (page 77), and/or Sweet Plantains (page 79).

CHARRED MACKEREL

Nigerians love their mackerel, which they call Titus fish, and they prefer it *spicy* in the sense of heat (thanks to the Scotch bonnet–laden obe ata din din and the cayenne) and *spiced* as in cumin and paprika. Here I temper the heat of the nigesco (thanks to Martel, one of my sous, for the punny nickname), a Nigerian spin on romesco sauce, with the tart sweetness of pickled grapes and a good char to give the dish balance. When I lived in Nigeria and when I return now to visit, it saddens me to know that though we have more than five hundred miles of coastline, the vast majority of mackerel is imported. Without governmental support, most Nigerian fishermen lack the resources to compete with the industrial fishing companies in the United States and Europe. Of course, there are some amazing fish markets like the Epe Market, which represent, I hope, the future of a homegrown fishing industry and offer thousands of species of local fish worth exploring.

ORIGIN: Nigeria
YIELD: 2 servings

For the nigesco sauce
2 tablespoons extra-virgin olive oil, divided
2 cups Obe Ata Din Din (page 22)
¼ cup raw Marcona almonds
2 teaspoons RGP (page 11)
1 teaspoon sweet paprika
1 teaspoon cayenne
½ teaspoon ground cumin
2 teaspoons sherry vinegar
Kosher salt, to taste

For the pickled white grapes and chilies
1 cup Spice Pickling Liquid (page 32), divided
10 green grapes, quartered
2 Fresno chilies (or other fruity, medium-heat red chilies), stemmed, seeded, and thinly sliced into rings

For the nigesco sauce

In a medium heavy-bottomed pot, heat 1 tablespoon olive oil over medium heat. Add the obe ata din din and simmer, stirring frequently, until brick red, the texture of tomato paste, and reduced to ¾ cup, about 20 minutes.

While the sauce reduces, heat the oven to 400°F. Spread the almonds on a sheet pan and toast for 5 minutes, until shiny and lightly toasted, shaking the pan halfway through. Transfer 3 tablespoons toasted almonds to a blender and blend. Roughly chop the remaining nuts and set aside to use as garnish.

Combine the reduced sauce, the ground toasted almonds, RGP, paprika, cayenne, cumin, vinegar, and the remaining 1 tablespoon olive oil in a blender and purée until smooth. Taste and adjust seasoning, then set aside.

For the pickled white grapes and chilies

Bring the spice pickling liquid to a boil in a small pot. Place the grapes in one small nonreactive container and the sliced chilies in another. Divide the hot spice pickling liquid between the two containers. Let cool for 1 hour, then refrigerate until cooled completely, at least 1 hour more.

For the charred mackerel

Heat the broiler to high and move the oven rack as close to the broiler as possible.

Pat the mackerel dry. Line a sheet tray with foil, then grease the foil and set the mackerel fillets on top, skin side up. Drizzle each fillet with a tablespoon of olive oil and season well with salt. Broil the mackerel, leaving the oven door cracked slightly, for 6 minutes, until blackened. You're looking for a good char here, so if your broiler isn't very strong, you can do this step in a pan on the stove: Heat 2 tablespoons of oil in a large nonstick pan over high heat until shimmering, then reduce the heat to medium-high and add the mackerel skin side down. Cook, pressing on the fish with a spatula periodically to keep it from curling, for 3 minutes, then carefully flip the fish and cook for 2 minutes more.

To assemble

While the mackerel is cooking, warm the nigesco sauce in a small saucepan over low heat.

Spoon the warm sauce over the surface of a single large plate. Place the broiled mackerel over the sauce, then garnish with the pickled grapes and chilies, herbs, and chopped almonds. Serve immediately with the Jollof Rice.

For the charred mackerel
2 **mackerel fillets** (about 8 ounces each)

2 tablespoons **extra-virgin olive oil**, plus more for greasing

Kosher salt, to taste

To assemble
¾ cup **nigesco sauce** (above)

3 tablespoons **pickled white grapes** (above)

1 tablespoon **pickled chilies** (above)

10 fresh **parsley leaves**

10 fresh **cilantro leaves**

Jollof Rice (page 57)

1 tablespoon toasted **Marcona almonds** (above), roughly chopped

---

Charred mackerel is best served immediately. The sauce may be made up to 3 days ahead, and the pickled grapes and chilies may be made up to 1 day ahead; both should be stored in airtight containers in the refrigerator.

CRAWFISH BOIL

Spring is crawfish season in Louisiana, a season marked by the sounds of buckets of bright red crawdads being spilled onto newspaper-lined tables and the ensuing scramble to eat them. Though Native Americans have been catching and eating crawfish in the freshwater streams and lakes of southern Louisiana for hundreds, if not thousands, of years, it was the Arcadians, exiled Canadians turned Cajuns, who popularized these creatures, the closest thing they could find to their beloved Nova Scotian lobster. Today, most of Louisiana's crawfish are farm raised, many by rice farmers who raise crawfish in their rice paddies. Even among friends and family, it is generally understood that it's a free-for-all as soon as the bodies tumble out onto the table. Grab the biggest ones you can, twist their bodies in half, and suck the yellow "fat" from the tail and the juice from the head. Repeat until there's none left, then wait for next spring.

Bring 5 gallons of water to a boil in an extra-large (at least 24-quart) pot. Add all ingredients except for the crawfish, squeezing in the juice of the lemons and oranges before adding the fruit itself.

Boil, covered, until the potatoes are nearly fork tender, about 30 minutes, then add the crawfish. Stir well to combine, then turn off the heat. Leave the crawfish in the broth to soak for 30 minutes before serving. Meanwhile, in anticipation of the boil, line an easily cleaned dining table with newspaper.

Remove the crawfish, potatoes, andouille, and corn from the pot and spread over the newspaper. Sprinkle with house spice.

Enjoy immediately.

ORIGIN: American South
YIELD: 6 to 8 servings

3 pounds golf-ball-sized Yukon Gold potatoes

7 andouille sausages, cut into thirds

5 ears **corn**, husked and quartered

1½ cups **House Spice** (page 6)

3 cups **Louisiana-Style Hot Sauce** (page 23)

¼ cup **white granulated sugar**

1 head **garlic**, halved crosswise

1½ ounces (about 2 large bunches) fresh **thyme sprigs**

5 **lemons**, halved crosswise

5 **oranges**, halved crosswise

5 pounds **live crawfish**

House Spice (page 6), to taste

CRAWFISH PIE

There are basically two ways of eating crawfish. One is fresh. The crawfish are boiled in an aromatic broth along with andouille, corn, and potatoes and then deposited in a large bright red pile, often on newspaper, with everyone fighting for as many crawfish as possible. That's a Crawfish Boil (page 127). The other is to use their tender meat in another preparation which leads to, on the whole, a more peaceful meal. Into the latter category goes this pie, a touchstone of Cajun and Creole kitchens. Basically an étouffée en croute, the pie swathes the spicy, bright flavors of the crawfish (plus the Holy Trinity of onions, bell peppers, and celery, and house spice, of course) in a flaky warm pie crust. Though a little less chaotic than the scramble of a boil, every time I make this for my family there's always fighting for a second serving.

ORIGIN: American South
YIELD: One 9-inch pie

For the pie filling
4 tablespoons unsalted butter
¼ cup all-purpose flour
½ medium yellow onion, diced
1 celery stalk, diced
½ large green bell pepper, diced
3 garlic cloves, roughly chopped
2 teaspoons House Spice (page 6)
1 fresh bay leaf
2 fresh thyme sprigs
1 teaspoon kosher salt, plus more to taste
2 cups cold Shrimp Stock (page 37)
2 tablespoons finely grated (or microplaned) Parmigiano Reggiano cheese
¼ cup shredded cheddar cheese
1 pound cooked crawfish tail meat

For the pie filling

In a large, heavy-bottomed pot, melt the butter over medium-high heat until foamy. Add the flour, then reduce the heat to medium-low and whisk mixture to a smooth, toasty-smelling paste, 1 to 2 minutes.

Add the onions, celery, bell peppers, and garlic. Sauté until the vegetables have begun to soften, about 6 minutes, then add the house spice, bay leaf, thyme, and 1 teaspoon salt. Cook for 1 minute more.

Whisking constantly, gradually add the shrimp stock to the pot. Cook, stirring often, until the sauce has reduced by half, about 15 minutes—it should be thick enough that your wooden spoon leaves a line behind it. Fold in the cheeses and taste, adjusting the salt as needed, then stir in the crawfish. Let cool slightly, then refrigerate until ready to assemble the pie (up to overnight), as it is essential that the filling be totally cooled.

For the dough

Place the flour, as well as the bowl and blade of your food processor, and a mixing bowl, in the freezer for 20 minutes. After 20 minutes, assemble the food processor, then add the flour and salt and pulse to combine. Add 8 tablespoons butter and shortening and pulse to a coarse meal. (The butter should now be in dime-sized pieces.) Transfer the mixture to the cold mixing bowl and add the ice water a tablespoon at a time, mixing gently with a rubber spatula until the dough begins to come together in large clumps. Knead the mixture a few times until it forms a smooth dough. If it's sticky, sprinkle in a bit more flour; if it doesn't come together, add a bit more water.

Cut the dough in half, flatten each half into a disc, and wrap them individually in plastic wrap. Refrigerate for at least 1 hour and up to overnight.

To assemble: Heat the oven to 400°F. Beat together the egg and milk in a small bowl to make an egg wash and set aside. Grease a 9-inch pie plate with the remaining 2 teaspoons butter.

On a lightly floured surface, roll one of the discs of pie dough into an ⅛-inch-thick circle. (Keep the other half of the dough in the fridge.) Transfer to the greased pie plate—the pie dough should hang over the dish's edge. Press the dough against the sides of the dish lightly to adhere, then add the crawfish filling. Roll out the second disc of pie dough and place it over the filling. Use a floured fork to crimp the dough all the way around the edge of the dish, then use scissors or a paring knife to trim away any excess dough. Use a sharp knife to trim a 1-inch slit in the top crust to allow steam to escape. Set the pie on a sheet pan.

Brush the pie with the egg wash and bake for 20 minutes, then reduce the heat to 350°F and bake for 20 to 25 minutes more, or until the pie is golden brown and crisp. If the edges or any part of the top crust are browning too quickly, tent them with foil. Let cool for 10 minutes, then serve.

For the dough

2¾ cups **all-purpose flour,** plus more as needed for dusting

1½ teaspoons **kosher salt**

8 tablespoons cold **unsalted butter,** cut into cubes, plus 2 teaspoons at room temperature for greasing the pie plate

¾ cup **vegetable shortening,** cold, diced

½ cup **ice water**

1 **egg**

1½ teaspoons **whole milk**

Crawfish pie is best the day it's made.

SALMON CAKES

Sunday mornings growing up meant salmon cakes, grits, and fresh biscuits on the table. Though the week was (usually) hard—frayed nerves and stretched budgets in small spaces yielded frequent conflict—Sunday morning was a balm. At the heart of these brunches were my mom's salmon cakes, crunchy on the outside but yielding within, whose smell sizzling in the pan often woke me up. Though she used canned salmon—and you can too in a pinch—the flavors of the Holy Trinity of onions, bell peppers, and celery, plus house spice, turned the fish, which can at times be almost a non-flavor, into a flavorful, lively, and memorable Creole centerpiece. Topped with remoulade and a dash of Calypso sauce, salmon cakes were the best part of my Sunday mornings, though now, as an adult, I'm free both to use fresh salmon and to cook them for easy lunches or dinners any day of the week.

For the roasted salmon

Heat the oven to 350°F. Set the salmon on a parchment-lined sheet tray and season with house spice, salt, and olive oil. Roast for 15 minutes or until the fish flakes easily with a fork, then set aside to cool. Reserve the sheet pan.

For the salmon cakes

Heat a medium pan over medium heat and add 2 tablespoons oil. Add the garlic and sauté until fragrant, 2 to 3 minutes, then add the onions, bell peppers, celery, thyme, and bay leaf. Cook, stirring occasionally, until the vegetables are tender, about 10 minutes. Remove and discard the thyme and bay leaf and transfer the vegetables to a medium bowl. Let cool slightly.

To the bowl with the vegetables add the salmon, breaking up the fillet into small pieces as you add it, along with the eggs, mayonnaise, house spice, breadcrumbs, Worcestershire sauce, parsley, lemon juice, and salt. Fold together gently until combined.

ORIGIN: American South
YIELD: 4 servings

For the roasted salmon
One 1-pound **salmon fillet**, skinned
1 tablespoon **House Spice** (page 6)
1 teaspoon **kosher salt**
2 tablespoons **extra-virgin olive oil**

For the salmon cakes
3 tablespoons **grapeseed oil**, divided, plus more as needed
2 **garlic cloves**, minced
½ medium **yellow onion**, finely diced
½ **green bell pepper**, finely diced
1 stalk **celery**, minced
2 fresh **thyme sprigs**
1 fresh **bay leaf**
1 pound **roasted salmon** (above)
2 **eggs**
2 tablespoons **mayonnaise**
2 teaspoons **House Spice** (page 6)
½ cup **panko breadcrumbs**
1 tablespoon **Worcestershire sauce**
1 tablespoon roughly chopped fresh **parsley**
Juice of 1 lemon
2 teaspoons **kosher salt**

Fry the salmon cakes: Add a bit of oil to a medium pan and set it over medium heat. When it shimmers, form 1 tablespoon of the salmon cake mixture into a small patty and cook for 2 minutes per side. Taste and adjust the seasoning of the uncooked mixture accordingly.

Divide the salmon cake mixture into 4 equal pieces and form each quarter of the mixture into a 1-inch-thick patty. Heat a tablespoon of oil in the pan over medium heat and cook the patties for 3 to 4 minutes per side, until deeply golden brown and cooked through. Carefully transfer to the reserved sheet pan and bake for 10 minutes. Let the cakes rest 5 minutes, then serve with Remoulade (page 19) and Calypso Sauce (page 24).

Salmon cakes are best served immediately, but leftovers will keep in an airtight container in the refrigerator for up to 3 days.

FRIED CATFISH

Fish fries were a regular event in my family growing up, especially on visits to my mother's childhood home in Beaumont, Texas, as they are in the houses and churches of Black people across the country. Catfish, plentiful in the waterways of the South, has a mellow, mild flesh that contrasts nicely with a crunchy cornmeal coating. This recipe is a variation I learned from my grandfather, Bertrand Russell. Bertrand spent his career in the kitchen galley of a ship in Beaumont. At least that's where I first met him, and a plate of insanely crunchy, surprisingly light, and piping hot fried catfish is what he was holding.

In a nonreactive bowl, combine the catfish, onions, mustard, 1 tablespoon house spice, and 1½ teaspoons salt. Cover with plastic wrap and marinate in the refrigerator for at least 1 hour and up to 4 hours.

When ready to cook, heat 2 inches oil in a Dutch oven over medium-high heat until it reaches 350°F.

While the oil heats, set up your breading station. In one shallow bowl, combine ½ cup all-purpose flour and ½ teaspoon kosher salt. In a second shallow bowl, place 2 cups buttermilk. In a third shallow bowl, stir together 1 cup all-purpose flour, the cornmeal, and 1 tablespoon + 1 teaspoon house spice.

Remove the catfish from the marinade and scrape off excess liquid and onions. Coat each piece of fish in flour, then buttermilk, then the cornmeal mixture, tapping off excess between bowls. Repeat until all the fish is breaded.

Working in batches as necessary, fry each piece of fish until crispy and cooked through, about 3 minutes. Remove to a paper towel–lined tray and season with salt, then repeat the same breading and frying process with the onions, frying until crispy and golden, 2 to 3 minutes.

Serve the fish and onions together with Remoulade (page 19) and lemon wedges.

ORIGIN: American South
YIELD: 2 to 4 servings

1 pound **catfish**, skinned and filleted, cut into 1-inch-thick strips

1 medium **yellow onion**, halved and sliced into ¼-inch-thick pieces

2 tablespoons **yellow mustard**

2 tablespoons + 1 teaspoon **House Spice** (page 6), divided

2 teaspoons **kosher salt**, divided, plus more to taste

Vegetable oil, such as canola, for frying

1½ cups **all-purpose flour**

2 cups **buttermilk**

1 cup **cornmeal**

Lemon wedges, to serve

Fried catfish is best served immediately.

SHRIMP ÉTOUFFÉE

Étouffée comes from the French word for "smothered," but to me étouffée means home. This recipe, in which the powers of roux, shrimp, the Holy Trinity of bell peppers, onions, and celery, and spices combine to form . . . Captain Planet. Or, at least, a superpowered shellfish stew that connects me back to my childhood, to my mother, who made this on special occasions, and through her to her mother, Cassie, and so on and so forth all the way back to ki-ngombo, the forerunner of gumbo, a cousin of étouffée, from West Africa. There are a few étouffée variants. Creole étouffée uses a lighter roux, in which the butter and flour is toasted but not darkened, and often includes tomatoes; Cajun étouffée uses a brown roux, in which the flour-and-butter mixture is brought to a darker, nuttier color, and never has tomatoes. Both use the smothering technique, in which the roux is infused with the trinity and other spices. (It is also used in many other Louisiana-style dishes like smothered chicken and the Smothered Pork Chops on page 212.) The hallmark of a good étouffée is the symphony of texture and flavor—silky, saline, spiced.

ORIGIN: American South

YIELD: 6 to 8 servings

8 tablespoons **unsalted butter**

½ cup **all-purpose flour**

1 medium **yellow onion**, diced

2 **celery** stalks, diced

1 large **green bell pepper**, diced

5 **garlic cloves**, roughly chopped

1 tablespoon **House Spice** (page 6)

1 fresh **bay leaf**

4 fresh **thyme sprigs**

1 quart cold **Shrimp Stock** (page 37), cold

2 pounds medium **shrimp**, peeled and deveined, tails removed

Kosher salt, to taste

Shrimp étouffée will keep in an airtight container in the refrigerator for up to 2 days.

In a heavy-bottomed pot, melt the butter over medium-high heat until foaming. Add the flour, reduce the heat to medium-low, and whisk into a smooth paste. Cook, stirring constantly, until it smells slightly toasty, about 3 minutes.

Add the onions, celery, bell peppers, and garlic. Cook, stirring frequently, until the vegetables have softened, about 6 minutes. Add the house spice, bay leaf, and thyme, and cook for 1 minute.

While whisking, add the shrimp stock to the pot a third at a time, whisking to combine completely before adding more. When all the stock is added, bring to a simmer and cook for 20 minutes, or until the broth has thickened somewhat. Stir in the shrimp and remove from the heat. Let sit, stirring occasionally, until cooked through, about 5 minutes. Season to taste with salt and serve with Perfectly Steamed Rice (page 46).

SHRIMP CREOLE

Tomatoes and, of course, shrimp are the stars in this New Orleans Creole classic. In fact, the presence of tomatoes distinguishes between Creole and Cajun recipes. Even though the two terms are often used interchangeably, Creole cuisine originated in the urban setting of New Orleans, as an evolution and hybridization of Spanish and French traditions, influenced by the flavor palates of the African women who often prepared the colonizers' food. The recipes reflect access to imported and luxurious ingredients such as tomatoes, butter, and cream. Cajun cuisine, on the other hand, emerges from the Acadian kitchens of the Louisiana backcountry and, though the original Acadians were French-speaking Canadian exiles, doesn't include as many French techniques nor as luxurious ingredients. It's humble but no less complex. This dish, a sort of tomato-kissed étouffée variant, is clearly Creole and a staple anywhere you go in New Orleans.

Season the shrimp all over with 1 tablespoon house spice and 1 teaspoon kosher salt. Heat 2 tablespoons of oil in a large pan over medium-high heat until it shimmers, then add the shrimp. Sear for 1 to 2 minutes per side, until golden brown. Remove to a bowl and set aside.

Decrease the heat to medium. Add another tablespoon of oil if the pan looks dry, then add the garlic and sauté until fragrant, 2 to 3 minutes. Add the onions, celery, and bell peppers, then sauté until the onions are translucent and the celery is tender, 5 to 7 minutes.

Add the tomato paste and RGP. Cook, stirring often, until the mixture is brick red, then add the crushed tomatoes, remaining 1 tablespoon house spice, thyme, bay leaves, and stock. Increase the heat to high and reduce the mixture by half, about 10 minutes. It should be thick and deep red, like tomato sauce.

Return the shrimp to the pan to finish cooking, about 2 minutes, then taste and adjust seasoning with salt and house spice. Serve with Perfectly Steamed Rice (page 46) and Louisiana-Style Hot Sauce (page 23).

ORIGIN: American South
YIELD: 6 servings

2 pounds medium (20–26 size) **shrimp**, peeled, deveined, and tails off

2 tablespoons **House Spice** (page 6), divided, plus more to taste

1 teaspoon **kosher salt**, plus more to taste

2 tablespoons **grapeseed oil**, plus more as needed

6 **garlic cloves**, minced

1 medium **yellow onion**, diced

2 stalks **celery**, diced

2 **green bell peppers**, diced

2½ tablespoons **tomato paste**

2 tablespoons **RGP** (page 11)

One 28-ounce can **crushed tomatoes**

8 fresh **thyme sprigs**

3 fresh **bay leaves**

3 cups **Shrimp Stock** (page 37)

Shrimp Creole will keep in an airtight container in the refrigerator for up to 1 day.

SHRIMP AND GRITS

No other dish has come to embody the growing influence of southern food than shrimp and grits. Originally confined to the areas in and around Charleston, South Carolina, and cooked in home kitchens but rarely in professional ones, these days you can't walk into a vaguely hip spot for brunch and not see some variation of shrimp and grits on the menu. It's popular, and I'm not immune to its charms either, even if this wasn't something I grew up making. (Grits, though popular throughout the South, grow in popularity the farther east you go. In eastern Texas and southwestern Louisiana, where my family is from, rice is more common.) If it's on the menu, I'll order it. No questions asked. In its best forms, cream and butter conspire to turn the grits into a lush backdrop for the shrimp, which I make here almost as an étouffée but with a bit of white wine to cut through the richness.

Season the shrimp generously to taste with salt and house spice. Heat a large pan over medium-high heat. Add 2 tablespoons of oil; when it shimmers, add the shrimp in a single layer. Sear the shrimp on both sides, 1 to 2 minutes total—they should be about halfway cooked. Remove from the pan and set aside.

In the same pan, heat the remaining 2 tablespoons of oil over medium heat. Add the ham for 2 minutes, then the garlic and sauté for 2 minutes, then add the onions, celery, and bell peppers. Cook until the onions become translucent, about 5 minutes.

Add paprika and house spice and cook, stirring frequently, for 2 minutes. Add the oregano, bay leaf, thyme, wine, stock, and cream. Bring to a simmer and reduce until nearly all of the liquid is gone, 2 to 3 minutes, then return the shrimp to the pan and stir well to combine. Remove the pan from the heat and allow to rest for 1 minute, then add the butter a cube at a time, stirring constantly to emulsify the sauce. Add hot sauce and season to taste with salt.

Remove the thyme sprigs and bay leaf before serving over grits.

ORIGIN: American South

YIELD: 2 to 4 servings

1 pound large (16–20 size) **shrimp**, peeled and deveined

Kosher salt, to taste

1 tablespoon **House Spice** (page 6), plus more for seasoning shrimp

4 tablespoons **grapeseed oil**, divided

4 tablespoons **tasso ham**, diced

3 **garlic cloves**, minced

½ **yellow onion**, finely diced

½ stalk **celery**, minced

½ **green bell pepper**, finely diced

½ **red bell pepper**, finely diced

2 teaspoons **smoked paprika**

2 teaspoons dried **oregano**

1 fresh **bay leaf**

4 fresh **thyme sprigs**

¾ cup dry **white wine**, such as Pinot Grigio

3 tablespoons **Shrimp Stock** (page 37)

¼ cup **heavy cream**

4 tablespoons cold **unsalted butter**, cubed

1 tablespoon **Louisiana-Style Hot Sauce** (page 23)

2 cups **Buttered Grits** (page 84), prepared with salt and pepper, warmed, to serve

Store the shrimp separately from the grits. The shrimp will keep in an airtight container in the refrigerator for 2 days, the grits for 5 days.

MOM DUKE'S SHRIMP

This is an homage to my own Mom Duke's, Jewel Robinson, and her supercharged version of the Peel-and-Eat Shrimp (page 140) I grew up with. I was inspired by that dish's addictive flavor and silky texture as well as New Orleans's famous barbecue shrimp. The Worcestershire sauce, beer, white wine, and butter—so. much. butter.—yield a highly aromatic glistening sauce, hovering right on the sea side of a traditional barbecue. I like to serve it with rice and torn French bread, though anything that sops up all that good sauce works.

Prep the shrimp: Peel and devein the shrimp, keeping the tails and heads on. (If you like, stash the shells in a ziplock bag and keep them in the freezer until you have enough to make Shrimp Stock, page 37.) Season the shrimp generously to taste with salt and house spice.

Sear the shrimp: Heat a large pan over medium-high heat. Add 2 tablespoons of oil and, when it shimmers, add the shrimp in a single layer. Sear the shrimp on both sides, 1 to 2 minutes total—they should be about halfway cooked. Remove from the pan and set aside.

Build the sauce: In the same pan, sauté the garlic, onions, celery, and bell peppers until translucent, about 5 minutes, adding more oil if needed. Add house spice, oregano, bay leaf, thyme, beer, orange juice, wine, stock, and Worcestershire sauce. Increase the heat to a brisk simmer and cook, stirring often. When about 80 percent reduced, after 2 to 3 minutes, return the shrimp to the pan and toss to coat. Continue to cook until the liquid is evaporated, then remove the thyme and bay leaf.

Remove the shrimp from the heat and add the cold butter a cube at a time, stirring constantly, until emulsified. Season to taste with salt and lemon juice, sprinkle with chives, and serve immediately, with additional house spice and Perfectly Steamed Rice (page 46) and/or torn French bread.

YIELD: 2 to 3 servings

10 large (16–20 size) raw Gulf shrimp, shell-on, head-on if possible

Kosher salt, to taste

1 tablespoon House Spice (page 6), plus more to taste

2 tablespoons grapeseed oil, plus more as needed

2 garlic cloves, minced

½ yellow onion, finely diced

½ stalk celery, minced

½ green bell pepper, finely diced

1 teaspoon dried oregano

1 fresh bay leaf

3 fresh thyme sprigs

3 tablespoons Abita Amber Lager or other amber lager

3 tablespoons freshly squeezed orange juice

3 tablespoons dry white wine, such as Pinot Grigio

3 tablespoons Shrimp Stock (page 37)

5 teaspoons Worcestershire sauce

8 tablespoons cold unsalted butter, cubed

Freshly squeezed lemon juice, to serve

2 teaspoons finely chopped chives

Mom Duke's Shrimp is best served immediately.

SEAFOOD GUMBO

Gumbo is my first love, and all my love, in one pot. A culmination of New Orleans's history, a fusion of the foods of the Germanic settlers who brought their spicy andouille sausage and the fishermen from the Canary Islands who furnished crabs, plus the Holy Trinity of onions, bell peppers, and celery, house spice, and shrimp stock.

I'm from a family of cooks; each relative has his or her special dish. Uncle Herm is Shrimp Étouffée (page 133). Papa Winston is Curried Goat (page 223). Grandma Cassie is chitlins. My sister Tatiana is cheesecake. And my mom has this. She's so damn good at it—and the ingredients so expensive for us growing up—that she made seafood gumbo as a literal gift for me and my sister on Christmas. Better than any PlayStation game, we ate it Christmas morning, and for the next few days as the gumbo got better and better with age.

ORIGIN: American South
YIELD: 6 to 8 servings

For the roux
1 pound **unsalted butter**
2 cups **all-purpose flour**

For the gumbo
5 live **blue crabs**
2 tablespoons **grapeseed oil**
1½ cups finely diced **yellow onions** (about 1 large onion)
1 cup finely diced **celery** (about 4 stalks)
¾ cup finely diced **green bell pepper** (about 1 small pepper)
2 tablespoons minced **garlic** (about 4 large cloves)
2 teaspoons **kosher salt**, plus more to taste
1½ tablespoons **House Spice** (page 6)
2 quarts **Shrimp Stock** (page 37)
1 quart **Chicken Stock** (page 33)
2 **andouille sausages**, 1 left whole and 1 sliced on the bias into ¼-inch pieces
1 whole **chicken** (about 3 pounds), skinned and quartered
2 cups **lump crabmeat**, picked through

For the roux

Heat the oven to 350°F. In a medium pot over medium heat, melt the butter. Gradually whisk in the flour until smooth, then transfer the mixture to a loaf pan. Bake uncovered, whisking every 30 minutes for 2 hours, until deeply browned and fragrant. You should have 3 cups of roux. Reserve 1½ cups for the gumbo; the remainder can be kept in an airtight container in the refrigerator for up to a week or the freezer for up to 3 months and used to make more gumbo later on.

For the gumbo

Place the live crabs in the freezer for 30 minutes—this will knock them out so that they won't move around (or feel much) when it's time to kill them. Working one at a time, remove a cold crab from the freezer and place it on its back on a cutting board. Break off the flap (aka the apron) at the back of the shell. This will leave a hole; place your thumb in the hole and lift up firmly, which should make the carapace break away. Use a spoon to scrape out the guts, then rinse thoroughly. Use a large sharp knife (or a cleaver if you have one) to cut right down the middle of the crab. Repeat with the remaining crabs. Set aside in the refrigerator until ready to use.

Heat the oil in a very large pot over medium heat. Add the onions, celery, bell peppers, and garlic with a pinch of salt and sauté until tender, about 10 minutes. Add 2 teaspoons kosher salt, house spice, shrimp stock, and chicken stock and bring to a simmer over medium-high heat, then slowly whisk in the roux to create a smooth, thick liquid. (If you're using frozen or cold roux, which will be solid, just add a few pieces at a time, whisking until incorporated before adding more.) Add the whole andouille and the chicken pieces and simmer gently for 20 minutes, then add the crab halves and simmer for 20 minutes more, skimming away excess fat from the surface as needed. Season to taste with salt, then remove the whole sausage and discard. Fold in the sliced sausage and the crabmeat.

Serve with Perfectly Steamed Rice (page 46).

Gumbo will keep in an airtight container in the refrigerator for up to 3 days. Roux will keep in an airtight container in the refrigerator for up to 1 week or in the freezer for up to 3 months.

PEEL-AND-EAT SHRIMP

Shrimping along the Louisiana coast isn't just a job. For many it's a way of life, one that stretches back to the eighteenth century. Today's shrimping communities are astonishingly diverse, made up of Vietnamese, Croatian, Arcadian, and Black shrimpers who harvest in both inland and federal waters. Regardless, though, it's an industry under threat from both natural and manmade disasters, as well as international competition. The price of a pound of shrimp has barely budged since the 1980s. Nevertheless, shrimp rules Louisiana, and that's good news for the hungry. Some of my best memories of living in Baton Rouge or visiting my mother in New Orleans were walking into a friend's house to find a mess of still-steaming peel-and-eat shrimp, ready for peeling and eating. Smothered in house spice, sweetened with garlic, and silky with melted butter, they burst with flavor with every bite. There are many, many ways to prepare the shrimp that come from these coastal waters, but this is perhaps the most fun, one of the easiest and quickest, and so damn delicious.

ORIGIN: American South
YIELD: 2 servings

3 tablespoons **grapeseed oil**

10 **garlic cloves**, crushed

12 large (16–20 size) **shrimp**, shell-on, head-on if possible, deveined

Kosher salt, to taste

1 tablespoon **House Spice** (page 6), plus more to taste

6 fresh **thyme sprigs**

4 tablespoons **unsalted butter**, cubed and cold

Freshly squeezed **lemon juice**, to taste

10 fresh **parsley leaves**, roughly chopped

Peel-and-eat shrimp are best served immediately.

In a large pan over medium heat, add the oil and the garlic. Sauté the garlic for about 3 minutes, until very fragrant. Meanwhile, heavily season the shrimp on both sides with salt and house spice.

Raise the heat to high. Keep sautéing the garlic so it doesn't brown too much or too quickly. Add the shrimp and thyme to the pan and sauté, moving the pan constantly, until the shrimp are fully cooked, about 2 minutes.

Remove the pan from the heat and let rest for 1 minute, then add the 4 tablespoons of butter a cube at a time, stirring constantly until emulsified. Season with salt, lemon, and more house spice to taste, then garnish with parsley. Serve with torn bread.

SALMON with CARROT ESCOVITCH SAUCE

The word escovitch carries with it the currents of time and human movement. At its root are the words sik, Persian for vinegar, and bah, Persian for sauce. This became the Arabic sikbaj and from there we get the Spanish variant escabeche, and then, moving west across eons and oceans, we arrive at escovitch, the Jamaican version of this vinegar-based sauce kicked in the pants with Scotch bonnet pepper and allspice. Though in other parts of the world this sauce itself is used to "cook" the protein—usually fish, and not unlike its cousin ceviche—in Jamaica we use it as a flavoring agent. We fry the fish, usually a white fish like snapper or pollock, first and then pour the sauce over it. But it doesn't need to be just fish. When I began making my own version, I loved it so much I put it on everything: fried chicken sandwiches, fresh tuna and avocado, tongues of uni, jollof rice. In this preparation I use the acidic escovitch to set off the smoky sweetness of the carrot purée to accompany the fish.

Note: If you can't find mesquite liquid smoke, hickory may be used.

For the escovitch sauce

In a medium pot over medium heat, sweat the GGP and peppa sauce in 2 tablespoons of NKO until very fragrant, stirring constantly, about 2 minutes. Add the spice pickling liquid, carrot juice, and sugar. Bring to a boil over medium-high heat, then reduce the heat to a simmer. Simmer, occasionally scraping the bottom and sides of the pot, until the mixture is syrupy, about 30 minutes. You should have 1 cup liquid. Purée in a blender, and set aside.

Meanwhile, in another medium pot or skillet over medium heat, sauté the onions and peppers in the remaining 2 tablespoons of NKO until translucent and just barely tender, about 5 minutes. Add the syrup and carrots and cook, stirring often, until the carrots are just tender and the mixture is mostly dry, 5 to 7 minutes. →

ORIGIN: Caribbean
YIELDS: 4 servings

For the escovitch sauce

¼ cup NKO (page 21), divided

¼ cup + 1 tablespoon GGP (page 5)

1 tablespoon + 1 teaspoon Peppa Sauce (page 25)

1½ cups Spice Pickling Liquid (page 32)

⅔ cup carrot juice

1¼ teaspoons white granulated sugar

1½ medium yellow onions, thinly sliced

½ medium red bell pepper, thinly sliced lengthwise

½ medium orange bell pepper, thinly sliced lengthwise

3 medium carrots, peeled, halved crosswise, and julienned

For the smoked carrot purée

2 tablespoons pimento (or mesquite) wood chips, soaked 30 minutes, for smoking, or 1 teaspoon mesquite liquid smoke

2 tablespoons NKO (page 21), plus more as needed

¾ medium carrot, peeled

1½ teaspoons GGP (page 5)

¼ medium yellow onion, thinly sliced

3 tablespoons + 1½ teaspoons carrot juice →

For the smoked carrot purée

If smoking, prepare a charcoal grill for low heat, with coals on just one side of the grill. Fill a small disposable foil pan with 2 cups water and place on the side of the grill opposite the heat, beneath the grate. When the grill is at about 350°F, drop the soaked wood chips on top of the coals, lightly grease the carrot with NKO, and place the carrot on the grate over the pan of water. Close the grill and smoke the carrot at 350°F for 1 hour, until very tender.

For a gas grill, light the burners on low on one side of the grill. Fill a small disposable foil aluminum pan with water and another with soaked wood chips. Place the pan of water and the carrot over the unlit burners and the pan of wood chips over the lit burners.

Alternatively, heat the oven to 450°F. Place the carrot on a sheet pan and roast until tender and beginning to char, 30 to 40 minutes.

Let the carrot cool enough to handle, then cut into 1-inch pieces.

In a small pot over medium heat, heat 2 tablespoons NKO until shimmering. Add GGP and sauté for 4 minutes, stirring constantly, until caramelized. Add the sliced onions and carrots and cook for 8 to 10 minutes, stirring frequently, until very tender. Add the carrot juice, cumin, peppa sauce, ½ teaspoon salt, and 1 teaspoon liquid smoke (if not smoking). Reduce the heat to medium-low and cover with a lid, leaving it slightly ajar so that steam may escape.

Let the mixture simmer for 3 to 4 minutes, then set aside to cool slightly. Transfer to a blender and purée until totally smooth, then cool completely. Season with the juice of half a lime, then taste and adjust seasoning with more lime juice and salt. You should have about ¼ cup. Set aside.

¼ teaspoon ground **cumin**

¼ teaspoon **Peppa Sauce** (page 25)

½ teaspoon **kosher salt**, plus more to taste

Freshly squeezed **juice of ½ lime**, plus to taste

To assemble

Four 5-ounce skinless **salmon fillets**

House Spice (page 6), to taste

1 teaspoon **kosher salt**, plus more to taste

1 cup **escovitch sauce** (see above)

2 tablespoons cold **unsalted butter**, cubed

Freshly squeezed **juice of 1 lime**, plus more to taste

2 tablespoons **NKO** (page 21)

Smoked carrot purée (above)

12 fresh **cilantro leaves**

Lime wedges, to serve

Escovitch sauce will keep in an airtight container in the refrigerator for up to 2 weeks.

Salmon with carrot escovitch sauce is best served immediately.

To assemble

Twenty minutes before cooking, season the salmon generously all over with salt and house spice. Meanwhile, in a small pot over low heat, warm the escovitch sauce with 1 teaspoon salt. Once warm, add the cold butter a cube at a time, stirring constantly so that the sauce emulsifies. Add the juice of 1 lime, then taste and adjust seasoning with more lime juice and salt. Cover to keep warm and set aside.

Heat a large sauté pan over medium-high and add the NKO. When it shimmers, add the salmon. For a fillet about 1½ inches thick, cook for 4 minutes, until deeply golden brown, then carefully flip and cook for 3 minutes more. The salmon should just start to flake when gently squeezed. (For thinner fillets, cook for 4 minutes on the first side, then flip and continue just until opaque and beginning to flake.) Remove to a plate.

To serve, swipe 1 tablespoon of smoked carrot purée onto a plate. Place the salmon over it, then top with 2 tablespoons escovitch sauce. Garnish with cilantro and serve immediately, with lime wedges.

FRIED SNAPPER WITH BROWN STEW SAUCE

This was one of the first dishes I developed at my second restaurant, Kith and Kin. I knew from the start that I wanted a whole fried fish on the menu, a show-stopping presentation that was actually easy to prepare and fun to share. (Although for the home cook, you don't absolutely need to serve it upright. Lying down is just fine.) I remember holiday dinners at my Uncle Rupert's house in the Bronx, the fried fish master of my father's side, and how my cousins and I used to fight over the eyes and tail, so crispy it resembled a potato chip. After just minutes, the fish would be picked clean, looking like an alley cat had eaten it. Uncle Rupert used to score the sides of the fish and slather it with jerk paste, letting the seasoning seep deeply into the flesh. For this preparation, not only do I follow Uncle Rupert's technique but I also draw inspiration from another Caribbean classic: brown stew. Here I use a version of the classic Browning sauce (page 13), most often used in Brown Stew Chicken (page 168), to add tangy sweetness to the fish. Then, using a technique I picked up in Thailand, I dredge the fish in cornstarch to turn it seriously crispy. One of the happiest memories I have of my time at Kith and Kin was emerging from the kitchen to see the bones of the snapper picked as clean as I remember from Uncle Rupert's house.

ORIGIN: Caribbean
YIELD: 6 servings

For the snapper and to assemble

2 whole **red snappers** (about 3 pounds each), scaled and gutted

½ cup **Jerk Paste** (page 17)

Vegetable oil, such as canola, for frying

1 cup **cornstarch**

Kosher salt, to taste

3 tablespoons chopped fresh **chives**

2 tablespoons chopped fresh **cilantro**

1 **lime**, cut into 8 wedges

For the brown stew sauce

6 tablespoons **grapeseed oil**, divided

⅔ cup **GGP** (page 5)

1¼ cups **turbinado (raw) sugar**

⅔ cup **ketchup**

1 tablespoon **Peppa Sauce** (page 25)

1¼ cups **water**

Kosher salt, to taste

3 large **yellow onions**, halved and sliced into ¼-inch-thick pieces

---

Fried snapper is best served immediately. Brown stew sauce will keep in an airtight container in the refrigerator for up to 5 days, or in the freezer for up to 2 months.

For the snapper

Using a sharp knife, score the skin in a crosshatch pattern on both sides of the fish. Rub the jerk paste evenly over the skin and cavities. Set the fish on a sheet pan and wrap the sheet tightly with plastic wrap. Refrigerate for 2 hours.

For the brown stew sauce

As the snapper marinates, heat 3 tablespoons of oil in a medium pot over medium heat. Add the GGP and cook, stirring often, until fragrant, about 5 minutes. Add the sugar, ketchup, peppa sauce, and water and bring to a simmer. Simmer, stirring often, for 30 minutes, until thick (almost jammy), glossy, and a deep →

reddish brown. Reduce the heat as necessary to keep from burning and spattering. Remove from the heat and let cool slightly, then transfer to a blender and purée until smooth. You should have about 2 cups of sauce. Season with salt and set aside.

In a separate pot, heat the remaining 3 tablespoons oil over medium heat. Add the onions and sauté, stirring often, until sweet and translucent but not browned at all, 12 to 15 minutes. Add the puréed sauce, taste, and adjust seasoning if necessary.

To assemble

When ready to cook the fish, fill a large Dutch oven (wide enough to fit a whole snapper horizontally) with vegetable oil to a depth of 4 inches. Heat over medium-high heat until the oil has reached 350°F. Warm the brown stew sauce in a small saucepan over low heat.

Remove the fish from the fridge and dredge in cornstarch. Fry one fish at a time until deeply browned and cooked through, about 10 minutes, carefully turning halfway through. Remove the fried fish to a paper towel–lined platter and sprinkle evenly with salt.

Transfer the fried fish to a serving platter and top with warm brown stew sauce, then garnish with chives and cilantro. Serve with lime wedges.

MARINATED SARDINES

Canned sardines are wildly popular in the Caribbean. They're versatile, have a long shelf life, are easy to prepare, and, importantly, are economical. A good Caribbean chef has a head full of sardine variations, from sardine fritters to pan-fried sardines to this super-simple marinade, which, thanks to the supercharged trio of spice pickling liquid, house spice, and peppa sauce, endows the fish with massive amounts of flavor. I used to eat canned sardines prepared this way with my grandfather for breakfast alongside a crunchy salty cracker.

Combine all the ingredients except the sardines in a medium bowl.

Drain the sardines. Use a paring knife to split each fish into two fillets and remove the bones. Place the sardines on a plate or in a shallow bowl and cover with the tomato mixture. Let marinate in the refrigerator for 1 hour before serving with Bake (page 246) or saltines.

ORIGIN: Jamaica
YIELD: 2 to 3 servings

¼ medium yellow onion, thinly sliced

2 Roma tomatoes, sliced

¼ cup Spice Pickling Liquid (page 32)

1 tablespoon yellow mustard

Juice of 1 lemon

1 teaspoon House Spice (page 6)

2 teaspoons Peppa Sauce (page 25)

2 tablespoons extra-virgin olive oil

Two 4.4-ounce cans sardines packed in oil

Marinated sardines will keep in an airtight container in the refrigerator for up to 3 days.

SNAPPER ESCOVITCH

When I began thinking about the menu for my second restaurant, Kith and Kin, I wanted to focus on the foods I grew up with. This wasn't soul food, per se, that designation given in the 1960s to a cast of American southern classics. But it was *my* soul food. One of the flavors that was a touchstone of my childhood was my grandmother's escovitch, a slightly sweet, slightly vinegary Jamaican marinade. But when I went to the kitchen, I quickly found that though the tastes were embedded in my body, the recipes were not. A little sheepishly I called home to ask, "Recipe?" My mom said, "We don't have a recipe!" Instead we just talked through the process, mixing in family memories with ingredient lists. This escovitch isn't the same one made by my grandma, or by my mother. It's a little—just a little—me. But the flavors ring out loud, a bright complement to snapper's mild taste.

For the escovitch

Combine all the ingredients in a large bowl and toss well to combine. Cover and refrigerate for at least 6 hours or up to 24 hours.

For the snapper

Combine 1 cup oil, garlic, house spice, thyme, and ginger in a blender or food processor. Purée until a smooth paste forms, about 2 minutes. Using a sharp knife, score the fish skin in a crosshatch pattern on both sides of the fish. Rub the marinade evenly over the skin and cavities. Place the fish on a sheet pan, wrap the sheet tightly with plastic wrap, and refrigerate for 2 hours.

When ready to cook the fish, fill a large Dutch oven (wide enough to fit a whole snapper horizontally) with oil to a depth of 4 inches. Heat over medium-high until the oil reaches 350°F.

Remove the fish from the fridge and sprinkle evenly with salt. Fry one fish at a time until deeply browned and cooked through, about 10 minutes, carefully turning halfway through. Remove fried fish to a serving platter and top with escovitch.

ORIGIN: Caribbean

YIELD: 6 servings

For the escovitch

2 red bell peppers, julienned

2 medium yellow onions, halved and thinly sliced

2 large carrots, peeled and julienned

¼ cup distilled white vinegar

5 garlic cloves, minced

4 teaspoons minced ginger

1 Scotch bonnet pepper, stemmed, seeded, and thinly sliced lengthwise

2 teaspoons freshly squeezed lime juice

2 teaspoons ground allspice

1 teaspoon kosher salt

For the snapper

1 cup vegetable oil, such as canola, plus more for frying

20 garlic cloves

2 tablespoons House Spice (page 6)

1 tablespoon fresh thyme leaves

One 2-inch piece ginger, peeled

2 whole red snappers (about 3 pounds each), scaled and gutted

2 teaspoons kosher salt

Snapper escovitch is best served immediately. Escovitch keeps in an airtight container in the refrigerator for up to 3 days.

ACKEE AND SALTFISH

It's easy to see why ackee and saltfish is Jamaica's national dish. Ackee, a bright red fruit with yellow flesh, is indigenous to West Africa and was brought to Jamaica along with West Africans. Saltfish, called salt cod or stockfish outside the Caribbean, was imported by plantation owners from Nova Scotia in the nineteenth century to feed their workforce. This dish has a painful history, one marked by suffering. But it is also a testament to the ingenuity of my ancestors to find sustenance and deliciousness even in these circumstances. Not only is it a perfect, if unlikely, combination yielding alchemical beauty—a West African fruit plus North Atlantic fish equals a Caribbean breakfast—but the ingredients embody the currents of Jamaican history.

Ackee, which because it can be poisonous if not prepared correctly is only available canned outside of Jamaica, absorbs the flavors, and softens the brininess of the saltfish. The mixture of flavors and textures yields a sort of nutty, subtly briny dish, laced with the heat of peppa sauce. Just make sure you add the sauce close to the end, to allow the fruit to retain its texture.

ORIGIN: Jamaica
YIELD: 4 servings

---

1 pound **salt cod**

2 tablespoons **grapeseed oil**, plus more as needed

3 **garlic cloves**, minced

1 medium **yellow onion**, diced

1 **green bell pepper**, diced

1 **red bell pepper**, diced

1 **Roma tomato**, diced

1½ teaspoons **Peppa Sauce** (page 25)

One 19-ounce can **ackee**, well drained and shredded

Kosher salt, to taste

Freshly ground **black pepper**, to taste

Ackee and saltfish is best served immediately.

Place the salt cod in a large bowl or dish and cover with boiling water. Let cool, then cover and store overnight in the refrigerator. The next day, drain and rinse the fish. Add to a large pot of water and boil for 20 minutes. Drain, let cool, then shred into medium-sized pieces and set aside.

Heat a large pan with the oil over high heat until almost smoking. Add the saltfish and cook until crispy on both sides, about 2 minutes per side. When crispy, lower the heat to medium and add the garlic, onions, bell peppers, tomatoes, and peppa sauce. Sauté until tender, 7 to 10 minutes, then fold in the ackee. Cook until warmed through, about 3 minutes, then season to taste with salt and pepper.

CALAMARI VERACRUZ

The story of African slavery in Mexico is generally overlooked. Growing up, I had never heard it or, honestly, thought about it enough to ask. But while researching diasporic cuisine in the run-up to opening my restaurant Kith and Kin, I discovered that when Hernán Cortés landed in Veracruz—a coastal state on the Gulf of Mexico and still one of Mexico's most important ports—in 1517, he brought with him an enslaved African, one of many who eventually found themselves in Spanish territory. West African slaves were brought largely to replace indigenous workers who had died working the sugar plantations of the Spaniards. Many slaves perished, many survived, and some, like Veracruz's Gaspar Yanga, rebelled. In 1570, Yanga, a Gabonian slave, established a long-standing and remote palenque, or settlement, in the Veracruz highlands which served as a beacon to escaped slaves. Forty years later, he repelled a Spanish attack and eventually earned independence for himself and his Maroons. But life remained tenuous for the Afro-Mexicans. In 1683, a Dutch pirate named Laurens de Graaf laid siege to Veracruz, eventually kidnapping and selling into slavery the entirety of that city's African population. (Many ended up in Charleston, South Carolina.)

But just as we've done in the United States, and everywhere the inhumane currents of slavery took us, Black people developed, safeguarded, and synthesized their own culture. In Veracruz, this can be seen in son jarocho, a musical-style wedding with Mexican and African rhythmic elements, and of course in the food, a combination of Spanish, indigenous, and African traditions. This dish, for instance, is a nod to snapper Veracruz (Huachinango a la Veracruzana). Instead of a whole red snapper, I use crispy. I love the richness of the sauce with the texture of the squid. Nigerian red sauce replaces the traditional tomato sauce, but I keep the olives, a signature element of Veracruz cuisine.

ORIGIN: Mexico
YIELD: 4 servings

For the Veracruz sauce
1¼ cups Obe Ata Din Din (page 22)
½ cup pitted Castelvetrano olives
1 teaspoon Peppa Sauce (page 25)
1 teaspoon dried oregano
Freshly squeezed lemon juice, to taste
Kosher salt, to taste

For the calamari seasoning
1 tablespoon House Spice (page 6)
1 tablespoon Curry Powder (page 10)
1 teaspoon ground cumin
2 tablespoons powdered sugar
2 teaspoons kosher salt

For the Veracruz sauce

Place the obe ata din din in a blender with the olives, peppa sauce, and oregano. Purée until smooth, then season to taste with lemon juice and salt. Refrigerate in an airtight container until ready to use.

For the calamari seasoning

Stir together all the seasoning ingredients in a small bowl and set aside.

To assemble

In a Dutch oven, add 4 inches of vegetable oil and heat over medium heat to 350°F.

Meanwhile, combine the flour, cornstarch, and 1 teaspoon salt in a large bowl. Marinate the calamari in buttermilk for 1 hour. Drain the calamari and coat generously in the flour mixture, then transfer to the hot oil, working in batches so as not to crowd the pot. Fry for 2 minutes, stirring occasionally, until light and crisp (it might not be browned). Toss the fried calamari immediately with the seasoning mixture. Taste and season with salt if necessary.

To serve, spoon 3 tablespoons of the Veracruz sauce over the bottom of each plate or shallow bowl. Divide the calamari between the dishes, setting it on top of the sauce, and garnish with sliced olives and cilantro. Serve immediately, with lemon wedges.

To assemble

Vegetable oil, such as canola, for frying

½ cup **all-purpose flour**

¼ cup **cornstarch**

1 teaspoon **kosher salt**, plus more to taste

1 pound **calamari**, thawed if frozen, cut into ½-inch rings

1 quart **buttermilk**

Calamari seasoning (above)

¼ cup pitted **Castelvetrano olives**, sliced into rings

1 tablespoon chopped fresh **cilantro**

1 **lemon**, cut into wedges

Calamari Veracruz is best served immediately, but the sauce may be made up to 2 days in advance and stored in an airtight container in the refrigerator.

BULJOL (SALTFISH SALAD)

Every time I went to visit my grandfather on Long Island, we'd have buljol, a saltfish salad from his native Trinidad, for breakfast, often served on bake, with johnnycakes, or with bread. "Kwame," he'd say, pulling me aside, "I'll tell you my secret. I *slice* the onions." I'm not sure why he thought that was the secret, or even *a* secret, but his buljol is some of the best I've had. My sister refused to eat it, but that just meant more for me and Papa. The dish, like Ackee and Saltfish (page 149), can be traced back to the colonial occupation of Trinidad by Europeans who provisioned themselves and their slaves with salt cod. Augmented with spice—in this case, peppa sauce—the salt cod basically became a vehicle for heat (even though the dish is served cold). In fact, the name comes from eighteenth-century French settlers. Brule (burned) and geule (mouth) became bu'n jaw and finally buljol.

Place the salt cod in a large bowl or dish and cover with boiling water. Let it cool, then cover and store overnight in the refrigerator. The next day, drain and rinse the fish. Add to a large pot of water and bring to a boil, then reduce the heat to medium. Simmer the saltfish for 40 minutes. Drain, let cool, then shred into medium-sized (1–2-inch) flakes and set aside.

In a medium nonreactive bowl, fold together all the remaining ingredients except for the avocado. Let marinate at room temperature for 30 minutes, then divide the salad between plates and top with sliced avocado. Serve with Bake (page 246) or saltine crackers.

ORIGIN: Trinidad and Tobago
YIELD: 2 servings

½ pound salt cod

¼ medium white onion, sliced

1 Roma tomato, diced

1 clove garlic, minced

1 teaspoon Peppa Sauce (page 25)

1 teaspoon freshly ground black pepper

1 teaspoon kosher salt

Juice of 1 lemon

Juice of 1 lime

½ ripe avocado, sliced

Buljol is best served immediately.

TUNA KITFO

Tuna kitfo is an example of how adaptable so much of Ethiopian cuisine is to the rest of the world. Kitfo, also called ketfo, is essentially Ethiopian beef tartare. Spicier than the regular American steakhouse version, both traditional beef kitfo and tuna kitfo are commonly found on the menus of many of Washington, D.C.'s hundreds of Ethiopian restaurants. And it's no surprise why. The flavor profile—NKO; mitmita, a cardamom spice blend; berbere; and the blazing heat of awaze, a spicy simmered sauce—works as beautifully on tuna as it does on beef. (Even though tuna can be found in the nearby Red Sea, Ethiopia is landlocked and thus, no tuna kitfo.) I love this preparation because it combines two undeniably appetizing classics—tuna tartare and kitfo—and helps us open our eyes to the possibilities of both.

For the awaze

Stir together all the ingredients, taste, adjust seasoning, and set aside.

For the tuna

Fill a medium bowl with ice and set a smaller bowl inside it. To the smaller bowl add the mitmita, black cardamom, NKO, and salt, stirring well to combine, then fold in the tuna. Cover with plastic wrap, transfer to the refrigerator, and let marinate for 1 hour, then stir in the lemon juice. To serve, dust very lightly with ground oregano and serve with awaze on the side.

ORIGIN: Ethiopia
YIELD: 2 to 4 servings

For the awaze
1½ teaspoons GGP (page 5)
½ cup NKO (page 21)
¼ cup freshly squeezed lemon juice
6 tablespoons Berbere (page 9)
2 teaspoons cayenne
Kosher salt, to taste

For the tuna
½ teaspoon mitmita
½ teaspoon ground black cardamom seeds (from 2 or 3 pods)
2 tablespoons NKO (page 21)
½ teaspoon kosher salt
½ pound skinless sushi-grade tuna, diced into ¼-inch cubes
Juice of 1 lemon
Ground dried oregano, to serve

Tuna kitfo is best served immediately, but awaze will keep in an airtight container in the refrigerator for up to 4 days.

FISHERMAN'S PIE

Fisherman's pie, like the Jamaican Beef Patty (page 191), is a culinary legacy of British colonialism in the Caribbean. It is a dish familiar to the English kitchen but wrung through the Caribbean wringer. In Jamaica, for instance, the potato-topped dish is made with cod or haddock and coconut milk and a burst of hot pepper. To Louisianians, like my mom, fisherman's pie is essentially a luxurious bisque, in which a bayou's worth of shrimp and crawfish swim in a cheesy beurre blanc sauce. But for Miss Fran, the mother of my two child-hood friends, a dyed-in-the-wool Irish American, fisherman's pie was a classic Irish American casserole, made with cod and scallops. Imagine how surprised Miss Fran was when she asked my mother to cater a party, only to find that my mom's fisherman's pie was radically different from—and, let's face it, much better than—her own. This Louisianian version, inspired by a similar dish from Pappadeaux Seafood Kitchen, a regional seafood chain in Louisiana and Texas, pretty much screams comfort. And the sheer amount of dairy—cream! butter! cheese! cream cheese!—makes a post-pie nap inevitable. But it's impossible not to eat a first serving, then a second, and quite possibly a third.

For the duchess potatoes

Place the potatoes in a large pot and cover with 2 inches cool water. Season with 2 teaspoons of salt, then cover and bring to a boil. Boil until fork tender, 10 to 15 minutes.

While the potatoes cook, combine the butter and cream in a small pan and heat over the lowest setting to keep warm until the potatoes are ready.

Drain the potatoes and spread on a sheet pan to steam out for 5 minutes—they should start to look a little chalky at the edges. Use a ricer or food mill to rice the warm potatoes (alternately, mash with a potato masher until smooth and fluffy). Transfer the butter and cream mixture to a medium-sized mixing bowl, then, using a wooden spoon, gently fold the potatoes into the warm cream mixture, along with the remaining 1 teaspoon salt. Taste

ORIGIN: American South
YIELD: 4 to 6 servings

For the duchess potatoes
2 pounds **Yukon Gold potatoes** (about 4 to 5 medium), peeled and cut into ½-inch dice
1 tablespoon **kosher salt**, divided, plus more to taste
4 tablespoons **unsalted butter**
¼ cup **heavy cream**
1 **egg**, lightly beaten

For the fisherman's pie
4 tablespoons **unsalted butter**, divided
5 **garlic cloves**, minced
¼ cup dry **white wine**
½ cup **heavy cream**
4 ounces **cream cheese**
2 tablespoons **House Spice** (page 6)
4 ounces **Parmigiano Reggiano cheese**, divided, grated on a microplane (about 3 loose cups)
1 pound medium **shrimp**, peeled, tailed, deveined
½ pound skinless **salmon fillet**, cut into 1-inch cubes
1 pound cooked **crawfish tails**, thawed if frozen
1 tablespoon **kosher salt**, plus more to taste

Fisherman's pie is best served immediately, but leftovers will keep in an airtight container in the refrigerator for up to 1 day.

and adjust seasoning, then let cool to room temperature, 20 to 30 minutes. Gently mix in the egg, being careful not to overmix or the potatoes will become gluey. Set aside.

For the fisherman's pie

Heat the oven to 350°F.

In a medium saucepan over medium-low heat, melt 3 tablespoons of the butter. Add the garlic and sauté until fragrant and pale golden, 2 to 3 minutes. Add the wine and let simmer for 3 minutes, then add the cream, cream cheese, and house spice. Bring to a gentle simmer, then fold in half of the Parmigiano. Remove from the heat and let cool to room temperature, 10 to 15 minutes, then fold in the seafood and 1 tablespoon of salt.

To assemble, grease a 11-x-7-inch (2-quart) baking dish with the remaining 1 tablespoon butter. Add the seafood mixture, then dollop with the potatoes, spreading into an even layer on top. Use a large spoon to make some peaks and valleys in the potatoes. Sprinkle with the remaining Parmigiano, then bake for 30 minutes, until potatoes are golden brown.

Let the pie rest 10 minutes before serving warm.

JAMAICA

The idea for my second restaurant, Kith and Kin, began at Jackie's West Indian Bakery, a narrow long-countered spot, tucked between a Popeye's and a dentist office on 233rd Street in the Bronx. From the oven at Jackie's emerged pillowy soft coco bread and half-moon beef patties, whose sun-colored wrappers were filled with ground beef studded with Scotch bonnet pepper. Jackie's is just one of many terrific Jamaican bakeries in the North Bronx, which, along with Flatbush, Brooklyn, form Little Jamaica, home to more than 300,000 Jamaican immigrants in the New York City area. I used to live for those patties, that bread, moments of pleasure during the long commute from my father's house to school in Mount Vernon.

My father's mother, Grandma Gloria, is Jamaican. But by the time I arrived in Jamaica a few months ago for the first time as an adult, I had realized exactly how complete my family's migration had been. Despite multiple attempts on Facebook, I couldn't locate any of my family still on the island. They had all left, some to England, and many more to the United States. I arrived in Montego

Bay as a secondhand third-generation Jamaican with no kith or kin to speak of.

I was here both to explore this country to which I owe such a huge culinary debt and to cook at the birthday of my friend Common's mother, who was turning seventy the day before I turned thirty. I got in late and had just enough time to grab some snapper at the resort's restaurant, Sugar Mill, before I passed out. The next morning, I met my friend Andre Fowles, the talented young chef at Miss Lilly's at the Skylark resort in Negril, on the beach. He was standing on the deck of a small boat holding a spear gun with a broad smile. "Ready to go fishing, bro?" he asked. "You have to ask?" I replied.

We sailed until the captain cut the engine a couple miles offshore. "Come with me," said Andre, thrusting a spear gun and a pair of goggles into my hand. We dove into the water. From above the surface, the Caribbean sea seems tranquil, but underneath, life teems: lobster, lionfish, and conch scatter and climb along the coral reefs. These are easy hunting, and I quickly bagged a couple good-sized lobster. Back at the beach, Andre had arranged for grills to be set up. We headed back and stuffed ourselves on fresh conch grilled with just a squeeze of lime.

More than almost any other country, Jamaica is read about in two different ways in two different places and rarely by the same person. Newspaper front pages tend to talk about crime and corruption, both of which

have plagued the country since independence in 1962. Travel stories wax lyrical about the beaches (snow white) and the ocean (deep blue) and the music (reggae, now on the UNESCO World Heritage list). And all of these things are true together but somehow false separately. Nowhere is this more clear than in Kingston, Jamaica's largest city.

After saying farewell to Andre, I drove three hours through the inland to Kingston to meet Jacqui Sinclair, a local food journalist who happens, I soon found out, to know every single restaurant in Kingston, every vendor at every food market, and nearly everyone else, too. We started our journey at Coronation Market, a vast farmer's market in an old wrought iron pavilion on the eastern edge of Tivoli Gardens. Inside the market, I walked by mountains of fiery Scotch bonnet peppers, mounds of dark crimson hibiscus blossoms, and technicolor displays of fresh ackee. We bought them all. "C'mon," Jacqui said, "we'll make this all at my house."

Shopping done, Jacqui took me to a stall for sprats and dumplings, fried silvery fish bathed in vinegary escovitch accompanied by flecks of fried dough. "Be careful," she cautioned, "don't fill up. We have a ways to go." What followed wasn't just a food tour—though it was that—but also a journey into Jamaica's colorful history. The curried goat at Moby Dick's was a reminder of the Indian influence still exerted centuries after British merchants first brought Indian slaves to the island in the seventeenth century. The bowls of steaming peanut porridge, touched with honey and cinnamon, made clear the connection with West African cuisine, where such ground crops are staples. The stew peas—with the long-simmered salt beef and pig tails—connect Jamaica to the rest of Latin America's rice-and-bean obsession.

It was late in the evening when we arrived, bags in hand, back at Jacqui's house, at the top of a steep mountain. She had invited a few friends over for dinner, including a Culinary Institute of America–trained chef who goes by the name Alex D-Great and who had bright green dreadlocks. "Kwame, brother," he said to me, "let me show you a thing or two." He led me back to the kitchen, where he was mid–mise en place, making brown stewed chicken. My nostrils flared as memories flowed into me. This was one of the dishes I remember from my childhood—not from my mother's kitchen but from my father's girlfriends—and it was a small bright spot of my time with him. Alex showed me how he first marinated the chicken with raw sugar, tomato and onions, garlic, scallions, allspice, Scotch bonnet peppers, and pickapeppa sauce, a sort of Jamaican Worcestershire sauce. As we stood side by side, we cooked together: marinating, then searing the chicken, adding stock and a bit of ketchup. The smells bloomed around us, and when I brought the spoon to taste the stew, I felt at home again.

POULTRY

*U*nfortunately for *Gallus gallus domesticus*, but fortunately for mankind, chickens are meal-sized. As opposed to hogs or cattle, one chicken yields one chicken dinner. They're a cinch to raise and easy to slaughter. (Well, as much as anything is. I remember the horror with which I greeted the task as a child in Nigeria, but those chickens running about the yard of my grandfather's compound weren't just any chickens, they were Red and Goofy, my friends!)

Today chicken is by far the most consumed animal on the planet, accounting for 23 billion of the 30 billion land animals living on farms. This is thanks largely to industrial chicken production, but even before Big Egg, Africans, Afro-Caribbeans, and African Americans—along, of course, with everyone else—made ample use of the bird.

Not only does their small nature make chickens affordable to raise and convenient to slaughter, but the high skin-to-meat ratio offers all sorts of benefits. The well-seasoned crunch of a rotisserie bird, like the ones dripping their fat into the crackling flame in the windows of the lechoneras of the Bronx, are, I think, poultry's highest form. But it would be crazy not to shout out fried chicken here, which, of all that is fried in the American South, is rightfully the most well known. Before fried chicken was injected into the national bloodstream, thanks to the transformation of Harland Sanders's roadside restaurant into a vast fast food empire built on dewy-eyed antebellum myth, and long before fried chicken was "rediscovered" by gourmets, it has been a staple for Black folks in the South and wherever we landed after the Great Migration.

As with so many foodways of the American South, fried chicken too has its roots in the slavery era. Chicken was one of the few livestock the African and African American families could raise on their own. Fried chicken requires little except chicken, lard—which was in ample supply—seasoning, some flour, and an iron vessel. That recipe has largely remained unchanged.

In Africa, where the chicken was introduced in the year 1000 by Arab traders, the bird was held in high regard as both a protein and a tool of divination. In the South, well into the twentieth century, this carried through as the Gospel Bird, served to preachers on Sundays. Today, still, the call of the chicken draws pilgrims from around the world to places like Nashville's Prince's Hot Chicken and the jerk joints of Portland, Jamaica.

The popularity of fried chicken rests on the bird itself. For instance, when brined, that fried chicken sucks up the buttermilk and brine until the meat is plump and juicy and can withstand the moisture being sucked out of it in the hot fat without becoming dry. As any kitchen-savvy chicken lover knows, the thighs, with their dark juicier meat, are much better in almost all cases than the lily-white breasts. Chicken's ability to bear flavor also makes it perfect for soups and stews, which are much more common in Africa and the Caribbean than fried chicken. The berbere spice of Ethiopia's doro wat or the red stew of Nigeria's chicken in red stew and even the sweetness of Jamaica's brown stew chicken or Senegal's chicken yassa are all made impossibly delicious thanks to chicken's willingness to play wingman. The same can be said for the garlicky, citrus-y, mojo sauced pollo asado. The call of the bird is strong and heard by all who are hungry.

POLLO ASADO

At the Culinary Institute of America, where I went to culinary school, the unit on rotisserie chicken was meant to blow our minds. Had we ever had skin so crispy or meat so succulent? The bird—prepared with thyme, lemon, mirepoix, and unfathomable amounts of butter—was indeed picture perfect. But the answer is, I grew up in the Bronx, eating $5 pollo asado from Dominican and Puerto Rican storefront restaurants—so yeah, I had had bird this good. I was impressed but not *that* impressed by a French poulet roti.

    This pollo asado is garlic-forward with a citrus punch and the reddish hue of ajiote (or annato) and adobo, the Latin American equivalents of house spice. Like so much chicken worthy of praise, this one takes time. Though the time in the oven is relatively short—an hour and change—the brine and marinade take 36 hours, plenty of time to build up an appetite.

For the brined chicken

Halve the lime and squeezing the juice into a large bowl, then toss in the lime halves. Add the remaining ingredients except the ice water and stir until the salt and sugar dissolve, then stir in the ice water. Set aside.

Rinse the chicken and remove and discard any giblets. Place the chicken in a 1-gallon ziplock bag and cover completely with the brine. Seal the bag, pressing out as much air as possible, then place in a large bowl. Refrigerate overnight.

For the marinade

Meanwhile, make the marinade by combining all the ingredients and set aside.

ORIGIN: Caribbean
YIELD: 4 to 6 servings

For the brined chicken
1 whole chicken
(about 3½ pounds)
1 lime
½ cup + 1 tablespoon kosher salt
4½ tablespoons white granulated sugar
6 garlic cloves
4 fresh bay leaves
3 cups boiling water
9 cups ice water

For the marinade
1 cup Mojo Sauce (page 31)
8 packets (or 3 tablespoons + 1 teaspoon) sazón con culantro y achiote
1 tablespoon adobo seasoning
½ cup GGP (page 5)

To assemble
Marinade (above)
Brined chicken (above)
10 fresh thyme sprigs
5 fresh oregano sprigs
1 orange, halved
1 lemon, halved

To assemble

Rinse the brined chicken and pat it dry with paper towels. Rub it inside and out with the marinade, then stuff with the thyme, oregano, and orange and lemon halves. Tuck the wing tips and tie the legs with kitchen twine. Line a sheet pan with foil. Set the chicken on a roasting rack (or a wire cooling rack) set in a lined sheet pan and refrigerate, uncovered, for 24 hours.

When ready to cook, take the chicken out of the fridge and let it sit out at room temperature for at least 30 minutes and up to 1 hour. Heat the oven to 300°F. Roast the chicken on its rack for 1 hour, then increase the heat to 500°F and roast for 15 minutes more.

Let the chicken rest for 10 minutes, then serve immediately, with Yellow Rice (page 51).

Pollo asado will keep in an airtight container in the refrigerator for up to 4 days.

CHICKEN IN RED STEW

My father had many sisters, and each had her own specialty. Chicken in red stew was my Aunt Theresa's. Like most Nigerian families, we ate the fragrant, slightly spicy, slightly sweet stew with jollof rice but, in an Onwuachi-only tradition, often also with fufu, which is a rather more uncommon swallow accompaniment. Chicken in red stew relies, naturally, on red stew, or obe ata din din, the Nigerian mother sauce. It can be used to braise a protein, as it is here, imbuing the rather tough meat of a chicken leg with flavor, or as a finishing sauce, or an element of a more complex sauce. When re-creating this dish for my restaurant Kith and Kin, I would have been a fool not to tap my aunt for her knowledge, particularly on the red stew. The first time I called "hands" at the pass—meaning it was time for the server to run the plate from the kitchen to the table—for an order of chicken in red stew, I teared up. To see this dish, vibrant, flavorful, so intrinsically a part of my own family history, exit the kitchen in a fine porcelain bowl felt like a triumph. That it was so often ordered was a validation not only that I had done right by my aunt but that these flavors, this dish, this history, could be appreciated by everyone.

ORIGIN: Nigeria
YIELD: 4 servings

2 tablespoons grapeseed oil
Kosher salt, to taste
4 chicken leg quarters
(2 to 2½ pounds total)
1 cup Chicken Stock (page 33)
3 cups Obe Ata Din Din
(page 22)

Chicken in red stew will keep in an airtight container in the refrigerator for up to 4 days, or in the freezer for up to 2 months.

Heat the oil in a Dutch oven over high heat. Season the chicken on both sides with salt, then sear, skin side first, until deep golden brown, about 7 minutes per side. Do this in batches if necessary so as not to crowd the pan. Remove the seared chicken to a bowl, then deglaze the pot with the chicken stock, stirring and scraping to pick up any browned bits. Stir in the obe ata din din, then add the chicken along with any juices. Bring to a simmer over medium heat and simmer gently, uncovered, until the chicken is tender, 25 to 30 minutes. Season with salt to taste.

Serve with Fufu (page 111) and/or Jollof Rice (page 57).

BROWN STEW CHICKEN

Brown stew, like Browning, is an outgrowth of Jamaica's sugar industry, which claimed the lives of hundreds of thousands of Africans forced to work on the plantations that dotted the island. Though the vast majority of sugar—in its finished form, as molasses or as rum—was exported, nevertheless some of it inevitably made its way into local kitchens. There it became caramelized into Browning, and it's used here in one of Jamaica's best-known dishes. Not so spicy it scares off children, not so sweet it turns off adults, everyone can agree on brown stew chicken. Not all families add additional sugar—recipes vary from region to region and from house to house—but I do, which yields even more caramelization. That means, this is browning on browning, browning squared, and I haven't had any complaints yet.

In a large nonreactive dish, combine all the ingredients except the grapeseed oil, ketchup, chicken stock, and Scotch bonnet. Cover and refrigerate for at least 24 hours and up to 48 hours.

When ready to cook, remove the chicken from the marinade, reserving the marinade with the vegetables. In a Dutch oven over high heat, heat 2 tablespoons oil. When it shimmers, add the chicken skin side down and sear until deeply golden brown on both sides, about 4 minutes per side. Work in batches as necessary to avoid crowding the pan. Remove to a plate and set aside. Reduce the heat to medium and add the vegetable-marinade mixture. Sauté, stirring occasionally, until tender, about 10 minutes, then stir in the ketchup, stock, and Scotch bonnet (leaving it whole). Return the chicken to the pot and bring to a gentle simmer over medium-low heat. Cook for 1 hour.

Remove the chicken from the pot and increase the heat to medium-high to bring the stew to a brisk simmer. Reduce to a thick, saucy consistency, 10 to 15 minutes, then remove and discard the Scotch bonnet (being careful not to puncture it) and return chicken to the pot. Serve with Rice and Peas (page 49) and Sweet Plantains (page 79).

ORIGIN: Jamaica
YIELD: 6 servings

6 **chicken leg quarters**

2 medium **yellow onions,** large dice

2 **plum tomatoes,** large dice

3 tablespoons **GGP** (page 5)

4 tablespoons **Peppa Sauce** (page 25)

3 tablespoons **Browning** (page 13)

2 teaspoons ground **allspice**

½ tablespoon **House Spice** (page 6)

3 fresh **thyme sprigs**

3 fresh **bay leaves**

2 tablespoons **turbinado (raw) sugar**

2 teaspoons **kosher salt,** plus more to taste

Grapeseed oil, as needed

1 cup **ketchup**

2 quarts **Chicken Stock** page 33)

1 **red Scotch bonnet pepper**

Brown stew chicken will keep in an airtight container in the refrigerator for up to 4 days, or in the freezer for up to 2 months.

CARIBBEAN CHICKEN SOUP

Every culture has a feel-better soup, a get-warm soup, a soup for comfort. This is Jamaica's. When I was sick as a kid, this is what my mother made me. It was so delicious I half looked forward to getting a cold. These days, I don't need that excuse to make a pot of this soup. The recipe is unique for its use of cho-cho, what Jamaicans call chayote, a member of the gourd family popular in the Caribbean, augmented here with other winter squash. Together with a packet of the ubiquitous Grace mix, the pop from the ginger, and the chorus of Caribbean aromatics, the soup is full of flavors that both comfort and cheer.

Season the chicken generously with house spice and salt. Let marinate at room temperature for 20 minutes.

Heat the oil in a Dutch oven or stock pot over medium-high heat. When it shimmers, add the chicken and sear until golden brown on both sides, about 4 minutes per side. Remove the chicken to a bowl and set aside.

Reduce heat to medium and add onions, garlic, and bell peppers. Sauté until the onions are beginning to turn translucent, 5 to 7 minutes, then add the tomato paste and cook, stirring often, 5 minutes more, until brick red. Add 1 tablespoon of house spice, the reserved chicken, and the remaining ingredients to the pot, stirring well to combine. Bring to a boil, then reduce to a gentle simmer. Simmer uncovered for 40 minutes.

Carefully remove the ginger, allspice berries, Scotch bonnet (being careful not to puncture it), bay leaves, and thyme sprigs. Taste and adjust seasoning, then serve.

ORIGIN: Jamaica

YIELD: 6 to 8 servings

---

1 whole **chicken** (3½ to 4 pounds), cut into 8 pieces

2 tablespoons **House Spice** (page 6), plus more to taste

Kosher salt, to taste

2 tablespoons **grapeseed oil**

2 medium **yellow onions**, diced

10 **garlic cloves**, minced

1 **green bell pepper**, diced

2 tablespoons **tomato paste**

1 **chayote squash**, cut into ½-inch dice

2 cups (about ¾ pound) ½-inch cubes peeled, seeded **pumpkin** or other hard **winter squash** (like butternut or kabocha)

One 1.76-ounce packet **Grace Cock Soup Mix**

2 large **Yukon Gold potatoes** (about 1 pound total), peeled and cut into ½-inch cubes

2 ears **corn**, each cut into 6 rounds

2 bunches **scallions**, sliced

Four 1-inch knobs **ginger**, peeled

12 whole **allspice** berries

1 **red Scotch bonnet pepper**

4 fresh **bay leaves**

10 fresh **thyme sprigs**

6 quarts **Chicken Stock** (page 33)

Caribbean chicken soup will keep in an airtight container in the refrigerator for up to 4 days, or in the freezer for up to 2 months.

DORO WAT

Ethiopia's national dish, doro wat is a brick-red chicken stew that combines two of Ethiopia and Eritrea's greatest contributions to the culinary world: the heat of berbere and the warmth of nitter kibbeh oil. The berbere works its spicy magic both as a marinade for the chicken (doro) and as a seasoning for the wat (stew), while the NKO is the fat in which the chicken is browned, imparting a spice profile that includes cinnamon, allspice, and cardamom. The other key component here is the caramelized onions, which soften the heat of the berbere. I've done all I can to complement these essential flavors with some tricks of my own, including the addition of GGP and the kick-in-the-pants of Maggi. To adjust the heat, go easy on the addition of berbere spice, making up the difference, if you wish, with paprika. Or, my preference, use injera as sweet soothing for a mouth on fire.

Combine 2½ tablespoons berbere and 1 tablespoon salt in a medium bowl. Season the chicken all over with the spice mixture, cover, and refrigerate for 24 hours.

When ready to cook, set a large heavy-bottomed pot over medium-high heat. Add enough NKO to cover the bottom in a thin layer. When it shimmers, add the chicken, skin side down. Sear the chicken on both sides until deep golden brown, about 4 minutes per side. Remove the chicken to a plate and set aside.

Add the puréed onions to the pot, reduce the heat to medium-low, and cook until the onions are sweet and beginning to look dry, about 2 minutes. Add the GGP and cook for 10 minutes more, stirring frequently, then add the tomato paste, the remaining 2 tablespoons of berbere, and the crushed Maggi, paprika, cardamom, and koseret (or oregano). Increase the heat to medium-high and cook, stirring often, until the mixture has caramelized to a brick-red color, 5 to 7 minutes.

ORIGIN: Ethiopia
YIELD: 4 servings

4½ tablespoons Berbere (page 9), divided

1 tablespoon kosher salt, plus more to taste

4 chicken leg quarters

2 tablespoons NKO (page 21), plus more as needed

3 medium yellow onions, puréed

¾ cup GGP (page 5)

6 tablespoons tomato paste

5 Maggi Seasoning cubes, crushed

1 tablespoon sweet paprika

2 teaspoons ground black cardamom

½ teaspoon koseret (or dried oregano)

6 cups Chicken Stock (page 33)

4 eggs

Injera, to serve (see note)

Note: Injera can be purchased at many grocery stores or ordered online.

Doro wat will keep in an airtight container in the refrigerator for up to 4 days.

Add 6 cups of chicken stock, scraping the pot to loosen any browned bits and stirring well to incorporate, then return the chicken to the pot. Bring to a simmer over medium-high heat, then add the eggs whole. Cook eggs 10 minutes, then remove to a bowl of ice water. Meanwhile, continue to cook the stew until the mixture has reduced by half, about 20 minutes more.

Once the eggs are cool, peel and prick them all over with a fork. Add the peeled eggs to the pot just before serving.

Taste and adjust the seasoning as necessary, adding more salt or berbere for more heat. Serve with injera.

JERK CHICKEN

Some dishes call to mind a flavor. Others sights or smells. Jerk chicken, though, is a sound memory. The whine of motorcycles, revved to wheelie, the rhythm of dance hall blasting, the beating heart of Little Jamaica. My father, whose mother was Jamaican and whose father was Nigerian, used to bring me up here at nights for dinner. In what was often a very tumultuous and difficult relationship, these nights were some of our most peaceful moments. We'd sit by the side of the road, with an open container of jerk chicken. Though I was a boy, I felt like a grown man, next to him, a man with a mouth on fire. Jerk chicken is spicy by nature. What was once a method of preparing food surreptitiously by Jamaican Maroons has become Jamaica's greatest contribution to the culinary canon: a tapestry of flavors, aromatics, and spices.

In Little Jamaica, these come alive in jerk shacks, in grocery stores, and in bakeries with freshly made beef patties and coco bread. Little Jamaica will always be my true Jamaica. So much so, in fact, that when I finally did go to the island, I remember thinking it just seemed like a bigger version of the Bronx. And when I had the jerk there, I was immediately transported back to those hot New York nights with my dad.

ORIGIN: Jamaica
YIELD: 4 servings

For the brine
2½ tablespoons kosher salt
1½ tablespoons white granulated sugar
1 clove garlic
1 tablespoon whole allspice berries
2 tablespoons Peppa Sauce (page 25)
8 fresh thyme sprigs
1 tablespoon sliced ginger (peel on)
1 fresh bay leaf
¼ lime
2 cups ice

For the chicken
4 bone-in, skin-on chicken leg quarters (2 to 2½ pounds)
¼ cup Jerk Paste (page 17)
2 tablespoons GGP (page 5)
Pimento (or mesquite) wood chips
½ cup Jerk BBQ Sauce (page 18), plus more to serve

Note: For the best result, you'll need a grill for this recipe.

Serve with additional jerk BBQ sauce, peppa sauce, Braised Cabbage and Carrots (page 85), and Rice and Peas (page 49).

For the brine

Combine all the ingredients but the ice, squeezing in the lime juice and dropping in the lime quarter, with 2 cups water in a medium pot over medium heat. Cook, stirring, until the salt and sugar have dissolved. Remove from heat, add the ice, and stir until all the ice has melted.

For the chicken

Place the chicken in a large ziplock bag and pour the brine over it. Seal the bag, pushing out as much air as possible, and place in a large bowl. Transfer to the refrigerator at least overnight and for up to 48 hours.

Discard the brine, then transfer the chicken to a large bowl. Toss with jerk paste and GGP, then cover the bowl and refrigerate for 24 hours.

One hour before you're ready to grill, soak the wood chips.

Heat the grill to medium heat. If using charcoal, pour the (soaked and drained) wood chips over it. If using a gas grill, pour the drained wood chips into a disposable foil pan, cover tightly with foil, and use a sharp knife to poke a few holes in the foil so smoke can escape. Set the pan of wood chips in the back corner of the grill. Once the chips begin smoking, remove the chicken from the marinade, letting any excess drip back into the bowl. Grill the chicken for 30 minutes, turning frequently to ensure a deep and even char. In the last 10 minutes, brush the chicken with jerk BBQ sauce each time you turn.

POLLO GUISADO

The soup all abuelitas make their grandchildren, cooking "a ojo," or by feel, with a million variations. I didn't have a Puerto Rican grandmother, so this version is a re-creation of the flavors I remember from places like Caridad and Louie's on Gun Hill Road, 188 Cuchifritos, and all the other lechonerias, cuchifritos, lunch counters, full-on restaurants, and street food vendors that nourish and restore the Bronx's massive Nuyorican population. The soup is a festival of comfort. At its base are the annatto and sofrito that define much of Puerto Rican cuisine, plus a touch of cumin and, because it's me who's making it, a bit of house spice to give just the merest hint of heat.

ORIGIN: Puerto Rico

YIELD: 4 servings

For the marinade

1 tablespoon **annatto powder**

1 medium **yellow onion**, sliced into ⅛-inch pieces

1 **Roma tomato**, chopped

10 **garlic cloves**, minced

1 tablespoon dried **oregano**

1 teaspoon **kosher salt**

Two 5-gram packets (or 2½ teaspoons) **sazón con culantro y achiote**

1½ teaspoons **House Spice** (page 6)

1 teaspoon ground **cumin**

4 **chicken leg quarters**

To assemble

2 tablespoons **grapeseed oil**

1 cup **Sofrito** (page 28)

3 cups **Chicken Stock** (page 33)

2 fresh **bay leaves**

One 6-gram cube powdered **chicken bouillon**, such as Knorr, crushed (or 1½ teaspoons powdered)

3 large **Yukon Gold potatoes** (about 1½ pounds total), peeled and cut into ½-inch cubes

2 **carrots**, peeled and diced

Kosher salt, to taste

Pollo guisado will keep in an airtight container in the refrigerator for up to 4 days.

For the marinade

Stir together all the ingredients for the marinade in a large bowl. Add the chicken leg quarters and toss to coat thoroughly. Cover and refrigerate overnight.

To assemble

When ready to cook, heat the oil in a large pan over medium-high heat. Scrape excess marinade from the chicken, reserving it in the bowl. When the oil shimmers, add the chicken and sear on both sides until golden brown, about 4 minutes per side. Remove the chicken to a plate and set aside.

Reduce the heat to medium and add the marinade and sofrito. Cook, stirring often, for 10 minutes, until caramelized and thick. Stir in the stock, bay leaves, bouillon, potatoes, and carrots, then return the chicken to the pot, skin side up. Bring to a gentle simmer and cook, uncovered and stirring often, for 40 minutes, until sauce is thick and deep reddish-brown and the potatoes and carrots are tender.

Remove bay leaves and discard. Season to taste with salt, then serve with Yellow Rice (page 51) or Perfectly Steamed Rice (page 46).

CURRIED CHICKEN

Americans like to think of America as a melting pot. But if they ever set foot on Trinidad and Tobago, they'd marvel at how so small a nation can be so vibrantly diverse. Curried chicken is a prime example. Obviously, curry is an East Indian staple; and the chicken, rather than pork or beef, a nod to the many Hindu and Muslim Trinbagonians for whom those meats are haram, or forbidden. The rest of the ingredients I include—the culantro-heavy green seasoning, house spice from my mom's kitchen, and the omnipresent peppa sauce—round out the dish, while the potatoes add starchy balance and serve as repositories of flavor.

Combine the salt, onions, green seasoning, curry powder, house spice, and chicken in a large bowl. Cover and refrigerate for 24 hours.

When ready to cook, add 2 tablespoons of oil to a large pot over high heat. When it shimmers, sear the chicken until deeply golden brown on both sides, about 4 minutes in total. Remove to a plate and set aside. Add ½ cup chicken stock to the pot, stirring to scrape up any browned bits, then return the chicken to the pan. Add any remaining marinade, the Scotch bonnet (leaving it whole), peppa sauce, and the rest of the chicken stock.

Bring the mixture to a boil over medium-high heat, then reduce the heat to medium-low. Simmer gently, uncovered, for 1 hour. Remove the chicken to a plate. Add the potatoes to the pot, cover partially, and simmer for 30 to 40 minutes, until just tender. Add up to ½ cup water as needed to keep saucy while the potatoes cook.

Remove and discard the Scotch bonnet (being careful not to puncture it), then return the chicken to the pot. Taste and adjust seasoning, then serve with Perfectly Steamed Rice (page 46).

ORIGIN: Trinidad and Tobago
YIELD: 4 servings

---

2 teaspoons **kosher salt**, plus more to taste

1 medium **yellow onion**, diced

1½ cups **Green Seasoning** (page 29)

4 tablespoons **Curry Powder** (page 10)

1½ teaspoons **House Spice** (page 6)

4 **chicken leg quarters**

2 tablespoons **grapeseed oil**, plus more as needed

1 quart **Chicken Stock** (page 33)

1 **red Scotch bonnet pepper**

2 teaspoons **Peppa Sauce** (page 25)

3 large **Yukon Gold potatoes** (about 1½ pounds), peeled and cut into ½-inch cubes

---

Curried chicken will keep in an airtight container in the refrigerator for up to 4 days, or in the freezer for up to 2 months.

CHICKEN AND WAFFLES

Chicken and waffles form a sort of continental divide between food scholars. On one side are those who regard the origin story of the combination—as a late-night/early-morning after-the-gig meal for jazz cats in early-twentieth-century Harlem, caught between dinner and breakfast—as nothing more than myth. They note, rightly, that chicken and waffles predates its Harlemite fame. On the other side are food historians who note, also rightly, that just because chicken and waffles have existed among the Pennsylvania Dutch since the seventeenth century, that doesn't in any way undermine the fact that they might also have spontaneously cropped up in late-night restaurants like Well's Supper Club. For my money, I'm betting both sides can be true. It makes sense that two disparate groups of people would cotton on to the sweet-and-crunchy combination of fried chicken and waffles independently. As for me, chicken and waffles will always be associated with the rare occasions we'd go out for family brunch at places like Sugar Hill Bistro and Sylvia's. In my family, at least, the adults ordered shrimp and grits while we children got chicken and waffles. The day you switched from one to the other was the day you became an adult, bar mitzvah through brunch.

As no doubt you'll notice, this recipe is different from the traditional fried chicken recipe (page 183). I love them both, of course. That one combines cornstarch and flour. This version relies only on cornstarch as a coating and places an emphasis on textured crunchiness, which holds the chili honey better.

For the fried chicken

Prep the chicken: Place the thighs in a bowl and add buttermilk. Stir to coat, then cover and refrigerate overnight.

For the crispy waffles

Sift together all the dry ingredients in a medium bowl. In another bowl, stir together the milk, melted butter, and whole egg. Stir

ORIGIN: American South
YIELD: 4 servings

For the fried chicken
4 boneless skinless chicken thighs
2 cups buttermilk
2 cups cornstarch
1 teaspoon kosher salt, plus more to taste
House Spice (page 6), to taste
Vegetable oil, such as canola, for frying

For the crispy waffles
1½ cups pastry flour
2½ tablespoons malted milk powder
1½ teaspoons instant dry yeast
2 tablespoons white granulated sugar
1 teaspoon kosher salt
½ teaspoon baking soda
1¼ cups whole milk, warmed
5½ tablespoons unsalted butter, melted
1 egg + 1 egg white

For the chili honey
1 cup honey
1 tablespoon red chili flakes
½ teaspoon kosher salt

the wet ingredients into the dry until just combined; let rest for at least 10 minutes and up to 2 hours so the yeast can bloom.

For the chili honey

While the batter rests, make the chili honey: Combine all the ingredients in a small saucepan set over low heat. Warm gently for 15 minutes, then remove from the heat and set aside to cool slightly. Transfer to a blender and purée until smooth, return to the saucepan, and set aside.

To assemble

When ready to cook, preheat a waffle iron. Heat the oven to 300°F. Place a wire cooling rack inside a sheet tray, and place the sheet tray in the oven. In a large, deep-sided cast-iron skillet or Dutch oven, heat 1½ inches of oil over medium heat to 350°F. Place the egg white in a third bowl. Using a handheld mixer (or a whisk and some elbow grease), whip the egg white to stiff peaks, then gently fold into the waffle batter.

Stir together the cornstarch and 1 teaspoon salt in a shallow bowl. Working in batches as necessary and being careful to shake off excess buttermilk, dredge the chicken in cornstarch, then fry until golden and cooked through, turning every 4 minutes or so, about 16 minutes total. Place the fried chicken on one side of the warmed sheet pan, seasoning each piece generously with house spice and salt, and return it to the oven while you finish making the remaining chicken and the waffles.

While the chicken fries, cook the waffles until deeply golden brown and crisp: Follow your waffle maker's instructions, using ¾ cup batter per waffle. Transfer the cooked waffles to the other side of the sheet pan in the oven.

To serve, warm the chili honey if desired. Place a fried chicken thigh on top of each waffle and drizzle with chili honey.

Fried chicken and waffles are best served immediately, though they'll each hold (unassembled) in the oven for 20 minutes. Chili honey may be made up to 1 month in advance and stored in an airtight container at room temperature. Any leftover chicken will keep in the refrigerator in an airtight container for up to 4 days. Any leftover waffles may be frozen for up to 1 month.

HOT CHICKEN SANDWICH

Nashville-style hot chicken, made famous by Prince's Hot Chicken, was originally invented as payback for the philandering ways of one James Thornton Prince. According to André Prince Jeffries, his great-niece, who now runs Prince's, one Saturday night in the 1930s the tall and handsome Thornton stepped out on his woman (one of them, anyway). Infuriated, she doused his chicken on Sunday morning with hot sauce. But pain mixed with pleasure when Thornton took a bite, and a classic was born. Soon thereafter, he and his brothers began selling the hot chicken recipe. Like any sane person, I stop by Prince's every time I'm in Nashville, willingly biting into the fiery sandwich, knowing the burn will last for hours and obliterate everything else I taste. It's worth it, though, for the heat is accompanied by hidden sweetness, intense juiciness, and lingering notes of spice. For this version, however, I wanted to dial down the heat so the underlying mix of spices isn't lost. Berbere strikes the right balance, while using NKO rather than oil or lard to season turns this chicken sandwich, once meant for revenge, into a reward.

ORIGIN: American South
YIELD: 4 sandwiches

For the pickles
2 **Persian cucumbers**
2 tablespoons freshly squeezed **lemon juice**
2 tablespoons **white balsamic vinegar**
4 teaspoons **Green Seasoning** (page 29)
1 tablespoon roughly chopped fresh **cilantro leaves**
½ teaspoon **kosher salt**

For the ginger-cabbage slaw
¼ small **green cabbage**, cored and shredded
¾ cup **white balsamic vinegar**
2 tablespoons **GGP** (page 5)
1 tablespoon plus 1½ teaspoons **white granulated sugar**
2 tablespoons **kosher salt**
1 teaspoon **Berbere** (page 9)

For the chili honey
1 cup **honey**
1 tablespoon **red chili flakes**
½ teaspoon **kosher salt**

For the house sauce
¼ cup **Hellmann's mayonnaise**
2 teaspoons **ketchup**
2 teaspoons **RGP** (page 11)
½ teaspoon **House Spice** (page 6)
¼ teaspoon **kosher salt**

For the pickles

Slice the cucumbers into ⅛-inch-thick coins. Combine the remaining ingredients in a blender and purée until smooth, then transfer to a ziplock bag along with the cucumbers. Toss to coat thoroughly, then press out as much air as possible and seal the bag. Place in a bowl and refrigerate for 24 hours.

For the slaw

Combine all the ingredients in a nonreactive bowl with ½ cup water, scrunching the cabbage gently with your hands. Cover tightly with plastic wrap and refrigerate for 24 hours.

For the chili honey

Combine all the ingredients in a small saucepan set over low heat. Warm gently for 15 minutes, then remove from the heat and set aside to cool slightly. Purée until smooth and set aside at room temperature.

For the house sauce

Stir together all the ingredients in a small bowl. Cover and refrigerate until ready to assemble.

For the fried hot chicken

Marinate the chicken: Place the chicken in a bowl and add buttermilk. Stir to coat, then cover and refrigerate overnight.

When ready to eat, fry your chicken: Set a wire rack inside a rimmed sheet pan. In a large, deep-sided cast-iron skillet or Dutch oven, heat 1½ inches of oil over medium heat to 350°F. Stir together the NKO, chili oil, berbere, and paprika in a medium bowl. Whisk together the cornstarch and 1 teaspoon salt in a shallow bowl. Working in batches as necessary and being careful to shake off excess buttermilk, dredge the chicken in the cornstarch, then fry until golden and cooked through, turning every 4 minutes or so, 16 minutes total. Immediately salt the chicken to taste and fully dunk in the spiced oil (stir the oil before dipping, since the spices will settle). Set the fried chicken on the wire rack to drain.

To assemble

Drain the slaw. Spread a teaspoon of butter on the cut sides of each bun. Heat a large pan over medium heat and toast the buns, cut side down, until golden. Then build the sandwich in the following order: bottom bun, 5 pickles, fried hot chicken, 1 tablespoon chili honey drizzled over the chicken, 2 leaves lettuce, about 2 tablespoons slaw, 1 tablespoon house sauce spread on the top bun, top bun. Season to taste with house spice and salt.

For the fried hot chicken
4 boneless skinless **chicken thighs**
2 cups **buttermilk**
Vegetable oil, such as canola, for frying
1 cup **NKO** (page 21)
1 cup store-bought **Chinese chili oil** (strained of any chili flakes, if necessary)
¼ cup **Berbere** (page 9)
¼ cup **sweet paprika**
2 cups **cornstarch**
1 teaspoon **kosher salt**, plus more to taste

To assemble
8 teaspoons **unsalted butter**, softened
4 **brioche burger buns**
8 leaves **Boston bibb lettuce**
House Spice (page 6), to taste
Kosher salt, to taste

Once assembled, hot chicken sandwiches are best served immediately. Fried hot chicken will keep in an airtight container in the refrigerator for up to 4 days. Pickles, slaw, and house sauce may be made up to 1 day in advance and stored in airtight containers in the refrigerator. Chili honey may be made up to 1 month in advance and stored in an airtight container at room temperature.

FRIED CHICKEN

Fried chicken is me. Fried chicken is my mom. Obviously, Black people aren't monolithic—do I really need to write that?—but fried chicken nevertheless has been closely associated with Blackness for years, rightfully occupying a privileged place within our culture. (It has also been used as a weapon by bigots outside of it—but then again, what hasn't?) Fried chicken came from the South, and there is a bridge between Africans in the South, who were able to raise their own chickens, and the West Africans, for whom chicken—first introduced by Arab traders in the year 1000—were sacred both as food and as tools for divination. By the time fried chicken made its way onto the Sunday dinner table, the time-consuming process of brining and marinating had itself become an almost religious ritual. There's no arguing with the holy spirit of a well-fried chicken. Starting with the Great Migration, fried chicken went wide, and since then, it has become more than just a Sunday dinner—it's a national treasure.

For the brine

Combine all the ingredients but the ice water in a large bowl and stir until the salt and sugar dissolve. Add the icy water and stir until the ice is melted.

For the fried chicken

Place the chicken pieces in a ziplock bag and cover completely with brine. Seal the bag, pressing out as much air as possible, then place the bag in a bowl and refrigerate overnight.

The next day, stir together the buttermilk and 1 tablespoon house spice. Drain the brined chicken, discarding the brine, then place in a bowl (or another ziplock plastic bag) and cover with the buttermilk mixture. Marinate in the refrigerator for at least 2 hours and up to 24 hours.

When ready to cook, stir together the cornstarch, flour, remaining 1 tablespoon house spice, and salt in a large bowl. Remove the chicken from the buttermilk, letting the buttermilk drip off, →

ORIGIN: American South
YIELD: 4 servings

For the brine
6 tablespoons **kosher salt**
3 tablespoons **white granulated sugar**
3 **garlic cloves**
3 fresh **bay leaves**
2 cups **boiling water**
6 cups **ice water**

For the fried chicken
1 whole **chicken** (3½ to 4 pounds), cut into 8 pieces
4 cups **buttermilk**
2 tablespoons **House Spice** (page 6), divided
1 cup **cornstarch**
1 cup **all-purpose flour**
2 teaspoons **kosher salt**
Vegetable oil, such as canola, for frying

Fried chicken will keep in an airtight container in the refrigerator for up to 4 days.

and coat thoroughly in the seasoned flour. Set aside on a plate, reserving the seasoned flour, for 20 minutes while you heat the oil.

In a large, deep-sided cast-iron skillet or Dutch oven, heat 1½ inches of oil over medium heat to 350°F. Working in batches as necessary, quickly dredge the chicken again in the seasoned flour, then fry until golden and cooked through, turning every 4 minutes or so, about 16 minutes total.

Let rest for 8 minutes before serving with Louisiana-Style Hot Sauce (page 23).

CHICKEN YASSA

What defines yassa, one of Senegal's most beloved dishes, is the interplay between the tartness of the lemon, the sweetness of the onion, and the heat of the chili. These are all bumped up in this version with various amplifiers, like red wine vinegar and Dijon mustard, remnants of Senegal's French influence; Maggi Seasoning, the West African obsession; and GGP, my own secret weapon.

Chicken yassa is one of the most common preparations, though you'll also find fish yassa in the Casamance region of Senegal. Even though I didn't grow up eating yassa except for trips to Le Petit Senegal on West 116th, when I opened my restaurant Kith and Kin, I knew the combination of flavors would be a hit. I was right. This version, which calls for chicken legs, is simple and easy to make, one reason yassa is a weeknight favorite at my house.

In a large bowl, combine the onions, garlic, Scotch bonnet (leaving it whole), ¼ cup mustard, GGP, vinegar, black pepper, Maggi, salt, bay leaves, and carrots. Add the chicken and stir to coat thoroughly. Cover and marinate overnight in the refrigerator.

In a large pan or Dutch oven, heat the oil over medium-high heat. Scrape as much marinade off each chicken piece as possible, reserving the marinade for later, then sear the chicken pieces until golden brown on both sides, about 4 minutes per side. Remove from the pot and set aside.

Reduce the heat to medium and add the marinade to the pot. Sauté for 10 minutes, then stir in the chicken stock. Return the chicken to the pan, skin side up.

Bring to a simmer over medium-high heat and cook, uncovered, for 30 minutes, stirring frequently until the sauce has thickened. Be careful not to pop the Scotch bonnet while stirring.

Remove the Scotch bonnet (being careful not to puncture it) and bay leaves and discard. Stir the remaining tablespoon of mustard plus the lemon juice into the sauce, taste, and adjust seasoning. Serve with Jollof Rice (page 57).

ORIGIN: Senegal

YIELD: 4 servings

---

6 medium **yellow onions,** thinly sliced

12 **garlic cloves,** minced

1 **red Scotch bonnet pepper**

¼ cup + 1 tablespoon **Dijon mustard,** divided

¼ cup **GGP** (page 5)

¼ cup **red wine vinegar**

1½ teaspoons freshly ground **black pepper**

5 **Maggi Seasoning cubes,** crushed

2 teaspoons **kosher salt,** plus more to taste

3 fresh **bay leaves**

2 **carrots,** peeled and cut into ½-inch dice

4 **chicken leg quarters**

2 tablespoons **grapeseed oil**

6 cups **Chicken Stock** (page 33)

Juice of 1 lemon

Chicken yassa will keep in an airtight container in the refrigerator for up to 4 days, or in the freezer for up to 2 months.

BOILED TURKEY NECKS

Oxtails, chitterlings (chitlins), and boiled turkey necks all belong to the pantry of the dispossessed. They speak to our ability as a people to turn discard desirable. Boiled turkey necks, which appear on many soul food menus year round and at my house on Thanksgiving, are a tradition handed down over the centuries from our ancestors, who learned to make do with whatever part of an animal they had. These are boiled with aromatics until what meat is there is infused with flavor. But the meat is just one part of the pleasure. Sucking on the bones is something I remember fondly from many Thanksgiving nights. Turkey necks can be gotten for around $1.20 a pound from most butcher shops.

Heat the oil in a large pot over medium-high heat. Season the turkey necks all over with salt, then add to the pot and sear on each side until golden brown, about 8 minutes total. Add the stock, stirring and scraping to loosen any browned bits at the bottom of the pot, then add the remaining ingredients.

Bring to a boil, then reduce the heat to a simmer and cook, uncovered, for 1½ hours, until the turkey necks are tender and the broth has reduced slightly.

Discard the aromatics, then serve the turkey necks warm, with a bit of broth.

ORIGIN: American South
YIELD: 2 servings, plus extra broth

---

2 tablespoons **neutral oil** (such as canola)

1 pound **turkey necks**

Kosher salt, to taste

4 quarts **Chicken Stock** (page 33)

2 **white onions**, quartered

2 heads **garlic**, halved crosswise

1 bunch fresh **thyme** (about 20 sprigs)

2 cups **white vinegar**

3 tablespoons **House Spice** (page 6)

5 fresh **bay leaves**

Boiled turkey necks will keep in an airtight container, refrigerated, for up to 4 days, or in the freezer for up to 2 months.

MEAT

The spice-laden smoke of suya wafting above a Lagos street. The sweet scent of freshly baked beef patty, wrapped in sunset-yellow dough, sweeping down the avenues of the Bronx. The tendrils of spice from baby back ribs like notes of a melody that come in from the fire escape smoker my mother set up. Meat—beef, pork, goat, lamb—is woven into all diasporic cuisine, as much-needed life-sustaining protein and as vessels of flavor. Growing up, for me at least, meat was an event, not a default setting of the table. We were more likely to have peel-and-eat shrimp than, for instance, smothered pork chop. But when I saw the pork chop marinating on Monday night, I wouldn't eat all day Tuesday in anticipation.

The diet of Africans in the American South contained relatively little meat, since meat is an expensive ration. Pigs, since they could and did forage outside the plantation, were the main protein. Killed in fall or winter, their bodies became bacon, hams, loins, trotters, hogshead, sweetbread, maw, jowl, and chitterlings too. Smoked, the bacon and ham lasted longer, though ham, along with the "choicer" cuts high on the hog, went to the slave owners. Many of our techniques are therefore meant to extract from the "lesser" parts their flavors and to imbue them, by brining, by marinating, by rubbing, by salting, by slowly smoking, with even more.

To augment their rations, my ancestors relied on the streams and forests for their protein. Rabbit, opossum, deer, and squirrel were commonly hunted and trapped in the rare minutes of free time. But by and large, pork—smothered or shredded, barbecued or fried, made into bacon or fragrant chitterlings—was and continues to be the protein of the Black experience in America.

This is far from the case, however, in Nigeria, the West Indies, and the Caribbean. In Nigeria, an almost infinite parade of beef makes its way onto the tables, in the form of spiced skewers of suya, or as oxtail, ox tongue, cow foot, and cow skin. Other than beef, I remember market days with my grandmother, whom we called Mother, when stall after stall bore freshly slaughtered goats used during feasts, as well as bushmeat like grasscutter (the greater cane rat) and antelope. And in Trinidad and Tobago, where the cuisine is an intoxicating hybridization of East Indian traditions and Afro-Caribbean tastes, where the descendants of West African slaves mix with the descendants of East Indian indentured laborers, many of whom were Muslim, pork is replaced instead by goat, lamb, and beef. Goat, an adaptable species easy to raise in tight quarters, predominates, giving curries and stews their hardy flavors. For most of my life, my experience of Caribbean and West Indian meat was had a few blocks from my house in the Bronx, eaten standing up at tiny restaurants with outsized flavors. Goat roti. Beef patty tucked into coco bread. When I did finally get a chance to explore the home countries, these flavors burst forth with even more vibrancy than I could have imagined.

JAMAICAN BEEF PATTY

No other entry in the Jamaican canon of cooking captures the island's history as tidily, or as deliciously, as the beef patty. Layer upon layer of history and immigration—some forced, others voluntary—can be found in this patty and its pastry casing. English immigrants from Cornwall, where meat pies called pasties are common, are responsible for the invention of the hand pie itself. Indentured Indian laborers, who often served in the houses of the English colonizers, introduced turmeric to the pastry and curry to the filling, as revolutionary an evolution as perspective is to painting. West Africans and their descendants sharpened the flavors with peppers, while Jamaica's own Scotch bonnet pepper brought additional heat. As Jamaicans moved abroad, they carried these patties with them from Brixton to the Bronx. The yeasty sweet smell of the dough baking rises from the end of the line of the 2 train, In Flatbush Avenue in Brooklyn, to the other in Wakefield, in the far North Bronx. Dancing images of beef patties tucked into pillows of Coco Bread (page 236) got me through endless church services on Sundays because I knew what awaited me, a divine reward.

ORIGIN: Jamaica
YIELD: 18 small patties

For the dough and to assemble
1½ cups all-purpose flour, plus more as needed for dusting
1 teaspoon ground turmeric
¼ teaspoon kosher salt
8 tablespoons unsalted butter, cubed and frozen
¼ cup + 3 tablespoons ice water
2 eggs
2 tablespoons whole milk

For the filling
2 tablespoons grapeseed oil
1 tablespoon GGP (page 5)
1 tablespoon Jerk Paste (page 17)
1 tablespoon Green Seasoning (page 29)
1 tablespoon Peppa Sauce (page 25)
1½ teaspoons Curry Powder (page 10)
¼ cup panko breadcrumbs
¼ cup Chicken Stock (page 33)
½ pound ground beef
1 teaspoon kosher salt, plus more to taste

For the dough

Prepare the dough by placing the flour, along with the bowl and blade of your food processor, in the freezer for 20 minutes. After 20 minutes, assemble the food processor, then add the flour, turmeric, and salt and pulse to combine. Add the butter and pulse to a coarse meal. (The butter should be in dime-sized pieces.) Add the ice water a tablespoon at a time, pulsing until the dough begins to come together in large clumps. Transfer to a lightly floured surface and knead a few times until it comes together into a smooth dough. If it's sticky, sprinkle in a bit more flour; if it doesn't come together, add a bit more water.

Flatten the dough into a disc and wrap tightly in plastic wrap. Refrigerate for 24 hours. →

For the filling

While the dough rests, make the filling: Heat the oil and GGP in a large pan over medium-high heat. Cook, stirring often, until very fragrant and beginning to brown, 2 to 3 minutes. Add the jerk paste, green seasoning, peppa sauce, and curry powder. Cook, stirring often, for 3 to 4 minutes, until deeply caramelized.

Stir in the breadcrumbs and chicken stock. Cook for 1 to 2 minutes, until the breadcrumbs are completely hydrated, then add the beef and 1 teaspoon salt. Cook until well browned, crumbly, and cooked through, 7 to 10 minutes. The liquid should be mostly cooked out but the pan shouldn't be totally dry. Taste and adjust seasoning, then remove from the heat to cool slightly. Refrigerate until completely cool, at least 2 hours and up to 24 hours.

To assemble

Cut the dough into quarters. Set 1 quarter on a well-floured work surface and return the rest of the dough to the refrigerator. Roll the dough as thinly as possible (⅛ inch) and use a 4½-inch round cookie cutter to cut it into discs. Set the discs on a sheet tray lined with parchment paper, and place a sheet of parchment between

each layer of discs. Keep the sheet tray in the refrigerator, and repeat this process until all of the dough is cut, combining and rerolling any leftover scraps until you have 18 discs.

Scoop 1 tablespoon of the filling into the palm of your hand and squeeze firmly to make a small ball. Repeat with the remaining filling—you should have 18 balls total.

Fill a small bowl with water. Place a portion of the filling onto the center of a disc of dough. Using your finger or a pastry brush, wet the edge of the dough halfway around, then fold the dry edge onto the wet edge and press down gently but firmly to seal, pushing out as much air as possible and spreading the filling around the inside of the patty. Crimp the edges with a fork, then place on a parchment paper–lined sheet tray. Repeat until all the patties have been shaped, then freeze for at least 30 minutes, or until ready to bake.

Heat the oven to 410°F. Beat the eggs and milk in a small bowl to make an egg wash. Brush the frozen patties with egg wash, then bake on a sheet tray until golden brown, about 15 minutes.

Beef patties are best served immediately, with Calypso Sauce (page 24), but the dough and the filling may both be made up to 2 days ahead and stored separately in the refrigerator. Unbaked patties may be frozen for up to 2 months. Thaw the frozen patties in the refrigerator, then bake as described above.

THE BURGER

I was weaned on $3 bodega cheeseburgers and Big Macs. Those are the spirits I summoned with this burger, although given a significant upgrade. It's a riff on an American classic that incorporates a whole world of flavor. The Mac sauce—a combination of ketchup and mayo—is augmented with house spice and RGP. The pickles bristle with Trini green seasoning. The flaccid strips of bacon on lesser burgers are here crisp and filled with jerk flavors, and the patty itself, a mixture of brisket, short rib, and chuck, is almost obscenely flavorful.

Note: The best way to grind meat is with a meat grinder. If you don't have one, ask your butcher to grind the burger blend for you.

For the pickles

Slice the cucumbers into ⅛-inch-thick coins. Combine the remaining ingredients in a blender and purée until smooth, then transfer to a ziplock bag along with the cucumbers. Toss to coat thoroughly, then press out as much air as possible, seal the bag, and place in a bowl. Refrigerate for 24 hours.

For the house sauce

Stir together all the ingredients in a small bowl. Cover and refrigerate until ready to assemble.

For the jerk bacon

Set a wire rack on a sheet pan. Coat the bacon on both sides with jerk powder and place on the rack. Refrigerate uncovered overnight.

For the caramelized onions

Stir together all the ingredients in a medium pot over medium heat. Cook, stirring and scraping frequently, for 25 minutes; the onions will be toffee colored at this point. Reduce the heat to low and continue cooking until the onions are chocolate colored, soft,

ORIGIN: Chef Special
YIELD: 4 burgers

For the pickles
2 Persian cucumbers
2 tablespoons freshly squeezed lemon juice
2 tablespoons white balsamic vinegar
4 teaspoons Green Seasoning (page 29)
1 tablespoon roughly chopped fresh cilantro leaves
½ teaspoon kosher salt

For the house sauce
¼ cup Hellmann's mayonnaise
2 teaspoons ketchup
2 teaspoons RGP (page 11)
½ teaspoon House Spice (page 6)
¼ teaspoon kosher salt

For the jerk bacon
8 slices thick-cut bacon
¼ cup Jerk Powder (page 16)

For the caramelized onions
4 medium yellow onions, sliced into ¼-inch-thick pieces
3 tablespoons vegetable oil
1 teaspoon kosher salt

and sweet, 20 to 25 minutes more. If at any point your onions start to stick or burn, reduce the heat a bit and/or add a splash of water and scrape to deglaze the pan. Transfer to an airtight container and refrigerate until ready to assemble.

For the burger patties

Line a sheet pan or plate with parchment paper. Combine the meats in a large bowl and mix gently but thoroughly with your hands. Divide into 8 portions and press into patties using a burger press (or press the patties between 2 plates—they should be about 5 inches in diameter and between ¼ and ½ inch thick). Transfer to the pan or plate, cover loosely with plastic wrap, and refrigerate until ready to cook.

To assemble

When ready to cook, heat the oven to 400°F. Season the burger patties generously with house spice and salt. Return the caramelized onions to a pan over low heat. Line a sheet pan with parchment paper and place the marinated bacon on it. Bake for 12 to 14 minutes, until just golden and crispy, then transfer to a paper towel–lined plate.

Heat a large pan with a little oil over medium-high heat. When it shimmers, and working in batches so as not to crowd the pan, sear the burgers for 3 minutes per side, smashing each patty down with a spatula as you add it to the pan. Add a slice of cheese to each burger in the last 30 seconds of cooking. Stack the burgers two high (if you've used both yellow and white American cheese, use one of each kind per stack), then transfer to a wire rack. Top each stack with 1 tablespoon warm caramelized onions.

While the burgers rest, spread a teaspoon of butter on the cut sides of each bun. Wipe the pan clean—or use a fresh large pan—and heat over medium heat to toast the buns, cut side down, until golden. Then assemble each burger in the following order: bottom bun, 5 pickles, double patties with cheese and onions, 2 slices bacon, ¼ cup shredded romaine, 1 tablespoon house sauce (spread on the top bun), top bun.

For the burger patties

1 pound **beef chuck**, medium grind (see headnote)

7 ounces **beef brisket**, medium grind (see headnote)

5 ounces **boneless beef short rib**, medium grind (see headnote)

To assemble

House Spice (page 6), to taste

Kosher salt, to taste

Grapeseed oil, as needed

8 slices **American cheese** (yellow or white—or, if you want to be really fancy, 4 slices of each)

4 **brioche burger buns**

8 teaspoons **unsalted butter**, softened

1 cup shredded **romaine lettuce**

Once assembled, burgers are best served immediately. Uncooked patties will keep in an airtight container in the refrigerator for up to 1 day in advance; cooked burgers are best served immediately. Pickles, caramelized onions, and house sauce may be made up to 1 day in advance and stored in airtight containers in the refrigerator.

AWAZE TIBS

Ethiopian cooking is a high-wire act. The heat of dark red berbere, the warmth of NKO, a panoply of peppers—Ethiopian chefs are not playing around. Especially not with awaze tibs, a roast frequently eaten in Ethiopia at feasts or parties. Usually the dish—awaze means a mixture of water, oil, and berbere; tibs means fried meat—is made with chunks of lamb or beef and prepared à la minute as a stir-fry. But when I first made it, I found myself longing for a different protein, and my mind immediately turned to short ribs. I prepare them a day ahead and let them rest, so the flavors of the berbere penetrate the meat. The result is a dish that Is both achingly tender and totally on fire.

ORIGIN: Ethiopia
YIELD: 4 servings

For the braised short ribs
2 pounds bone-in **beef short ribs**
Berbere (page 9), to taste
Kosher salt, to taste
2 tablespoons **NKO** (page 21)
1 **Roma tomato**, halved
1 medium **red onion**, halved
1 head **garlic**, halved crosswise
One 3-inch knob **ginger**, peeled and halved
4 cups **Chicken Stock** (page 33)

To assemble
Braised short ribs (above)
2 tablespoons **NKO** (page 21), plus more as needed
Berbere (page 9), to taste
Kosher salt, to taste
1 medium **yellow onion**, thinly sliced
1 **green bell pepper**, thinly sliced lengthwise
1 **red bell pepper**, thinly sliced lengthwise
2 **jalapeños**, thinly sliced into rings
2 **Roma tomatoes**, cut into ½-inch dice

For the braised short ribs

Place the short ribs on a cutting board or large plate and season generously all over with berbere and kosher salt. Let sit at room temperature for 30 minutes.

When ready to cook, heat the oven to 300°F. Heat the NKO in a large Dutch oven over high heat until almost smoking. Add the short ribs and sear until deeply browned on all sides, 3 to 4 minutes per side. Add the tomatoes, red onions, garlic, and ginger around the meat, then pour over the chicken stock. It should just cover the meat and vegetables (if it doesn't, add a bit more stock or water). Place a sheet of parchment paper over the pot, then cover tightly with the lid and place in the oven.

Braise for 3 hours, until short ribs are very tender, then remove from the oven and set the lid ajar so the steam can escape. Let cool completely, then remove the short ribs, discarding the bones (which should come out easily). Discard the braising liquid (or save it for another use—it's amazing as a stock). Wrap each short rib individually in plastic wrap, doing your best to maintain its rectangular shape, and refrigerate overnight.

To assemble

When ready to prepare the awaze tibs, cut the ribs into 1-inch cubes. Heat the NKO over high heat in a pan large enough to fit all the short ribs in an even layer. Season the short ribs generously with berbere and salt and then, when the NKO is nearly smoking, add the ribs to the pan. Sear until deeply browned on all sides, about 1 minute per side. Remove the seared short ribs to a serving platter and set aside.

Reduce the heat to medium-high. If the pan looks dry, add 1 to 2 tablespoons more NKO, then add the onions, bell peppers, and jalapeños. Season with salt and cook, stirring constantly, for 3 minutes. Add the tomatoes and cook for 1 minute more.

Taste and add more salt if desired, then pour the seared vegetables over the short ribs. Dust with berbere and serve.

Awaze tibs is best served immediately, but short ribs may be made (and kept tightly wrapped in plastic in the refrigerator) up to 4 days before assembling.

SUYA

Suya is the grandfather of American BBQ. In Nigeria, the spices draw out and fire up the meats, often cooked over an open flame. Here I do the same. But if you don't have a grill, use a well-oiled cast-iron skillet over high heat in a kitchen with open windows. The open windows are very important, unless you find the blare of a smoke alarm harmonious and enjoy fits of sneezing. I find the sweetness of the char plus the heat of the spice totally irresistible. I did when I first smelled it from beyond the walls of my grandfather's compound in Nigeria, or when we went to market when I could sneak a skewer. (Since my grandfather was an obi, or chief, there were many customs and rules around what he and his family could eat.) When I opened my second restaurant, Kith and Kin, I wanted to suya everything. The reaction from the diners, at least initially, was mixed. Many Nigerians scoffed at the idea that suya could be applied to, for instance, brussels sprouts. They were, on the whole, proud that Nigerian cuisine was being given the attention it so much deserved but arrived at the table with some strong opinions. Judging from the empty bowls that came back to the kitchen, I think I won them over. But it was always a battle.

In this recipe, I stick to the traditional proteins—steak, chicken, and shrimp. In Nigeria, suya is served with sliced tomatoes and onions, which help mellow the heat. Here that role is played by a tomato-ginger soubise and a traditional onion cream sauce from France, and I keep the tomatoes and onions in the form of pickles, whose burst of acidity rounds out the flavors.

For the suya

Place the shrimp, steak, and chicken in three separate bowls. Season each with 1½ tablespoons of suya spice and ½ teaspoon salt, mixing well to combine. Cover with plastic wrap and refrigerate for at least 1 hour. (You can marinate the shrimp for up to 12 hours, and the steak and chicken for up to 48 hours.)

ORIGIN: Nigeria
YIELD: 6 to 8 servings

For the suya and to assemble
1 pound large (16–20 size) **shrimp**, peeled and deveined
1 pound boneless **ribeye steak**, excess fat trimmed, sliced into ¼-inch strips
1 pound boneless, skinless **chicken thighs**, sliced into ¼-inch strips
4½ tablespoons **Suya Spice** (page 8), divided, plus more to garnish
1½ teaspoons **kosher salt**, divided
¼ cup roughly chopped fresh **parsley**, to serve
Tomato-ginger soubise (below), to serve
Pickled tomatoes and **onions** (below), to serve
Lime wedges, to serve

For the tomato-ginger soubise
1 **Roma tomato**, roughly chopped
2 teaspoons **extra-virgin olive oil**
Kosher salt, to taste
2 tablespoons **grapeseed oil**
3 tablespoons **GGP** (page 5)
1 **yellow onion**, thinly sliced
1 cup **heavy cream**
1 cup **whole milk**

For the tomato-ginger soubise

Heat the oven to 400°F. Line a sheet pan with parchment paper. Toss the tomatoes with olive oil and season with salt. Spread evenly over the sheet pan and bake for 15 minutes, until deep red and a little wrinkly.

Meanwhile, heat the grapeseed oil in a medium pot over medium heat. When it shimmers, add the GGP and cook until fragrant, 2 to 3 minutes. Add the onions and cook until translucent and soft, 7 to 10 minutes. Add the roasted tomatoes, along with the cream and milk. Bring to a simmer and cook, stirring often, until reduced to about 1 cup—watch carefully, as cream has a tendency to boil over, so reduce the heat as necessary to keep it from sputtering or burning—about 1 hour. Remove from the heat and let cool slightly, then transfer to a blender and purée until velvety smooth. Season to taste with salt and set aside. You should have 1 cup of soubise.

For the pickled tomatoes and onions

Bring the spice pickling liquid to a boil in a small pot. Place the onions and tomatoes in a nonreactive bowl and pour the hot liquid over them, stirring to combine well. Let cool to room temperature, about 1 hour, before serving. You should have about 3 cups of pickled tomatoes and onions.

To assemble

When ready to cook, prepare a grill for high heat. Let it heat for 10 minutes. Grill the shrimp, steak, and chicken, turning occasionally, until deeply browned and cooked through, about 3 minutes for shrimp and steak and 4 to 5 minutes for the chicken.

In a small pot, warm the soubise over low heat. Place the grilled items on a platter, dust with extra suya spice, and sprinkle with parsley. Serve with warm soubise, pickled tomatoes and onions, lime wedges for squeezing, and Jollof Rice (page 57).

For the pickled tomatoes and onions
1 cup **Spice Pickling Liquid** (page 32)
1 medium **red onion**, large dice
1 medium ripe **tomato**, large dice

Cooked suya shrimp will keep in an airtight container in the refrigerator for up to 1 day, chicken and beef suya for up to 4 days. Tomato-ginger soubise will keep in an airtight container in the refrigerator for up to 3 days. Pickled tomatoes and onions will keep in an airtight container in the refrigerator for up to 3 days.

TRIPE AND BEAN

Tripe is a criminally underused ingredient. The honeycomb-patterned protein has a delicate flavor and a soft yielding texture. I've always been a fan of chitlins, which is how tripe was usually cooked in my family, growing up. I, alone among cousins, would join the older generation. This recipe, on the other hand, shown to me by Alex D-Great, a Jamaican chef whom I met on a recent visit to the island, is abundantly flavored with curry powder and a whole mess of aromatics and is served with a flavorful kidney bean stew. I like my tripe spicy, especially here, but be careful not to let the whole Scotch bonnet pepper pop or it'll get so hot only the most masochistic pepper-heads will want to eat it.

For the marinated tripe

Rinse the tripe thoroughly in cold water while bringing a large pot of generously salted water to a boil. Boil the tripe for 10 minutes, then drain and rinse again.

Stir together the remaining ingredients in a medium bowl. Cut the tripe into 1-inch-thick strips, then toss with the remaining ingredients. Cover and refrigerate overnight.

For the stew

Place the kidney beans in a large bowl and cover with cold water by 2 inches. Let sit overnight.

When ready to cook, heat the oil in a Dutch oven over medium heat. When it shimmers, add the GGP and cook for 3 minutes, then add the house spice and curry powder and sauté until the spices and GGP are fragrant and just beginning to toast, 5 minutes more. Add the tripe and its marinade and cook, stirring often, until the onions are translucent, 7 to 10 minutes.

ORIGIN: Jamaica
YIELD: 4 to 6 servings

For the marinated tripe
2 pounds **honeycomb beef tripe**
Kosher salt, to taste
2 tablespoons **Curry Powder** (page 10)
1 tablespoon **House Spice** (page 6)
2 tablespoons **GGP** (page 5)
1 medium **yellow onion**, diced
1 bunch **scallions**, sliced
2 fresh **bay leaves**
5 fresh **thyme sprigs**

For the stew
2 cups dried **kidney beans**
2 tablespoons **grapeseed oil**
2 tablespoons **GGP** (page 5)
1 tablespoon **House Spice** (page 6)
1 tablespoon **Curry Powder** (page 10)
Marinated tripe (above)
3 quarts **Chicken Stock** (page 33)
1 **red Scotch bonnet pepper**
Kosher salt, to taste

Tripe and bean will keep in an airtight container in the refrigerator for up to 4 days, or in the freezer for up to 2 months.

Add all the soaked beans and the remaining ingredients but salt and bring to a boil, then reduce the heat to a gentle simmer. Simmer uncovered until the tripe and beans are both completely tender, 60 to 90 minutes, and reduced until the tripe and beans are thick enough to coat the back of a spoon. Carefully remove the Scotch bonnet (without popping it!), then season to taste with salt. Serve with Perfectly Steamed Rice (page 46).

CRACKLINS

Growing up, my mother, sister, and I greeted the cracklins—along with boudin, hot links, and crayfish in their fat—that were part of Grandma Cassie's annual care packages from Beaumont, Texas, with an electric joy. And why not? Cracklins are all crunch, salt, fat, and flavor. What could be better? An outgrowth of South Louisianians' horror at waste, cracklins are traditionally pork skin fried in its own rendered fat. Here I've added a bit more meat to the fat by using pork belly, but the idea stays the same: a delirious, addictive crunch is what you're looking for. Cracklins, also called grattons, scratchings, and pork rinds, take patience to make. They're marinated and then braised, to drive the flavors in. Then they're fried and fried again, until they're like little pork potato chips you can't stop eating.

Season the pork belly all over with the house spice and salt. Place it in a large bowl, cover with plastic wrap, and marinate overnight in the refrigerator.

Heat the oven to 300°F. Place the pork belly, onion, garlic, thyme, and bay leaves in a roasting pan and add chicken stock to just cover the pork belly. Cover with a sheet of parchment paper, then wrap the pan tightly with foil. Place in the oven and braise for 3 hours.

Remove from the oven and puncture the foil with a knife to allow steam to escape. Let cool, then remove the belly (discarding the braising liquid), wrap in plastic wrap, and refrigerate overnight.

Fill a large Dutch oven halfway with vegetable oil and heat over medium heat to 350°F. (If you have a mesh spatter guard, this is the time to use it. If not, be careful and stand back—the cracklins will spit and pop as they fry.) Cut the pork into 1-inch cubes. Working in batches and letting the oil return to 350°F between batches, fry for 10 minutes, stirring occasionally, until reddish brown, crisp, and floating to the surface of the oil. The cubes of pork belly will have gotten quite a bit smaller. Use a slotted spoon

ORIGIN: American South
YIELD: 4 to 6 servings

2 pounds skin-on **pork belly**

1½ tablespoons **House Spice** (page 6), plus more to serve

2 teaspoons **kosher salt**

1 medium **yellow onion**, halved

1 head **garlic**, halved crosswise

8 fresh **thyme sprigs**

3 fresh **bay leaves**

2 quarts **Chicken Stock** (page 33), or more as needed to cover

Vegetable oil, such as canola, for frying

Serve immediately.

to transfer the fried belly to a paper towel–lined sheet tray and let cool completely.

When all of the pork belly has been fried and cooled, increase the heat of the oil to 425°F. Working in batches and letting the oil return to 425°F between batches, fry the pork again for 3 minutes, stirring often, then remove to a fresh paper towel–lined sheet tray and season with house spice and salt.

BABY BACK RIBS

I have early memories of fragrant hickory smoke wafting in from the fire escape as my mom smoked ribs, low and slow just like her parents did in a smoker at their own barbecue joint in Texas. To me, ribs mean home. So much so that the first place I ate after two years living in Nigeria as a kid was a joint called Pan Pan's on Lenox Avenue. Sweet, sticky, tender meat falling off the bone, baby back ribs are synonymous with barbecue. And though these days the rib belt spans much of the South—or really anywhere where there's barbecue—baby back ribs were originally a product of the rapid industrialization of meat processing in the late nineteenth century and the Great Migration in the early twentieth.

Starting in the late nineteenth century, baby back ribs were deemed unsellable since they didn't fit into the pork barrels in which meat was transported. Meatpackers would literally give them away or sell them for pennies. This suited the Black families fleeing from Jim Crow, who arrived in towns like Chicago, Cleveland, and St. Louis, just fine. As resourceful (and economically disenfranchised) as ever, Black émigrés from the South did what they had done for years, turning the overlooked and cast-out into the lusted-after and valued. In the right hands, patiently cooked baby back ribs yield perfectly bite-sized fall-off-the-bone morsels, glazed in a deep sweet and spicy sauce. As addictive as Doritos but without the white-coated food scientists to reverse-engineer them, they are God's snacks. Today, baby back ribs are, to my mind, the ultimate barbecue, but they are also the perfect embodiment of what binds so much diasporic food together: the alchemy of forbearance, skill, perseverance, and, of course, house spice.

But baby back ribs without mac and cheese is like Jay-Z without Beyoncé: great, of course, but not yet at its full potential. So be sure to serve these with a side of the recipe that follows (page 208). Mac and cheese is the creamy co-equal partner to ribs and has a powerful history of its own. (Also, to be honest, where else could we stick the recipe but here?)

ORIGIN: American South
YIELD: 4 to 6 servings

For the baby back ribs
2 racks **baby back ribs** (2 to 2½ pounds each)
2 tablespoons **House Spice** (page 6)
2 teaspoons **kosher salt**
Mesquite BBQ sauce (below)

For the mesquite BBQ sauce
¼ cup **grapeseed oil**
10 **garlic cloves**, minced
3 cups diced **yellow onion** (about 2 medium **onions**)
½ cup **light brown sugar**
1¾ cups **ketchup**
¼ cup **Worcestershire sauce**
1 tablespoon **House Spice** (page 6)
1 tablespoon **mesquite liquid smoke**
Kosher salt, to taste

Note: To cook the ribs without a grill, broil them on a foil-lined sheet pan, turning every 2 to 3 minutes and brushing with BBQ sauce each time you turn, until glistening and browned in spots, 5 to 8 minutes total.

Heat the oven to 300°F.

For the baby back ribs

Season each rack of ribs with 1 tablespoon house spice and 1 teaspoon salt. Place the ribs in a roasting pan or on a rimmed sheet pan and cover with a sheet of parchment, then wrap tightly in aluminum foil. Cook for 3 hours, or until you can easily slide a paring knife between the ribs. Remove the ribs from the oven, puncture the foil to allow steam to escape, and let cool. Refrigerate overnight.

For the mesquite BBQ sauce

Meanwhile, heat the oil in a medium pot over medium heat. Add the garlic and sauté until fragrant, 2 to 3 minutes, then add the onions and cook until totally sweet and translucent, 15 minutes more. Add the remaining ingredients and simmer gently for 1 hour, until thick. Remove from the heat and let cool slightly, then transfer to a blender and purée until totally smooth. Season with additional salt to taste and set aside.

When ready to eat, prepare a grill for high heat. While the grill heats, glaze the ribs with the mesquite BBQ sauce. Grill the ribs until charred on both sides, brushing occasionally with BBQ sauce, approximately 4 to 5 minutes per side. Serve the charred ribs with additional mesquite BBQ sauce alongside. (To finish the ribs without a grill, see note above.)

Baby back ribs will keep in an airtight container in the refrigerator for up to 4 days—but they're best charred right before eating. Mesquite BBQ sauce will keep in an airtight container in the refrigerator for up to 1 week.

MAC AND CHEESE

Macaroni and cheese's journey to becoming perhaps the best-known example of soul food is a long one, moving from Italy in the fourteenth century to the royal courts of Paris in the sixteenth. Like so many in this book, it is a journey that is inexorably tied to the overlooked contributions of enslaved people—in this case, the contributions of one man, James Hemmings.

Though Thomas Jefferson often gets the credit for bringing mac and cheese from Paris, where he first tried it in the 1780s, it was actually his chef, Hemmings, who did that work. It was Hemmings's recipe—then sometimes called macaroni pie—that was served in the White House in 1802, after which it became a status symbol in the plantation houses of southern slave owners. For years mac and cheese remained the food of rich folks, but with Emancipation and the Industrial Revolution, and the newfound affordability of processed cheese, mac and cheese took off. Soon it was on the table at both celebrations and weekday dinners. Like anyone who has ever been a kid, I love the cheap stuff too, but this version is on the more luxurious side of the mac and cheese spectrum. I use Mornay sauce—a béchamel with the addition of Gruyère and Parmigiano Reggiano—and cavatappi, a corkscrew-shaped pasta that holds all that delicious sauce.

ORIGIN: American South
YIELD: 6 servings

For the Mornay sauce
1 cup unsalted butter
2 tablespoons chopped garlic
6 tablespoons all-purpose flour
8 cups cold whole milk
2 teaspoons freshly ground black pepper
1 cup (8 ounces) cream cheese
1½ cups (6 ounces) shredded Gruyère cheese
2 tablespoons (⅓ ounce) grated Parmigiano Reggiano cheese
1 cup (5 ounces) shredded mild yellow cheddar cheese

For the breadcrumbs
4 tablespoons unsalted butter
4 garlic cloves, crushed
1 cup panko breadcrumbs
20 leaves fresh parsley, finely chopped
½ teaspoon kosher salt

For the Mornay sauce

Melt the butter in a medium pot over medium-low heat. Add the garlic and sauté until fragrant but without browning, about 2 minutes. Add the flour and stir constantly with a rubber spatula until beginning to turn a pale golden color, about 5 minutes.

Swap your spatula for a whisk. Whisking constantly, gradually pour in the cold milk. Bring to a simmer over medium heat and simmer for 15 minutes, whisking occasionally. Stir in the pepper and all the cheeses, then transfer to a blender. Purée until smooth. Be careful of the splatter, as the sauce will still be hot.

For the breadcrumbs

In a medium pan over medium heat, melt the butter. Add the garlic and sauté until fragrant, 2 minutes. Add the breadcrumbs, parsley, and salt and cook, stirring often, until toasted and golden brown, 3 to 4 minutes. Transfer the crumbs to a paper towel–lined plate or sheet tray to cool, then remove the garlic and discard it.

To assemble

Heat the oven to 400°F. Combine the shredded cheeses in a bowl.

Bring a large pot of salted water to a boil and cook the cavatappi until al dente, according to the package instructions. Drain the pasta well, return to the pot, then toss with the Mornay sauce and half the cheese. Season with house spice to taste.

Transfer to a baking pan and sprinkle the remaining cheese over the top. Top evenly with the breadcrumbs. Place into the oven and bake uncovered for 20 minutes until bubbling and golden brown.

To assemble

1 cup (5 ounces) shredded **Monterey Jack cheese**

1 cup (6 ounces) shredded **Asadero cheese** (or substitute low-moisture mozzarella)

1 cup (5 ounces) shredded **mild yellow cheddar cheese**

Kosher salt, to taste

1 pound dried **cavatappi**

1 recipe **breadcrumbs** (above)

1 recipe **Mornay sauce** (above)

House Spice (page 6), to taste

Mac and cheese will keep in the refrigerator for up to 1 week and in the freezer for up to 2 months.

PORK BELLY GEERAH

Liming—or to "coast a lime"—is a Trinidadian national pastime. "Pastime," though, doesn't quite capture the importance of liming. As an activity, it doesn't look like much: just hanging out, swapping stories with friends, dancing, playing music, often in parks, yards, malls, and on the streets of Port of Spain, or wherever the Trini diaspora lands. But it's also an enactment of cultural identity, an exercise in story-telling, a historical resistance to colonialism, and an excuse to eat. When I visited Trinidad recently with my grandfather, Papa Winston, we went liming. To see him return to the streets of his youth, to the activities of his youth, with me alongside him is a memory I'll always carry with me. And it's a memory this dish summons. Not every lime with food is good, but no good limes don't have at least something to snack on. Eating, critiquing, fighting over, and sharing food is clutch to any good lime.

Geerah, or geera—the word means "cumin" in Urdu, Bengali, and a slew of other languages spoken in India—is, alongside roti, a contribution of the East Indians who arrived on the island in the mid-nineteenth century. The dish is often made with turkey neck or pork shoulder, and the meat is marinated and then cooked slowly with a bouquet of aromatics, until it ends up super tender and super tasty. Accompanied by a few wedges of lime, it's a Trini staple. In this recipe, I use pork belly, a rather fattier cut of meat, which just adds to the richness and succulence of the geerah.

ORIGIN: Trinidad and Tobago
YIELD: 6 servings

---

3 pounds **pork belly**, cut into 1½-inch cubes

1 **Roma tomato**, roughly chopped

¼ cup **Green Seasoning** (page 29)

2 tablespoons **Curry Powder** (page 10)

3 tablespoons **grapeseed oil**, divided

1 tablespoon **Peppa Sauce** (page 25)

1 medium **yellow onion**, finely diced

5 **garlic cloves**, minced

2 tablespoons ground **cumin**

1 tablespoon **white granulated sugar**

1 cup **Chicken Stock** (page 33)

1½ tablespoons freshly squeezed **lime juice**

Kosher salt, to taste

1 tablespoon chopped fresh **cilantro**

Pork belly geerah will keep in an airtight container in the refrigerator for up to 4 days, or in the freezer for up to 2 months.

Combine the pork, tomatoes, green seasoning, curry powder, 2 tablespoons oil, and peppa sauce in a large ziplock bag and seal tightly, pressing out as much air as possible. Squish the bag to evenly coat the pork with the marinade and set the bag in a large bowl. Refrigerate at least 3 hours and up to 24 hours.

When ready to cook, heat the remaining 1 tablespoon oil in a large Dutch oven over medium heat. Add the onions, garlic, cumin, and sugar. Sauté, stirring often, until the onions begin to soften, 5 to 7 minutes, then add the pork and marinade, along with the chicken stock. Reduce the heat to medium-low, then cover with a sheet of parchment followed by the pot lid. Cook for 2 hours, stirring halfway through, then uncover. Bring the geerah to a simmer and cook for 20 minutes, until the pork is completely tender.

Stir in lime juice and season to taste with salt, then transfer to a serving platter and sprinkle with cilantro.

SMOTHERED PORK CHOPS

Smothering is the Louisiana-born technique of slowly cooking a protein in a roux, or gravy, until the roux reduces and the shrimp, pork, chicken, or whatever is fully imbued with its silken deliciousness, which itself is the recipient of the flavors of the Holy Trinity of onions, bell peppers, and celery. The fundamentals of smothering I learned from my mother, including frying the pork chops *before* smothering, which adds a layer of crispness that allows the sauce to better stick to the pork. But I've adapted the brine and the marinade to make these extra juicy, which increases the prep time to thirty-six hours—the vast majority of it passive—but pays dividends at dinner.

For the brine

Squeeze the lemon half into a large bowl and then toss in the fruit itself. Add the remaining ingredients except the ice water and pork chops and stir until the salt and sugar dissolve, then stir in the ice water. Place the pork chops in a large ziplock bag and add brine to cover completely. Press out as much air as possible, then seal the bag and place in a large bowl. Refrigerate for 24 hours.

For the marinade

Stir together all the ingredients in a large bowl. Remove the pork chops from brine (discarding the brine) and add to the marinade, tossing to combine well. Cover and refrigerate overnight.

For the gravy

An hour before you're ready to cook the pork, make the gravy: Melt the butter in a large pot over medium heat. Add the garlic and sauté until fragrant, 2 to 3 minutes, then add the onions, bell peppers, and celery. Sauté until translucent, about 10 minutes.

Add the flour and cook, stirring constantly, until the mixture smells a little toasty, 6 to 8 minutes. Whisk in the chicken stock, then add the browning, thyme, bay leaves, and house spice. Sim-

ORIGIN: American South
YIELD: 4 servings

For the brine

½ lemon

6 tablespoons kosher salt

3 tablespoons white granulated sugar

3 garlic cloves

3 fresh bay leaves

2 cups boiling water

6 cups ice water

4 one-inch-thick, center-cut, bone-in pork chops

For the marinade

1 tablespoon House Spice (page 6)

1 cup buttermilk

12 garlic cloves, minced

1 teaspoon freshly ground black pepper

For the gravy

8 tablespoons unsalted butter

5 garlic cloves, minced

1 medium yellow onion, diced

1 green bell pepper, diced

1 stalk celery, diced

3 tablespoons all-purpose flour

6 cups Chicken Stock (page 33)

1 teaspoon Browning (page 13)

3 fresh thyme sprigs

2 fresh bay leaves

1½ teaspoons House Spice (page 6)

mer gently, stirring frequently, until the gravy is reduced by a third, about 35 to 45 minutes—you should have about 4 cups gravy. It will still be relatively loose, about the texture of a thin chowder. Remove from the heat and set aside.

To assemble

While the gravy simmers, heat ½ inch oil in a large pan or pot over medium heat until it reaches 350°F. Stir together the flour, house spice, black pepper, and salt to taste in a shallow bowl. Dredge the marinated pork chops in the seasoned flour. Working in batches as necessary to avoid crowding the pan, fry until golden brown, about 3 minutes per side. Set aside on a paper towel–lined tray.

Add the fried pork chops to the reduced gravy, turn them to coat, and simmer for 15 minutes, until the gravy has thickened. Serve with Perfectly Steamed Rice (page 46) and fresh parsley.

To assemble

Vegetable oil, such as canola, for frying

1 cup all-purpose flour

2 teaspoons House Spice (page 6)

½ teaspoon freshly ground black pepper

Kosher salt, to taste

Chopped fresh parsley, to serve

Smothered pork chops are best served immediately.

LAMB SAMBUSAS WITH SHIRO WAT

Growing up steeped in the curries and roti of West Indian cuisine, I've long been accustomed to the presence of the Indian spice pantry in the Caribbean. But Ethiopian sambusas illustrate that India itself was and has been subject to the winds of trade and flavor flowing east, not west. What in India is called a samosa started out in Persia in the ninth century as sanbusaj, a triangular pocket of fried dough, often stuffed with meat and vegetables. That same snack also traveled west from Central Asia to Northeast Africa. (It hasn't made it across the Sahara.) In Ethiopia, Somalia, and Kenya, samosas live as sambusas. In Ethiopia, they become, in my opinion, their best selves, thanks, in no small part, to the presence of both NKO and berbere, which add warmth and heat, respectively. In this recipe, the spice of the sambusas is paired with a luscious and rich chickpea shiro wat, another example of Ethiopia's culinary brilliance.

Make the sambusas

Heat the NKO in a medium pan over medium heat. When it shimmers, add GGP and cook, stirring constantly, until fragrant and just beginning to toast, 5 to 8 minutes. Add the onions and cook for 10 minutes more, until the onions are soft and translucent. Add lamb, spices, salt, and peppa sauce and cook for 10 minutes, stirring frequently and breaking up any large pieces of lamb, until browned and crumbly. Taste and adjust seasoning with salt. Remove lamb to a bowl to cool.

While the lamb cools, make the shiro wat

In a medium pot, heat the NKO over medium heat. When it shimmers, add GGP and sauté, stirring constantly, until fragrant and toasted, 7 to 10 minutes. Add the water, scraping the bottom of the pot to loosen any browned bits, then whisk in the chickpea flour and berbere. Cook for 10 to 15 minutes, whisking often, until thick and mostly smooth. Let cool slightly, then transfer to a blender (or use an immersion blender) and purée on high until velvety smooth. →

ORIGIN: Ethiopia
YIELD: 8 sambusas,
    plus 1 quart shiro wat

For the sambusas and to assemble

2 tablespoons NKO (page 21)
3 tablespoons GGP (page 5)
½ medium **white onion**, diced
½ pound ground **lamb**
1 teaspoon ground **cumin**
¼ teaspoon ground **cardamom**
¼ teaspoon ground **cinnamon**
2 teaspoons **Berbere** (page 9)
1 teaspoon **kosher salt**
1 teaspoon **Peppa Sauce** (page 25)
⅓ of a 1-pound package frozen **phyllo dough**, thawed and cut into 16 (4⅔-x-18-inch) strips
Vegetable oil, for frying

For the shiro wat

2 tablespoons NKO (page 21)
¼ cup GGP (page 5)
2 cups **water**
½ cup **chickpea flour**
1 tablespoon **Berbere** (page 9)
1½ cups **unsalted butter**, cubed
Kosher salt, to taste

To assemble the sambusas

Fill a medium pot with 3 inches of vegetable oil and, over medium heat, heat to 350°F. Fill a small bowl with water and set aside.

Lay a strip of phyllo on a clean surface, then brush all over with water and stack another strip of phyllo on top. Arrange a scant ¼ cup of lamb on one end of the phyllo strip, toward a corner. Fold the corner of phyllo nearest the filling over the filling to meet the opposite edge of the phyllo, making a triangle-shaped fold. Repeat this fold, moving down the strip of phyllo. When you have one fold to go, brush the exposed end of the phyllo strip with egg

Shiro wat will keep in the refrigerator for up to 2 days. Once baked, sambusas are best the day they're made, but you can freeze them after shaping. To bake them from frozen, simply place on a lined sheet pan and bake as instructed (though you may need a few extra minutes).

wash, then complete the fold, sealing the sambusa. Repeat with the remaining phyllo and filling.

Fry the sambusas for 3 to 4 minutes until golden brown. Transfer to a paper towel–lined sheet pan. Brush the outsides with egg wash, then bake for 15 to 20 minutes, until deeply golden brown.

While the sambusas bake, finish the shiro wat

Return the mixture to the pot over low heat. Add the butter a few cubes at a time, whisking to melt between additions, until all the butter is incorporated and the shiro wat is thick, glossy, and pudding-like. Remove from heat, season with salt to taste, and cover to keep warm.

Serve the sambusas beside the shiro wat while piping hot.

LAMB SHEPHERD'S PIE

In all honesty, I'm not sure how shepherd's pie became a staple in my house or why it fits so neatly into the African American kitchen, or at least my African American kitchen. I suspect I was first exposed to the classic Irish-Anglo dish at my childhood friends Michael and Patrick Gallagher's house in the Bronx. But this version, pumped up with house spice, is definitely inspired by my mother, who also loved making it. It is true that pot pies are part of many Caribbean cuisines—a less portable version of a patty and an outgrowth of the English settlement in the area. Many of those are curried, but here I've opted for the more classic use of stout, which adds a nice slightly malty flavor to the lamb. Everywhere and every time I've made it, no matter for whom, the pot pie has been a hit. I guess that explains why it is a staple. Who doesn't love delicious?

For the seasoned ground lamb

In a large pan, heat the oil over medium heat until shimmering. Add the garlic and cook, stirring, until fragrant and pale golden, about 6 minutes, then add the onions and carrots and sauté until the onions are translucent, 7 to 10 minutes.

Add the tomato paste and sauté until brick red, 3 to 5 minutes more. Increase the heat to medium-high and add the lamb. Let it cook, breaking it into small pieces with your spoon, until well browned, about 10 minutes.

Add the stock, Worcestershire sauce, beer, thyme, rosemary, peas, and salt and simmer until the liquid has almost completely evaporated, 7 to 10 minutes—it should be almost syrupy, and coat the lamb and vegetables. Taste and adjust seasoning, then set aside.

For the whipped potatoes

Cut the potatoes into ½-inch pieces and place in a medium pot. Cover with water by 1 inch and add 1 teaspoon salt. Bring to a boil over high heat and cook until fork tender, 10 to 15 minutes.

ORIGIN: American South
YIELD: 4 servings

For the seasoned ground lamb

2 tablespoons **extra-virgin olive oil**

5 **garlic cloves,** minced

2 medium **yellow onions,** finely diced

1 medium **carrot,** peeled and finely diced

2 tablespoons **tomato paste**

1 pound ground **lamb**

1 cup **Chicken Stock** (page 33)

1 tablespoon **Worcestershire sauce**

½ cup **stout beer** such as Guinness Draught or similar

2 teaspoons chopped fresh **thyme leaves**

1 teaspoon finely chopped fresh **rosemary leaves**

½ cup fresh or frozen **English peas**

1 teaspoon **kosher salt,** plus more to taste

While the potatoes cook, melt the butter in a medium pan over medium heat. Add the garlic and sauté until fragrant, 2 to 3 minutes. Pour in the cream and reduce the heat to the lowest setting to keep warm until potatoes are ready.

Drain the potatoes and spread on a sheet pan to steam out for 5 minutes. Use a ricer or food mill to rice the warm potatoes (alternately, mash with a potato masher until smooth and fluffy). Use a wooden spoon to gently fold the potatoes into the warm cream mixture. Taste and adjust seasoning, then remove from the heat.

Heat the oven to 400°F.

In an 8-x-8-inch baking dish, spread the seasoned ground lamb in an even layer. Dollop the whipped potatoes over the lamb and use a large spoon to spread them into an even layer.

Bake until the potatoes are browned in places, 20 to 30 minutes. Sprinkle with parsley and serve immediately.

For the whipped potatoes

1 pound **Yukon Gold potatoes**, peeled

1 teaspoon **kosher salt**, plus more to taste

8 tablespoons **unsalted butter**

6 **garlic cloves**, minced

½ cup **heavy cream**

1 tablespoon chopped fresh **parsley leaves**, to serve

Lamb shepherd's pie will keep in an airtight container in the refrigerator for up to 4 days.

BRAISED OXTAILS

Oxtails are a staple not just in the kitchens of the American South but also in kitchens from Iran to Italy to China and Korea. Oxtails fall into the bucket of cheap cuts of meat that reward patience. It takes time to free the gelatin-rich chunks of tail, each with their own segment of bone, but when freed, the flavors are released into a rich stew. The classic preparation from the American South is smothered with garlic and onion gravy. But this version is more akin to the Jamaican version I grew up with, in which jerk, curry, and brown sugar combine for a deep dark rich flavorful stew, studded with glazed carrots and chayote squash.

For the oxtails

Combine the jerk paste, GGP, curry powder, and brown sugar in a large bowl. Add the oxtails and toss to coat well, then cover tightly with plastic wrap and refrigerate for at least 24 hours and up to 48 hours.

For the oxtail braise

When you're ready to cook, heat the oven to 250°F. Heat 2 tablespoons oil in a large Dutch oven over high heat. When it shimmers, add the marinated oxtails, working in batches as necessary—you don't want to crowd the pan. Sear until deeply browned all over, about 4 minutes per side. Once all the oxtail is seared, add the green onions, garlic, ginger, thyme, allspice, and bay leaves. Pour in the chicken stock—It should just cover the oxtails (if not, add a little more).

Bring to a boil over high heat. When boiling, remove from the heat, place a sheet of parchment over the pot, then cover tightly with the pot's lid. Transfer to the oven and braise until the oxtails are tender and succulent, about 7 hours.

Carefully remove the oxtails from the pot and set aside. Strain the braising liquid through a fine-mesh sieve, discard the aromatics, and return the liquid to the pot. Bring to a simmer over →

ORIGIN: American South
YIELD: 6 servings

For the marinated oxtails
1 cup Jerk Paste (page 17)
½ cup GGP (page 5)
¼ cup Curry Powder (page 10)
¼ cup + 1½ teaspoons dark brown sugar
5 pounds oxtails

For the oxtail braise
2 tablespoons grapeseed oil, plus more as needed
1 bunch green onions (about 6), ends trimmed, cut into thirds
20 garlic cloves
Three 1-inch knobs ginger, peeled and cut in half
20 fresh thyme sprigs
10 whole allspice berries
2 fresh bay leaves
4 quarts Chicken Stock (page 33), plus more as needed
Jerk Paste (page 17), to taste
Dark brown sugar, to taste
Curry Powder (page 10), to taste
Kosher salt, to taste

For the glazed carrots and squash
1 cup Chicken Stock (page 33)
2 cups freshly squeezed orange juice, strained (or no-pulp store-bought)
½ pound carrots, peeled and cut into ¾-inch dice →

medium-high heat and cook until reduced to a quarter of its original volume—you should have about 2 cups. Taste the liquid and season with jerk paste, brown sugar, curry powder, and salt, but keep in mind that you'll reduce it even further, so don't overseason!

For the glazed carrots and roasted squash

While the braising liquid reduces, make the glaze and roast the vegetables. To make the glaze, combine the stock and orange juice in a small pot. Bring to a boil and reduce, stirring occasionally, until syrupy. You should have ¼ cup glaze. To roast the carrots and chayote squash, heat the oven to 425°F. On one side of a rimmed sheet pan, toss together the carrots with the oil, GGP, herbs, and salt; repeat with the chayote on the other half of the same sheet pan. Roast without stirring until just tender, about 8 minutes. Place the sheet pan on a cooling rack and reserve until ready to assemble.

To assemble

Return the oxtails to the pot and continue to reduce, stirring often but gently, until the liquid is thick and coats the oxtails. Cover to keep warm while you glaze the vegetables.

In a large pan, combine the glazed carrots and squash, vegetable glaze, and ¼ cup warm chicken stock. Bring to a brisk simmer over medium-high heat, and cook until syrupy, about 3 minutes. Reduce heat to low and add butter a cube at a time, stirring constantly, until sauce is emulsified. Season to taste with lemon juice and salt.

To serve, place the oxtails in shallow bowls (or on a large platter to share), then top with the glazed vegetables. Garnish with scallions and chives. Serve immediately, with Rice and Peas (page 49).

½ pound **chayote squash,** cut into ¾-inch dice

2 tablespoons **grapeseed oil**

3 tablespoons **GGP** (page 5)

10 fresh **thyme sprigs**

2 fresh **bay leaves**

1 teaspoon **kosher salt**

To assemble

¼ cup **chicken stock**

1 tablespoon cold **unsalted butter,** cubed

Freshly squeezed **lemon juice,** to taste

Kosher salt, to taste

2 tablespoons thinly sliced on the bias **scallions**

1 tablespoon finely chopped fresh **chives**

Braised oxtails (unassembled) will keep in an airtight container in the refrigerator for up to 4 days, or in the freezer for up to 1 month. Roasted vegetables are best cooked right before serving. Glaze may be made up to 1 week in advance and stored in an airtight container in the refrigerator.

CURRIED GOAT

Goat is perhaps the most underutilized and underappreciated protein in America. Around the world, from Greece to Venezuela to Sudan, the highest consumers of goat per capita, goat meat is the G.O.A.T., highly prized for its slightly sweet flavor—not to mention that goats are cheap to raise and that, as weed eaters, they leave the environment better off than the way they found it. And yet, when I was growing up, often the only places to find goat meat were at the African butchers up on Webster Avenue in the Bronx. Goat was an outer-borough meat.

When I visited my family in the Caribbean, this was not the case. Goat is at the center of many of Jamaica's best dishes, from mannish water (goat head soup) to this curry, which clearly exhibits the influences of the Indian subcontinent. The same can be said in Trinidad, where goat doesn't just make a cameo but has a starring role. This curried goat is actually a hybrid of the Trini and Jamaican versions I remember. I've used Jamaican curry powder along with Trinidad's heavily aromatic green seasoning.

Combine the goat, onions, green seasoning, curry powder, house spice, and 2 teaspoons salt in a medium bowl. Cover and refrigerate for 24 hours.

In a deep-sided sauté pan (or large pot) over high heat, add the oil. When it shimmers, add the goat meat, tapping off excess marinade and working in batches as necessary—do not crowd the pan. Deeply brown the meat on all sides, 8 to 10 minutes total, then remove to a bowl. When all of the goat has been seared, deglaze the pan with ¼ cup chicken stock, stirring and scraping up any browned bits from the bottom. Return the goat to the pan and add the peppa sauce. Add the remaining chicken broth, plus more as needed to cover. →

ORIGIN: Trinidad
YIELD: 4 servings

1½ pounds **goat stew meat** or **goat shoulder**, cut into 1-inch cubes

1 **yellow onion**, diced

1½ cups **Green Seasoning** (page 29)

¼ cup **Curry Powder** (page 10)

1½ teaspoons **House Spice** (page 6)

2 teaspoons **kosher salt**, plus more to taste

2 tablespoons **grapeseed oil**

4 cups **Chicken Stock** (page 33), divided, plus more as needed

2 teaspoons **Peppa Sauce** (page 25)

3 large **Yukon Gold potatoes** (about 1½ pounds), peeled and cut into ½-inch dice

Lime wedges, to serve

Curried goat will keep in an airtight container in the refrigerator for up to 4 days, or in the freezer for up to 2 months.

Bring the mixture to a boil, then reduce the heat to medium-low and simmer, partially covered, until the goat is tender and the sauce has started to thicken, about 3½ hours. Add the potatoes in the last 30 minutes of cooking, plus an additional ½ cup stock if the pot seems dry.

Season to taste with salt. Serve with Perfectly Steamed Rice (page 46) and lime wedges.

EGUSI STEW WITH GOAT

Egusi stew, a hearty Nigerian stew thickened with egusi (melon seed), was one of the few Nigerian recipes from outside the Caribbean and African American canon that my mother made. She learned it from my father's cousin, Ozubike, and cooked it frequently, even after my parents divorced. There's something so tasty about the faint bitterness of the egusi seeds, the really unmistakable taste of palm oil—used frequently in Nigerian cooking—and the flavor of the crayfish powder which is, actually, just dried shrimp. Each element summons a memory. I remember trips to the Nigerian grocery stores on Arthur Avenue, coming home with bags full of fufu powder, egusi, and iru (fermented locust) seeds, and packages of crayfish powder. We'd stop by a halal shop for goat meat, whose distinct flavor I learned to love from an early age, and then spend the rest of the afternoon with the unmistakable smell of egusi stew coming off the stovetop. Happily, you don't need to live near a Nigerian supermarket to access these ingredients now. All are easily available online—though, if possible, a trip to the store is always worth it.

ORIGIN: Nigeria
YIELD: 4 servings

¼ cup **palm oil**

2 pounds **goat shoulder,** cut into 1-inch cubes

Kosher salt, to taste

3 tablespoons **GGP** (page 5)

1 medium **yellow onion,** diced

½ cup ground **egusi seeds**

1 teaspoon **Peppa Sauce** (page 25)

¼ teaspoon **crayfish powder**

2 **Maggi Seasoning cubes,** crushed

½ teaspoon ground **iru seeds**

8 cups **Chicken Stock** (page 33)

1 cup stemmed, blanched, squeezed **pumpkin leaves** (or mature spinach), about 1 pound fresh greens

Fufu (page 111), to serve

Egusi stew will keep in an airtight container in the refrigerator for up to 4 days, or in the freezer for up to 2 months.

In a Dutch oven over medium-high heat, heat the palm oil until shimmering. Generously season the goat shoulder on all sides with salt, then sear until deeply golden brown, about 10 minutes. Use a slotted spoon to remove the goat to a bowl and set aside.

Reduce heat to medium and add the GGP. Sauté until fragrant and just beginning to toast, 5 to 8 minutes, then add the onions and cook until soft and translucent, 5 to 7 minutes.

Add the egusi and cook for 5 minutes, stirring often, then return the goat to the pan, along with any juices from the bowl. Add the peppa sauce, crayfish powder, Maggi, iru, and stock. Bring to a boil, then reduce to a simmer and cook, uncovered, for 2 to 2½ hours, until the goat is completely tender and the liquid is reduced by about half.

Remove from heat, stir in the pumpkin leaves, and taste, adjusting with salt as needed. Serve with fufu.

NEW YORK

January 20, 2021, was a day of change and transformation. Down in Washington, D.C., Joe Biden was being sworn in on the steps of the Capitol building, not too far from where I once lived. Kamala Harris—the first Black, first female, first Jamaican, first East Indian VP—sat in her bright purple outfit. Next to her sat the very first second gentleman. Near them, Barack was back, and Michelle, in an epic plum ensemble by Sergio Hudson, looked radiant. Bernie was there, too, in his now-famous handmade wool mittens. It was a bright, cold day in America. "The dawn is ours / before we knew it," recited Amanda Gorman, the young Black poet laureate. I listened on the radio as I drove up to say goodbye to the Bronx, where I was born and raised and which forms the source of so many of my early memories.

I had been living in New York for a few months, contemplating opening a restaurant, but, in the last year, the city had been transformed by a pandemic and the pandemic had made clear just how broken the restaurant industry is. I might be crazy, but I wasn't crazy enough to open here. Now I was leaving, moving to Los

Angeles, with its space, sunlight, and the siren call of Hollywood. But before I left, I yearned to return to the hills of the Bronx, to the storefront restaurants whose trays of lechon and pernil are obscured by steam, to the Jamaican bakeries in whose windows sit neat rows of beef and curried chicken patties, and to the closet-sized roti shops that kept me fed as a kid.

When I was too young to have been doing so, I used to walk down the hill from my father's home—a modest brick house with a yellow awning on a quiet street—to Jackie's West Indian Bakery. With fifteen cents in my pocket, I knew I could get a cloud of coco bread, Jamaica's answer to brioche yet so much more, more often than not still steaming. I remember Jackie, who was ancient even when I was young, and who knew my father and whose smiling face is part of the bakery's logo. Now, years later, as I pushed open the door of the bakery, I wondered if she was there. Nothing else had changed. The place, with that delicious yeasty scent of coco bread, was exactly as I remembered it. A painting of Bob Marley on one wall, a faded poster of the famous Jamaica girl next to him. There had been some additions, or perhaps details I hadn't remembered. A sign in front of the register that read, "I literally can't even." The ackee and saltfish had been *reduced* in price, perhaps a nod to how badly the community had been hit by the economic downturn brought on by COVID-19. But the bread was still there: loaves of hardo (hard dough) and

end bread, and the all-important coco bread, which could be had plain or stuffed with jerk chicken, a hot dog, or curried goat. I asked for Jackie, though I knew she wouldn't remember me. "Jackie is around, but she isn't available," said the woman behind the counter, in a voice that made clear she would not be made available. I nodded, and got myself a patty and a coco bread and headed outside, into the bitter cold.

I remembered when the parking lot was full at night, and my dad and I would listen to the dance hall music booming through impossibly loud speakers. The air was thick with smoke from the jerk barrels set up along 233rd. Motorcycles and dirt bikes zoomed up and down and past us. Cars, with their windows open, poured forth music. My dad and I sat on the curb and watched and ate our beef patties and coco bread. These were some of the precious few good memories I had with him. Now, under the bright sun of the morning, the parking lot was less festive, more workaday, almost sober. Whether this was a function of the pandemic or time or simply the time of day, I don't know, but I prefer to carry with me the memory of long-ago hot, loud, joyous nights, coco bread and patty in hand.

Jamaicans began settling in the North Bronx in the late 1940s and early '50s, as part of a larger influx to satisfy the labor market, which was hungry for workers after the end of World War II. Today, Jamaicans are just behind Dominicans as the largest immigrant population here. But on the walk from Jackie's to my next stop, every car that drove past had the green and black flag of Jamaica either hanging on the rearview mirror or affixed as a bumper sticker. Of course, the Dominicans hold a virtual monopoly on hair salons in the Bronx, but the bakeries are Jamaican. The heat—both temperature and spice—of the beef patty kept me warm as I walked along windswept 233rd to Wave Hill Road. Past a karate studio, past the Seventh-day Adventists, past the line of folks waiting for the food pantry at the church, past the old folks' home, and the gas stations, and the houses of aunts and uncles on my father's side with whom I had lost touch when he and I had gone our separate ways and whom I might never see again.

I was lost in thought and nearly got lost among these blocks I hadn't been to in years. But the *clickity-clack* of the elevated 2 train that runs north to south from the South Bronx along White Plains Road led me back on track. Walking south, I remembered how vibrant this stretch was when I was younger. How every store's front door was cast open and life spilled in and out from the sidewalk. The day I was there, it seemed muted. Every block or so a cluster of botanica candles and a photograph taped to a street sign marked the passing of someone, informal shrines of lives flickered out. I was heading to comfort, toward the Kingston Tropical Bakery, but

confronting a much-transformed neighborhood in the process.

Some things had not changed. There was still a line in front of the bakery, a sun-flooded corner spot that opened in 1970, when the neighborhood was still primarily Jewish and Italian. By the time I was growing up here, Kingston had become a neighborhood institution. I remember Sunday mornings, when my father sent me to pick up a loaf of hardo bread. The line curled up the block, and the loaf was so hot out of the oven it filled the plastic bag it came in with steam. Hardo is our Wonder bread, a slightly sweet, spongy loaf I used for my school sandwiches and, at home, to sop up stews and soups, sometimes even hot cocoa on cold days. Originally invented by a Chinese baker named Chin Bwang, who came to Jamaica, like so many Asians, with false hopes only to find themselves exploited, hardo bread carries with its sweetness sadness, too.

Whether the bakers at Kingston Tropical know this or not, I don't know. But they're damn good at the subtle art of hardo. (Underworked, it's chewy; overworked, it's dry.) At Kingston, there is, happily, only joy. The cases are still filled with loaves upon loaves of not just hardo bread but coco bread, too, here split open with a pat of butter melting inside, as well as the beef patties for which the bakery is famous. I couldn't resist and got a perfectly crimped prodigiously stuffed beef patty. Patty into coco bread, a loaf of hardo under my arm, I noticed with pleasure that it was still so fresh it steamed. When I bit into it, I could see the Scotch bonnet seeds and the fresh thyme, and feel the heat, and sense the love that had gone into making the patty. I recognized the flavors, but mostly I recognized that the feeling I had—of eating something made in a specific place for a community of people—was what I have always been looking for when I cook.

In the flavor map of my memory, the Southwest Bronx is full of curries and patties, ackee and saltfish, doubles, and curried goat. But the Northeast Bronx, up near Jerome Avenue and Burnside, under yet another elevated train and closer to my mother's house, these were Dominican and Puerto Rican flavors. Instead of jerk patties, there was pollo asado, pollo guisado, hunks of pernil, sweet plantains, and endless beans and rice. I had fixed in my mind that my last taste of the Bronx would be at Liberato, a large restaurant on a steep stretch of hill on Burnside. I remember the pollo asado being some of the best I've ever had and the oxtail so unctuous. But when I showed up, the place was dark, closed due to COVID-19, according to a sign on the window.

I wasn't hungry anymore—not for food, at least. But for nostalgia, I still had an appetite. Around the corner, Don Panchoco wasn't a place you would go on dates; it was a place you went when you were hungry and broke, where $7.50 bought you a pollo asado platter—dark meat only, please—and enough rice and beans to fill you up all day. So much has changed since those days, with me more than with the Bronx. The chafing trays in the window, at least, labeled to entice passersby, were the same I remembered: yellow-hued rice, golden chunks of pernil, neatly arranged alcapurria, taro-and-plantain fritters, and glistening maduros. I went inside and ordered as much as I could carry. I knew I couldn't finish it all before leaving the city. But leftovers are memories, and memories are something I'll always carry with me.

BREADS, PASTRIES, AND DESSERTS

That bread is universal is obvious. Everywhere food is, some sort of bread—flat or risen—exists. Types of bread are as numerous as the types of grain from which they're made. And in Africa, which the author Adrian Miller divided into carbohydrate zones including corn, yams, wheat, and sorghum, the range is extraordinary. In East Africa, Ethiopians rely on fermented teff for their famous njera, a slightly sour velvety flatbread. Sudan's flatbread kisra and Mali's ngome are made with millet. Corn, first introduced during the Columbian Exchange by Portuguese colonizers, was familiar to West Africans. This, like rice, was another bridge built between Africa and the Americas, and made into bread. During the darkness of enslavement, for instance, wheat was largely reserved for whites while my people made ash pone, a sort of rudimentary cornbread, from cornmeal distributed weekly. There's a direct line from the cornbread on my grandma's table to the terror of the antebellum South straight through to the maize fields of West Africa. So when the bread crumbles and the butter melts, it's a bittersweet bite. I've long been enchanted by the seemingly endless variations of breads. So many of my own explorations begin with selecting an unknown type of loaf from a bakery shelf, be it Jamaican hardo bread or Moroccan m'semen. Most are good enough to be eaten on their own but often play a supporting role to other proteins as sops or sidemen. And though I've tried to listen to my mom when she says *Don't fill up on bread*, sometimes the allure is too strong to resist.

But if I do show restraint, the reward often comes at the end of the meal with dessert. The desserts of the American South are notoriously sweet. From sweet potato pie to banana pudding, sugar is given free rein. As a chef, I've always preferred to restrain the hand of sweetness. Not because it's healthier, necessarily, but because it allows all the nuance of flavors to be heard. There is, however, no denying the supersaturated over-the-top pleasure of red velvet cake, which whisks me right back to Harlem bakeries where it beckons in pre-cut Saran Wrap, or the golden rum cake that transports me to Christmas with every bite. At other times, with other family members, desserts tend more toward the pastry. Such is the case in the Trini Currants Roll (page 252) of my Grandpa Winston, which borrows from the snack-loving British. No matter which, these desserts have, probably more than any other food, the ability to summon the past, with all its wonderful memories of family gatherings around the table.

COCO BREAD

The sweet smell of coco bread, so fragrant it's almost visible, streams from the Jamaican bakeries on 233rd Street in the Bronx. Some people describe coco bread as the Jamaican Parker House roll, or a Caribbean brioche. And though it is true that coco bread bears some of the Parker House roll's fluffiness and a brioche's crumb, this coconut milk–sweetened bread is in a class by itself. The best coco bread has a texture almost like memory foam and a sweet, yeasty taste. And though coco bread is an addictive snack on its own, the pro move is to use it as a holder of sorts for the patties—beef, chicken, goat, etc.—that are often served alongside them.

ORIGIN: Jamaica
YIELD: 12 buns

¼ cup warm **water**

5 tablespoons **white granulated sugar**

4¼ teaspoons **active dry yeast**

3½ cups **all-purpose flour,** plus more as needed for dusting

1½ teaspoons **kosher salt**

1¼ teaspoons **baking powder**

10 tablespoons **unsalted butter,** cubed, room temperature, divided

6½ tablespoons **whole milk**

6 tablespoons **coconut milk**

1 **egg**

Maldon salt (or other flaky sea salt), to taste

Coco bread is best served the day it's baked, but leftovers will keep in an airtight container at room temperature for up to 3 days.

In a small bowl, combine the water, sugar, and yeast. Let sit for 3 minutes, or until foamy.

Meanwhile, in the bowl of a stand mixer fitted with the dough hook, combine the flour, salt, and baking powder and mix to combine. Add the yeast mixture, 8½ tablespoons of the butter (reserve the remaining 1½ tablespoons of butter for finishing the buns), the whole milk, the coconut milk, and the egg. Slowly increase the mixing speed to medium and stir until the dough is smooth, elastic, and climbing up the dough hook, about 10 minutes. (If you stretch a piece of dough between your fingers, you should be able to see light through it without it tearing.) Cover the bowl tightly with plastic wrap and let rise for 1 hour in a warm part of your kitchen, until doubled in size.

Gently punch down the dough to remove excess air. Divide it into 12 pieces, then shape each piece into a bun on a very lightly floured surface by placing a piece of dough on the surface, then making a round claw shape with your dominant hand—the dough should be beneath your palm. Pressing down lightly, briskly roll the dough into a tight bun shape. Transfer the balls to 2 parchment paper–lined sheet pans, 6 buns per sheet, leaving 4 inches between each bun. Cover loosely with plastic wrap and let rise for 30 minutes, until puffy. Carefully peel off the plastic.

Heat the oven to 400°F. Place a baking dish (such as a loaf pan) filled with 2 cups of water on the floor of the oven to create steam (this will allow the buns to rise and remain soft). Place the coco bread in the oven and bake for 8 to 12 minutes, until golden brown. While the coco bread bakes, melt the remaining 1½ tablespoons butter in a saucepan. As soon as you remove the coco bread from the oven, brush with melted butter and sprinkle with Maldon salt. Let cool slightly, then serve.

DHAL PURI ROTI

Trinidad and Tobago, like the rest of the West Indies, are roti heaven. Roti, a type of Indian flatbread, arrived with East Indian laborers in the mid-nineteenth century and has become an integral part of the West Indian kitchen. Paratha roti, or plain roti, called "buss up shot" in Trinidad because it resembles a busted-up T-shirt; aloo roti, roti stuffed with potato; and saba roti, a thicker version often served plain, all serve as both sops for the stews, soups, and curries that form the backbone of Trini cooking and as snacks in themselves. But the King of All Roti, in my book at least, is dhal puri roti, a feat of culinary engineering and a symphony of texture. A two-layered roti with a thin layer of yellow split pea in the middle, dhal puri roti can be eaten alone but finds its higher calling as a wrapper for curries in the form of a roti wrap. In these cases, the inner roti serves as an absorbent layer for the curry inside, the dhal puri (split peas) add flavor and insulation, while the outer roti remains as soft and clean as a set of linen sheets.

ORIGIN: Trinidad and Tobago
YIELD: 6 servings

For the filling
¼ cup yellow split peas
¼ teaspoon ground cumin
¼ teaspoon ground turmeric
Pinch kosher salt

For the dough
2 cups all-purpose flour, plus more for dusting
½ teaspoon baking powder
1 teaspoon kosher salt
½ teaspoon white granulated sugar
½ cup + 3 tablespoons warm water
2 tablespoons canola oil, plus more for greasing

Once cooked, dhal puri roti are best served immediately. Uncooked, they'll keep tightly wrapped for up to 24 hours.

For the filling

Place the split peas in a bowl, cover with 2 inches of water, and soak overnight; the next day, drain and rinse. Bring 4 cups of water to a boil in a medium pot over high heat, then add the split peas and cook for 6 minutes, until translucent but not tender. Drain, then season with cumin, turmeric, and salt. Spread on a paper towel–lined sheet pan and refrigerate overnight.

Transfer the split peas to the bowl of a food processor and pulse to a sandy texture. Set aside.

For the dough

In the bowl of a stand mixer fitted with the paddle attachment, add the dry ingredients and stir to combine. Add the water and oil and stir on low until the dough is smooth and elastic, 8 to 10 minutes. Gather the dough into a ball, lightly grease it with oil, and wrap in plastic. Let rest at room temperature for 30 minutes. →

Divide the dough into 6 pieces, then shape them on a very lightly floured work surface: Place a piece of dough on the surface, then make a round claw shape with your dominant hand—the dough should be beneath your palm. Pressing down lightly, briskly roll the dough into a tight bun shape. (The dough should travel between your thumb and index finger as you roll it.) Cover loosely with plastic wrap and let rest on the floured work surface for 30 minutes more.

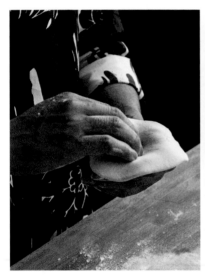  

When ready to cook, use your palm to flatten a ball of dough into a disc about 2½ inches in diameter. With your nondominant hand, make a fist as if holding an ice cream cone. Place the dough disc over the hole made by your thumb and index fingers, then gently push down to make a pocket. Stuff the pocket with 4 teaspoons of split pea mixture, then pinch the edges together to seal. The goal is to fill the middle of the dough ball with split peas, while keeping a perfectly even layer of dough around it. Repeat with the remaining dough and split pea filling.

Line a sheet pan with parchment paper and grease well with nonstick cooking spray. On a well-floured work surface, coat a dough ball with flour and flatten with your palm into a disc. Use a floured rolling pin to gently roll the roti into a 9-inch circle, flipping the circle every few rolls. Don't apply too much pressure—you want to be careful not to tear the dough or compress it too much.

Transfer the roti to the greased parchment paper. Repeat with the remaining dough, layering the finished roti between greased sheets of parchment. At this point, you can wrap the tray tightly in plastic wrap and refrigerate until ready to cook, up to 24 hours. (Be sure not to stack anything on top of the tray or you'll smush your rotis.)

When ready to cook, heat a large pan over medium heat. Place a roti in the hot, dry pan and cook for 1 minute on each side, until charred freckles appear. Serve immediately, either alone or with Curried Goat (page 223), Curried Chicken (page 177), or Channa (page 103).

M'SEMEN

M'semen, a crispy flatbread, is among the many culinary gifts from the Berbere people, who ruled over much of northern Africa including Morocco, Tunisia, and Algeria. The name itself means "well baked," and the bread, a mix of flour and semolina, is, to my taste at least, the perfect accompaniment for, well, everything. I use it as a sort of delicious carbolic shovel for the vegetarian dulet on page 89, but it is a good and quick substitute anytime you're in the need of its slightly puffier eastern cousin, pita.

Stir together the flour, 3 tablespoons semolina, yeast, sugar, and salt in a large bowl, then add the water. Stir together until a dry, shaggy dough forms. Knead by hand (or in the bowl of a stand mixer fitted with the dough hook, on low speed) until the dough is smooth and elastic, about 4 minutes.

Divide the dough in half, then transfer both halves to an oiled sheet pan. Cover loosely with plastic wrap and let rest for 15 minutes at room temperature.

While the dough rests, set up your work area: You'll need a large, flat, clean surface for spreading and folding the dough. Set the canola oil, remaining ¼ cup semolina, and softened butter in 3 separate bowls.

Generously oil the work surface and your hands. Dip one ball of dough in the bowl of oil and place in the center of your work surface. Using a light touch and a quick sweeping motion from the center outward, gently spread the dough into a paper-thin, roughly shaped circle about 12 to 14 inches in diameter. Oil your hands as often as needed so they slide easily over the dough.

ORIGIN: Northern Africa
SERVES: 8

1¾ cups all-purpose flour, plus more as needed for dusting

3 tablespoons + ¼ cup semolina flour, divided

¼ teaspoon active dry yeast

1 teaspoon white granulated sugar

1 teaspoon kosher salt

¾ cup warm water

¾ cup canola oil, plus more as needed for greasing

4 tablespoons unsalted butter, softened

M'semen will keep for up to 2 days before cooking, or freeze after rolling out for up to 2 weeks.

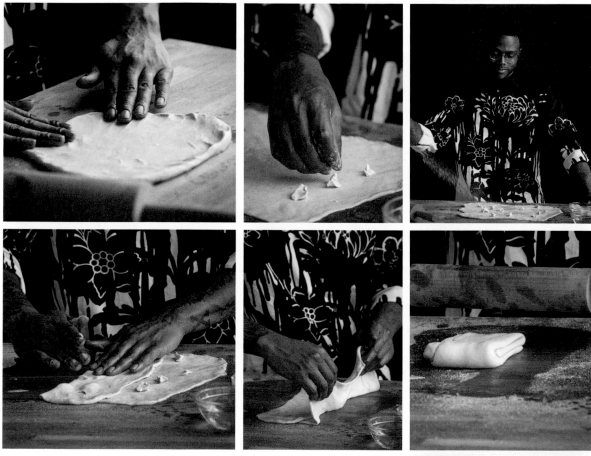

Dot the flattened dough with 1 tablespoon butter and sprinkle with 1 tablespoon semolina. Fold the dough into thirds like a letter to fold an elongated rectangle. Dot again with 1 tablespoon butter and sprinkle with 1 tablespoon semolina, then fold again into thirds to form a square.

With a rolling pin, roll the square into a long rectangle about 5½ x 12 inches, then cut into 4 even pieces, each 5½ x 3 inches. Repeat with the remaining dough ball. Place all 8 pieces of dough on a well-oiled sheet pan, with greased parchment paper between layers of m'semen. Wrap tightly in plastic wrap and refrigerate until ready to cook (or as many as 2 days in advance). →

When ready to assemble, cook the m'semen: Heat the oven to 200°F and place a sheet pan inside. Heat a large pan with 1 teaspoon oil over medium heat. When it shimmers, add one m'semen and cook for 90 seconds, then flip and cook for another 90 seconds. Flip the m'semen and repeat, cooking for 30 to 45 seconds per side. The outside should be golden brown, and the inside pillowy and fully cooked; reduce the heat if they seem to be browning too quickly. Transfer cooked m'semen to the sheet pan in oven until ready to serve. Repeat with remaining m'semen, adding 1 teaspoon oil to the pan for each piece.

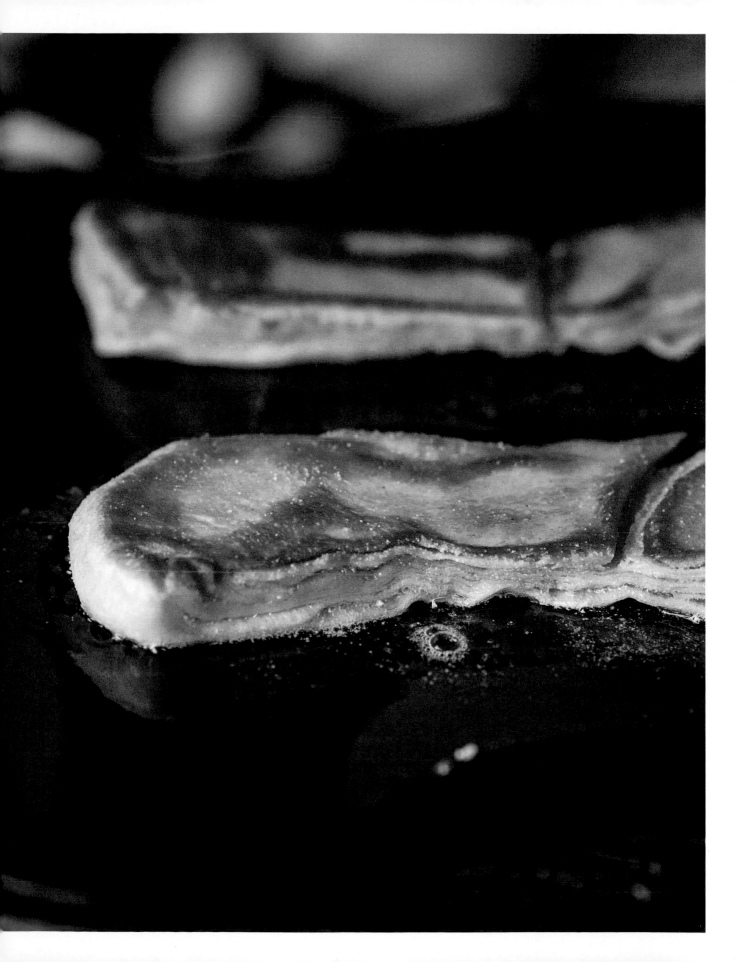

BAKE

One of the most precious memories I have of my Papa Winston is of sitting on the beach in Trinidad feasting on bake and shark toward the end of his life. The water was blue, the sun was hot, the sand into which we pressed our feet was cool, and the sandwich, succulent fried morsels of black tip shark, was enveloped in freshly made bake. To say it was perfect is no exaggeration. Bake in the Caribbean refers to an entire class of fried dough that includes this Jamaican version, often eaten for breakfast as an accompaniment with Buljol (page 154). Fried bread is not a complicated thing to make, but the reward, as a snack or a sop or a sandwich, is indelible.

In the bowl of a stand mixer fitted with the dough hook attachment, stir together the dry ingredients. Add the butter and water and knead on medium speed until smooth and elastic, about 3 minutes. (If you stretch a piece of dough between your fingers, you should be able to see light through it without it tearing.) Lightly grease the dough ball and mixing bowl with oil, then cover the bowl tightly with plastic wrap and let rest at room temperature for 20 minutes.

Divide the dough into 10 pieces (about 2½ ounces each). Place each piece of dough on a well-floured surface, then make a round claw shape with your dominant hand—the dough should be beneath your palm. Pressing down lightly, briskly roll the dough into a tight bun shape. Cover the dough balls with a damp kitchen towel. Working with one dough ball at a time, use a rolling pin to roll each ball into a circle ¼ inch thick and 5½ inches in diameter. Cover the rolled-out circles with another damp kitchen towel. Repeat until all the dough has been rolled. Let rest, covered, for 20 minutes.

While the dough discs rest, heat 2 inches of canola oil to 350°F in a Dutch oven over medium heat. Working with one disc at a time, fry each for 3 to 4 minutes, turning once halfway through, until puffed and golden all over. Carefully remove to a paper towel–lined plate. Serve immediately.

ORIGIN: Caribbean

YIELD: 10 servings

3⅔ cups all-purpose flour, plus more as needed for dusting

2 tablespoons + 1 teaspoon white granulated sugar

3¼ teaspoons baking powder

1 teaspoon kosher salt

3½ tablespoons unsalted butter, room temperature

1 cup + 1 teaspoon warm water

Canola oil as needed for greasing and frying

Bake is best served the day it's fried. Dough can be rolled out and reserved on a lightly greased sheet tray, tightly wrapped in plastic, in the refrigerator for up to 2 days before frying.

PLANTAIN BREAD

As someone who has never had much of a sweet tooth, the appeal of banana bread has always left me cold, but I find plantain bread, in which the plantains retain a bit of their starchiness, to be slightly more savory and much more compelling. It has just the right amount of sweetness and, thanks to the brown sugar and vanilla, is warmly aromatic. Plus, the texture has that firmness plantain lovers across the Caribbean—and the smart ones in the States—die for.

Note: This recipe calls for a 10-x-5-inch loaf pan. If you only have a 9-x-5-inch pan, use one cup of the batter to make three muffins and bake the rest in the loaf pan as directed (check for doneness at fifty minutes). To bake the muffins, grease a muffin tin (or line with muffin liners) and bake for eighteen to twenty minutes, until the muffin tops are puffed and a toothpick inserted into the center comes out clean.

ORIGIN: Caribbean
YIELD: One 10-x-5-inch loaf

4 or 5 large, overripe (totally black) **plantains**
2 cups **all-purpose flour**
1 teaspoon **baking soda**
½ teaspoon **kosher salt**
8 tablespoons **unsalted butter**, room temperature
½ cup virgin **coconut oil**, room temperature
¾ cup dark **brown sugar**
2 **eggs**
1 tablespoon **vanilla bean paste**
1 tablespoon ground **cinnamon**

Plantain bread will keep tightly wrapped at room temperature for up to 1 week, or in the freezer for up to 2 months.

Heat the oven to 350°F. Lightly grease a 10-x-5-inch loaf pan and line with parchment paper so it hangs over the 2 long edges.

Peel and halve 1 plantain lengthwise. Peel the remaining plantains and mash enough to have 2½ cups very smooth mash.

In a medium bowl, whisk together the flour, baking soda, and salt.

In the bowl of a stand mixer fitted with the paddle attachment (or in a large bowl with an electric hand mixer), cream the butter, coconut oil, and brown sugar on medium speed until light and fluffy, 2 to 3 minutes. Add the eggs one at a time, beating to combine between additions, then add the vanilla, cinnamon, and mashed plantains. Beat until completely incorporated. Fold the dry mixture into the wet, stirring until just combined, then transfer the batter to the prepared pan.

Place the sliced plantain on top of the batter, cut side up. Bake for 60 to 65 minutes, rotating the pan halfway through, until a toothpick inserted into the center comes out clean. Let cool in the pan for 10 minutes, then transfer to a wire rack to cool completely.

PUFF PUFF

The grandmother of beignets and a distant cousin of zeppole, West Africa's most popular form of fried dough, puff puff, is, as the name suggests, fried pillows of airy dough. On the streets of Lagos in Nigeria, in Cameroon and in Ghana, where this is just as popular, puff puff sellers grab a handful of dough, roll it into a ball, and thrust it into the fryer with one lightning-fast motion. What emerges is rolled in cinnamon sugar, and what you pop into your mouth is like a funnel cake ball crossed with a churro.

ORIGIN: Nigeria
YIELD: 25 to 30 pieces

For the puff puff
6 eggs
¾ cup **white granulated sugar**
1 cup **whole milk**
¼ teaspoon **vanilla bean paste**
3 cups **all-purpose flour**
1½ teaspoons **kosher salt**
1 tablespoon **baking powder**
½ teaspoon **freshly grated nutmeg**
¼ teaspoon **ground cinnamon**
Canola oil, for frying

For the cinnamon sugar
3 tablespoons **white granulated sugar**
2 teaspoons **ground cinnamon**

Puff puff are best served immediately (but the batter may be made up to 24 hours ahead).

For the puff puff

In a large bowl, whisk together the eggs, sugar, milk, and vanilla bean paste until well combined and smooth. In a separate bowl, combine the flour, salt, baking powder, nutmeg, and cinnamon. Gently fold the dry mixture into the wet mixture with a silicone spatula until you have a thick, smooth batter. Cover the bowl and refrigerate for at least 1 hour and up to 24 hours.

Fill a medium pot with 3 inches canola oil. Heat over medium heat to 350°F.

For the cinnamon sugar

While the oil heats, stir together the cinnamon sugar mixture.

Using a #30 (2½-tablespoon) cookie scoop or 2 large spoons, carefully drop a few balls of batter into the hot oil, being careful not to crowd the pot—the balls will puff up as the batter cooks. Fry for 3 to 4 minutes, then flip the puff puff and fry for another 3 minutes. They should be evenly and deeply golden brown, smooth, and light.

Remove the puff puff from the oil and immediately toss with cinnamon sugar. Serve right away.

CHIN CHIN

The streets of Lagos Island are crowded with street vendors. Everything from pillowcases to magazines to shoes to radios and wristwatches is for sale from informal stalls. The cries of hawkers are as much a part of the cityscape as the mega-mansions with their guard houses. When I was a child, the cacophony was both intimidating and exhilarating and reminded me of certain blocks in Harlem, around 125th Street, in which the street commerce was just as lively. In Nigeria, I could walk by most vendors without being tempted, but there were two exceptions. Both the suya men who presided over hot grills sizzling with meat, and the chin chin stalls, generally run by women, were nearly impossible to resist. (My very strict grandfather would yank my hand if I even paused for a moment.) But I got a taste. Chin chin are nutmeg-riddled fried puffs of dough, the Nigerian contribution to filling mankind's desire for crunchy, sweet snacks. From behind their tables, the chin chin sellers sold not just these addictive cookies but a whole menagerie of fried foods, foods whose crunch does double duty by helping to maintain their longevity in the hot sun. These include shuk shuk, balls of fried coconut flakes; elongated strands of fried cornmeal called kokoro; sweet fried dough called Puff Puff (page 248), and coconut cookie tuiles called gurundi. But it was the chin chin I ordered, hastily, whenever I could.

ORIGIN: Nigeria
YIELD: 10 cups ½-inch puffs

3½ cups all-purpose flour, plus more for dusting

¾ cup white granulated sugar

½ cup coconut sugar

½ teaspoon kosher salt

¼ teaspoon baking powder

1 teaspoon freshly grated nutmeg

4 tablespoons unsalted butter, cubed, room temperature

¾ cup heavy cream

¼ cup unsweetened coconut cream

1 egg

Vegetable oil, such as canola, for frying

Chin chin will keep in an airtight container at room temperature for up to 1 month. Dough may be frozen after being cut for up to 3 months.

In a large bowl, whisk together the flour, sugars, salt, baking powder, and nutmeg. Add the butter and rub with your fingers until well incorporated with the flour. Whisk in the cream, coconut cream, and egg, eventually switching from a whisk to your hands when the mixture becomes too thick to whisk. Mix until you have a sticky dough ball.

On a lightly floured surface, knead the dough until it is smooth, elastic, even in color, and no longer sticky, adding flour as needed, 2 to 3 minutes.

Divide the dough in half. Working on a floured surface with 1 piece at a time, roll half the piece into a rectangle ⅛-inch thick. (Feel free to use a pasta roller if you have one.) Trim away any uneven edges, then cut the dough into ½-inch squares. Occasionally flouring the blade of your knife will keep the dough from sticking. Repeat with the remaining dough. (At this point, you can freeze the dough for later if you like: Place the cut chin chin in a single layer on a parchment paper–lined sheet tray and freeze until solid, then transfer to a ziplock bag and store for up to 3 months. To cook from frozen, let thaw in a single layer at room temperature, then fry as instructed below.)

To fry: Heat 3 inches of oil to 375°F in a large Dutch oven over medium heat. Working in batches, fry the chin chin until golden, puffed, and crisp, about 1 to 2 minutes, stirring often with a slotted spoon—this goes quickly, so watch carefully. (Don't worry if the chin chin squares are a little stuck together. They'll separate once they hit the oil.) Remove to a paper towel–lined sheet tray, let cool slightly, then serve.

CURRANTS ROLL

Though the indentured laborers brought from India in the nineteenth century might have contributed the most to Trinbagonian food, the British, who ruled the island from 1802 until independence in 1962, left their mark too. This is perhaps most apparent in my Papa Winston's favorite pastry, currants roll. With a buttery, flaky dough enveloping plump currants, the currants roll is a descendant of the eccles cake, a traditional British dessert. Eccles cakes resemble small pies, but in Trinidad, we make them as rolls, almost more like a rugelach. On our last trip to Port of Spain, I'll never forget how happy my grandfather was to walk into a bakery and order a fresh currants roll. It was gone by the time we had even pushed open the shop's door to leave.

For the dough

Place the flour, along with the bowl and blade of your food processor, and a mixing bowl, in the freezer for 20 minutes. After 20 minutes, assemble the food processor, then add the flour, shortening, and butter. Pulse until the mixture resembles tiny pebbles. Add the vinegar and pulse again, then add the water 1 tablespoon at a time until the dough just comes together. (You may not need all the water.)

Transfer the dough to a lightly floured surface. Working quickly, roll the dough into a 10-x-16-inch rectangle. Fold the long ends of the dough toward the center, then fold in half from left to right, bringing the short ends together. With the smooth end on your left, roll the dough again into a 10-x-16-inch rectangle and repeat the fold. Turn the dough and repeat the roll and fold for a third time. Place the dough on a parchment paper–lined sheet tray and set in the freezer for 30 minutes. If the dough starts to feel warm or sticky, refrigerate it for 15 minutes—it's important to keep the fat as cold as possible.

For the filling

While the dough chills, make the filling by stirring together all the ingredients in a small bowl.

ORIGIN: Trinidad and Tobago
YIELD: 12 rolls

For the dough

2 cups **all-purpose flour**, plus more for dusting

½ cup **shortening**, cubed and cold

12 tablespoons cold **unsalted butter**, cubed

1 tablespoon **white vinegar**

½ cup **ice water**

For the filling

1 cup dried **currants**

1 tablespoon ground **cinnamon**

1 teaspoon ground **allspice**

¼ cup **coconut sugar**

3 tablespoons **unsalted butter**, melted

To assemble

1 **egg**

1 teaspoon **whole milk**

1 tablespoon **coconut sugar**

Currants roll will keep in an airtight container at room temperature for up to 1 week.

To assemble

Whisk together the egg and milk in another small bowl to make an egg wash.

Heat the oven to 375°F. On a very lightly floured work surface, reroll the dough into a 10-x-16-inch rectangle (it should be about ¼ inch thick) if it has shrunk. Sprinkle evenly with the filling mixture and press gently to adhere. Starting with one of the long ends, roll the dough into a tight spiral and pinch the ends to seal them closed. Place the roll on the lined sheet tray with the seam side down. Brush all over with the egg wash and bake for 45 to 50 minutes, until golden brown. Remove and immediately dust with 1 tablespoon coconut sugar. Let cool for 20 to 25 minutes, until cool enough to handle, then slice diagonally into 1½-inch pieces. It's best to do this right on the sheet tray, as the roll is flaky and delicate. Place the slices swirl side up and bake for 5 to 10 minutes more, until the swirls appear dry. Let cool completely before serving.

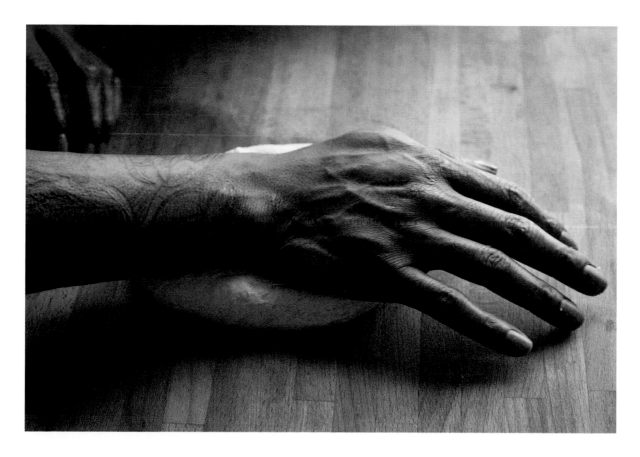

GOLDEN RUM CAKE

The Caribbean is the birthplace of rum, which is derived from molasses, which is made from the sugarcane that once dominated the region's economy. It was one leg of the hellacious triangular trade, a three-legged scar across the Atlantic Ocean. The sugar from the islands was shipped to New England or to Europe, where it was distilled into rum, and the rum was then shipped to West Africa, where it was sold for more slaves, who were taken to the Caribbean to work the sugar plantations. And although it is a bitter story indeed, sugar has a special place in the West Indian kitchen, from Browning (page 13) to both this cake and the Black Cake (page 258). Both are Christmas traditions that, like many aunties and uncles at the holidays, are soaked in booze. And both are delicious. Golden rum cake is often made in a Bundt pan, and emerges, as the name suggests, a beautiful golden color.

Heat the oven to 325°F. Grease a 10-to-12-cup Bundt pan with nonstick cooking spray.

For the cake

In the bowl of a stand mixer fitted with the paddle attachment, combine the flour, sugars, dry pudding mix, baking powder, salt, butter, and oil. Mix at medium speed until thoroughly combined—the batter should appear sandy in texture. Add the coconut cream and vanilla bean paste and mix to combine, then add the eggs one at a time, mixing to combine completely between additions. Use a rubber spatula to scrape the sides of the bowl and stir in the rum.

Scrape the batter into the prepared pan and bake for 55 to 60 minutes, rotating halfway through, until a toothpick inserted into the center comes out clean. Let the cake cool slightly while you prepare the soak.

For the soak

Combine all the ingredients in a medium saucepan over medium heat. Bring to a simmer and cook, stirring occasionally, until →

ORIGIN: Caribbean
YIELD: 8 to 10 servings
(8½-inch cake)

For the cake

2 cups **cake flour**

1 cup **white granulated sugar**

½ cup **turbinado (raw) sugar**

One 3.4-ounce package **instant vanilla pudding**

2 teaspoons **baking powder**

1 teaspoon **kosher salt**

8 tablespoons **unsalted butter**, room temperature, cubed

½ cup **vegetable oil**, such as canola

½ cup **unsweetened coconut cream**, room temperature

1 tablespoon **vanilla bean paste**

4 **eggs**, room temperature

½ cup **spiced rum**

For the soak

8 tablespoons **unsalted butter**

¼ cup **water**

1 cup **coconut sugar**

½ teaspoon **salt**

1 cup **spiced rum**

2 teaspoons **vanilla bean paste**

Golden rum cake will keep tightly wrapped at room temperature for up to 1 week, or in the freezer for up to 2 months.

it thickens into a syrup, 5 to 8 minutes. Reduce the heat as needed to keep from boiling over. You should have 1½ cups of syrup.

Keeping the cake in the pan, use a skewer to poke deep holes all over its surface. Pour ¼ cup warm soak over the warm cake. Once absorbed, repeat until all the soak has been used. Cover the pan loosely with plastic wrap and let the cake sit overnight at room temperature to cool completely and soak up the syrup.

When ready to serve, use a paring knife to loosen the edges of the cake from the pan and invert onto a serving plate. If the cake won't release, don't force it. Heat the oven to 350°F and return the cake to the oven for 10 minutes to soften the sticky syrup before tipping the warm cake onto the serving plate.

ZUCCHINI BREAD

An even more savory variation of Plantain Bread (page 247), zucchini bread is the answer to the dilemma faced by thousands of gardeners, whose zucchini patches during the peak of the summer season offer an almost diabolical amount of zucchini. Among them was my grandmother Cassie Philips, from whom this recipe comes. Though the pineapple isn't, strictly speaking, traditional, I have discovered that she—like a whole generation of cooks—was inspired by a 1974 recipe from *Sunset* magazine, which wisely added the fruit for moisture and sweetness.

Heat the oven to 350°F. Grease two 9-x-5-inch loaf pans, line each with parchment paper (it should hang over the pans' long sides), then grease the parchment. Lightly flour the greased, lined pans, tapping out any excess flour.

In a large bowl, whisk the eggs with the sugar until light and foamy, 2 to 3 minutes. Whisk in the oil and vanilla bean paste, then fold in the zucchini and pineapple, stirring until completely combined.

In a medium bowl, sift together the flour, baking soda, and baking powder. Whisk in the cinnamon, nutmeg, and salt. Gradually add the dry ingredients to the wet ingredients, folding gently until just combined. Divide the batter between the prepared loaf pans.

Bake the loaves for 1 hour, rotating halfway through, until golden brown and a toothpick inserted into the center of a loaf comes out clean.

Remove from the oven and let the loaves cool in their pans for 1 hour, then transfer to a wire rack to cool completely.

ORIGIN: American South
YIELD: Two 9-x-5-inch loaves

3 **eggs**

2 cups **white granulated sugar**

1 cup **canola oil**, plus more for greasing pans

1½ tablespoons **vanilla bean paste**

2 loosely packed cups shredded **zucchini** (from 9 ounces zucchini, about 1½ medium), squeezed of as much liquid as possible

One 8-ounce can **crushed pineapple**, drained

3 cups **all-purpose flour**, plus more for flouring pans

2 teaspoons **baking soda**

½ teaspoon **baking powder**

2½ teaspoons ground **cinnamon**

1 teaspoon freshly grated **nutmeg**

1 teaspoon **kosher salt**

Zucchini bread will keep tightly wrapped in plastic at room temperature for up to 1 week, or in the freezer for up to 2 months.

BLACK CAKE

Unlike Golden Rum Cake (page 255), which is traditionally found throughout the Caribbean, black cake is most closely associated with Trinidad and Tobago. It's called black cake because, if you do it right, all that dark sugar, wine, and spices turn the cake inky black, and it's the most decadent fruit cake in the world.

Every Trini family has either an undisputed black cake master or a lively debate about naming one. Some folks soak their fruit for days, others up to a year. Some pour nearly a whole liquor shelf into the batter, others are more restrained. I've split the difference here. I'm generous with the rum, but you can still drive home after.

Heat the oven to 350°F. Grease two 9-inch cake pans with non-stick baking spray.

For the cake

Combine the dates and water in a medium saucepan and place over high heat. Bring to a boil and reduce by three-quarters, 25 to 30 minutes. Let cool slightly, then transfer to a blender and purée until smooth. You should have 1¼ cups date purée. Set aside to cool completely.

In the bowl of a stand mixer fitted with the paddle attachment, cream together the butter, coconut sugar, and almond paste until fluffy, 2 to 3 minutes. Beat in the eggs one by one, then add the rum, vinegar, vanilla bean paste, and lime zest. Mix on medium speed until just combined, then add the date purée, wine, brown sugar, nutmeg, allspice, cinnamon, and salt. Scrape down the sides of the bowl as necessary.

Sift the cake flour, cocoa powder, and baking powder into a medium bowl, then gently fold into the wet mixture until just combined—you don't want to overmix.

Divide the batter evenly between the 2 prepared cake pans. Bake for 40 to 45 minutes, rotating halfway through, until a toothpick

ORIGIN: Trinidad and Tobago
YIELD: Two 9-inch cakes

For the cake
2 cups (8 ounces) **pitted Medjool dates**
4 cups **water**
2¼ cups **unsalted butter,** room temperature
2 cups **coconut sugar**
1 tablespoon **almond paste**
9 **eggs**, room temperature
¼ cup **dark rum**
1 tablespoon **white vinegar**
1 tablespoon **vanilla bean paste**
Zest from 1 **lime**
1 cup dry, fruity **red wine**
1 cup **dark brown sugar**
½ teaspoon freshly ground **nutmeg**
1 teaspoon ground **allspice**
1 teaspoon ground **cinnamon**
¼ teaspoon **kosher salt**
2½ cups **cake flour**
1 cup **cocoa powder**
1 tablespoon **baking powder**

inserted into the center comes out clean. Let cool for 10 minutes in the pans, then carefully flip onto a wire rack set over a rimmed sheet pan to cool completely.

For the soak

When the cakes are nearly cooled, make the soak: Combine all the ingredients in a large saucepan over medium heat. Bring to a simmer and reduce to a loose syrup consistency, about 10 minutes. The syrup will tighten as it cools, so don't overcook. Remove from the heat and let cool for about 5 minutes. You should have 3½ cups syrup.

Pour half the syrup into a large, flat-bottomed pan or dish (like a pie plate). Use a spatula to gently place one of the cakes in the syrup and let sit for 5 minutes, then carefully flip and soak for another 5 minutes. Transfer the cake back to the wire rack to drain and set. Repeat with the other cake and the remaining syrup.

Let the cakes rest for at least 1 hour before serving warm or at room temperature.

For the soak

1 cup **unsalted butter**

2 cups **coconut sugar**

1 teaspoon **salt**

2 cups **dark rum**

1½ tablespoons **vanilla bean paste**

1½ tablespoons **almond paste**

½ cup **water**

Black cake will keep tightly wrapped, loosely covered, or in an airtight container at room temperature for up to 1 week, or in the freezer for up to 2 months.

RED VELVET CAKE

When it comes to food, the division between what is "southern" and what is "Black" is as blurred as the boundary between where Harlem ends and Sugar Hill begins. (I'm inclined to say, though I'm sure others will argue, that just as all of Sugar Hill is in Harlem but not all Harlem is Sugar Hill, all southern cuisine is Black food, though not all Black food is southern.) This is an especially salient point when it comes to red velvet cake, which holds the distinction of being perhaps the most popular dessert in the soul food kitchen. Never mind the fact that it isn't really southern and doesn't have deep roots in Black culture.

How a cake that was, as most scholars agree, invented at New York's Waldorf Astoria in the 1920s, made popular by a man who sold red food coloring in the 1930s, and spread nationally in the 1950s came to be seen as the ultimate soul food dessert is unclear. But by the time I was growing up in the Bronx and spending time in East Harlem, red velvet cake was on the menu of every soul food restaurant on 125th. Perhaps none was as well known as the Kool-Aid red version made by Sylvia Woods of the iconic Sylvia's.

Luckily for me, at the time, my mother was working at the now-closed Sugar Hill Bistro, a restaurant that served upscale soul food which included, naturally, a version of red velvet. Whereas Sylvia uses food coloring, this recipe uses beetroot to give the cake its supernaturally silken texture and a deep crimson hue. It was this recipe, along with Seafood Gumbo (page 138), that I'd ask my mother to make every birthday and still do, up to this day.

For the cake

Peel and dice the beet. Transfer to a blender and purée until completely smooth. Reserve in the refrigerator until ready to bake. Beet purée may be made up to 1 day in advance.

Heat the oven to 350°F. Grease two 9-inch round cake pans with nonstick cooking spray and line with parchment paper.

ORIGIN: American South

YIELD: 10 to 12 servings

For the cake

1 small red beet

8 tablespoons unsalted butter, room temperature

1 cup white granulated sugar

½ cup coconut sugar

2 eggs

2 tablespoons cocoa powder

1 teaspoon kosher salt

1 tablespoon vanilla bean paste

1 cup buttermilk

2½ cups cake flour

1½ teaspoons baking powder

1 tablespoon white vinegar

For the icing

5 tablespoons all-purpose flour

1 cup whole milk

1 cup coconut sugar

8 tablespoons unsalted butter, room temperature

1 tablespoon vanilla bean paste

Two 8-ounce blocks cream cheese, room temperature

Red velvet cake will keep in the refrigerator, loosely wrapped in plastic wrap, for up to 1 week. The cake layers and the icing may each be made up to 2 days in advance and stored separately in the refrigerator before assembling; let the icing come to room temperature before assembling.

In the bowl of a stand mixer fitted with the paddle attachment, cream the butter and sugars together until fluffy, 2 to 3 minutes. Add the eggs one by one, beating to combine completely between additions, then scrape down the sides of the bowl.

In a small bowl, stir together the cocoa powder with 4 tablespoons beet purée to make a paste. Add to the stand mixer and beat to combine.

In a measuring cup, stir together the salt, vanilla bean paste, and buttermilk. In a medium bowl, sift together the cake flour and baking powder. Add ½ cup flour mixture to the batter and mix on low until just combined, then add ¼ cup buttermilk mixture, mixing until just combined. Repeat until both mixtures have been used up. Scrape down the bowl with a rubber spatula, then gently fold in the vinegar and stop stirring.

Divide the batter evenly between the prepared cake pans. Bake, rotating halfway through, for 30 minutes, or until a toothpick inserted into the center comes out clean. Let cool in pans for 10 minutes, then invert onto a wire rack, peel off the parchment paper, and cool completely.

For the icing

Combine flour and milk in a small saucepan over low heat. Stir constantly until the mixture thickens, then remove from the heat and let cool completely.

Beat the coconut sugar, butter, and vanilla bean paste in the bowl of a stand mixer fitted with the paddle attachment on medium speed until light and fluffy, 2 to 3 minutes. Add the cream cheese and beat again until fluffy, 1 to 2 minutes more. Add the cooled flour mixture and beat again until the frosting is silky and spreadable, a final 1 to 2 minutes.

To assemble

When the cakes are completely cool, set one on a serving plate. Frost the top of it, then place the second cake on top, bottom side up. (This will give you a flat top surface.) Frost the top and sides with the remaining icing, then serve.

SATSUMA CHESS PIE

Chess pie is really just buttermilk custard in pie crust. Quintessentially southern, chess pie has nothing to do with chess, either. Some think the name is a derivation of "cheese," and certainly the recipe can be traced back to English desserts like lemon curd pies, so that makes sense. Others suggest that the name comes from "chest," as in the pie has so much sugar it could be stored in the pie chest, not the refrigerator. The truth is probably somewhere in between, but there's no confusion about what makes chess pie irresistible: the rich custard flecked with cornmeal. (A chess pie without cornmeal is a buttermilk pie.) This chess pie is almost identical to the ones my aunties would make when I visited them in Louisiana. The satsuma, a winter citrus that grows in abundance down there, gives the sweet pie a touch of citric acid.

ORIGIN: American South
YIELD: One 9-inch pie

For the dough
1¼ cups + 2 tablespoons **all-purpose flour**, plus more for dusting

¾ teaspoon **kosher salt**

4 tablespoons cold **unsalted butter**, cubed

6 tablespoons cold **shortening**, diced

¼ cup **ice water**

For the dough

Place the flour, along with the bowl and blade of your food processor, and a mixing bowl, in the freezer for 20 minutes. After 20 minutes, assemble the food processor, then add the flour and salt and pulse to combine. Add the butter and shortening and pulse to a coarse meal. (The butter should be in dime-sized pieces.) Transfer the mixture to the cold mixing bowl and add the ice water a tablespoon at a time, mixing gently with a rubber spatula until the dough begins to come together in large clumps. (You may not need all the water.) Knead the mixture a few times until it comes together into a smooth dough. If it's sticky, sprinkle in a bit more flour; if it doesn't come together, add a bit more water.

Flatten into a disc and wrap in plastic wrap. Refrigerate for at least 1 hour and up to overnight.

Heat the oven to 425°F. Lightly flour a piece of parchment paper slightly larger than your pie dish, then roll the dough into a 12-inch circle about ⅛ inch thick directly on the paper. Use the parchment to transfer the dough to a 9-inch pie dish, then carefully peel off the paper and reserve. Fold the edges of the dough under itself, leaving a ½-inch-tall lip. Gently press the dough against the sides of the pie dish to adhere, then crimp the edges. Prick the dough a few times with a fork. If the dough ever begins to feel soft or warm, move it to the fridge for 10 to 15 minutes, until firm again.

Place the square of parchment paper on top of the pie dough and fill with pie weights (or dried beans). Bake for 10 to 15 minutes, until the dough starts to look dry, then remove the pie weights and parchment and bake until just turning golden, about 5 minutes more. Cool on a wire rack and reduce the oven temperature to 350°F.

For the filling

Whisk together all the ingredients except the eggs and powdered sugar in a large bowl. Slowly add the eggs in a steady stream, whisking thoroughly to combine. Place the crust on a sheet tray, then transfer the filling to the crust (it's okay if the crust is still a little warm, but it shouldn't be hot). Bake for 45 to 50 minutes, rotating halfway through, until the crust is golden and the filling is mostly set, with a slight jiggle. If the crust is browning too quickly, tent with foil.

Cool completely on a wire rack, then sprinkle with powdered sugar and serve.

For the filling

7 tablespoons **unsalted butter,** melted and slightly cooled

1½ cups **white granulated sugar**

1 tablespoon **vanilla bean paste**

3½ tablespoons **whole milk**

2¼ teaspoons **white balsamic vinegar** (or white wine vinegar)

5 teaspoons **medium-grind cornmeal**

2¼ teaspoons **all-purpose flour**

¼ teaspoon **kosher salt**

1 tablespoon **satsuma zest** (from 2 to 3 satsumas)

6½ tablespoons freshly squeezed **satsuma juice** (from 2 to 3 satsumas)

4 **eggs** + 1 **egg yolk,** lightly beaten

Powdered sugar, to serve

Satsuma chess pie is best served the day it's made, but leftovers will keep in the refrigerator, loosely covered with plastic, for up to 3 days.

BANANA PUDDING

If there was a Mount Rushmore of soul food, banana pudding, along with peach cobbler, pound cake, and sweet potato pie, would be etched in its granite. And the model for the carving would be found in my Aunt Yolanda's kitchen in Beaumont, Texas, where her fluffy, eye-poppingly sweet pudding is the stuff of family legend. A uniquely American descendant of the English trifle, most historians think the dessert was born in Jamaica, as British colonials incorporated locally grown bananas. By the turn of the twentieth century, America's hunger for bananas had made the once-exotic fruit common and, just as mac and cheese migrated from Big House kitchens to the estates of white gentry and finally to the kitchens of the African Americans, so too did banana pudding become *our* food, *our* dessert, *our* sweetness. Later on in the twentieth century, industrial food manufacturing made banana pudding even easier to make. Sure, some purists might deride the instant pudding or the Nilla Wafers, but by now both are integral aspects of this dessert. More importantly, it's what Aunt Yolanda uses and I'm not about to trouble a good thing.

ORIGIN: American South

YIELD: One 9-x-13-inch pan

One 3.4-ounce package instant vanilla pudding

2 cups whole milk

3 cups heavy cream

¼ cup powdered sugar

¾ cup + 2 tablespoons sweetened condensed milk

2 teaspoons vanilla extract

12 ounces Biscoff cookies (about 45 cookies, from two 8.8-ounce boxes)

8 ripe, freckly bananas, sliced into ⅛-inch-thick coins

One 11-ounce box Nilla Wafers

Maldon salt (or other flaky sea salt), to taste

Banana pudding will keep in the refrigerator for up to 4 days.

Following the package instructions, make the vanilla pudding with the milk. Set aside to cool completely.

When the pudding is cool, combine cream and powdered sugar in the bowl of a stand mixer. Whip until stiff peaks have formed, then fold in the sweetened condensed milk, vanilla, and pudding.

In a 9-x-13-inch pan, lay a quarter of the Biscoff cookies in an even layer. Top with about a quarter of the banana slices, spread with a quarter of the custard, then top with a quarter of the Nilla Wafers. Repeat 3 times, ending with a layer of custard. Line the edge of the pan with Nilla Wafers, with the top half of the cookie sticking out. Crush the remaining Biscoff and Nilla Wafers into coarse crumbs in a food processor or in a ziplock bag with a rolling pin, then sprinkle evenly over the top layer of custard.

Cover the pie loosely with plastic wrap and refrigerate for at least 3 hours and up to 2 days then finish with Maldon salt before serving.

SWEET POTATO CINNAMON ROLLS

If you are my mom or my aunties, you've probably landed on this recipe after searching this book for your famous candied yams. Kwame, how could you not include candied yams? A) They're delicious. B) They're important to the diasporic kitchen. Have some respect. Well, I don't want to cause any family fights, but I've never been a fan of candied yams. Not only are they not yams at all—what Americans call yams are actually sweet potatoes—but, as a dish, candied yams are too sweet to be on the dinner table at all. Marshmallows? Come on, now.

But I am not only a chef and an author but also a son and a nephew and I want to be invited back for Thanksgiving and Christmas so . . . here's a compromise: sweet potato cinnamon rolls. Why not lean into the sweet potato's sweetness, combining it in icing form with a chewy dough—not unlike the brioche-like cinnamon rolls from the Jamaican bakeries where I grew up—and a spice-rich cinnamon filling? You want sweet, Mom? You got sweet *and* sweet potatoes.

For the dough

Place the cream and coconut cream in a small microwave-safe bowl. Microwave for 15 to 30 seconds, until warm to the touch but not steaming. Transfer to the bowl of a stand mixer fitted with the dough hook, then add the yeast and sugar and stir to combine. Let stand until foamy, about 5 minutes.

With the mixer on medium, add the eggs one at a time until fully combined, then slowly add the flour and salt. Mix on medium speed until a sticky dough forms, then add the butter 2 tablespoons at a time, waiting until it's fully incorporated before adding more. Once all the butter has been incorporated, mix for 10 minutes. The dough should be soft, supple, and a little shiny.

Shape the dough into a ball, place it in a large, lightly oiled bowl, and cover tightly with plastic wrap. Transfer to the refrigerator for at least 8 hours and up to overnight. It will double in size.

ORIGIN: American South
YIELD: 8 rolls

For the dough
½ cup **heavy cream**
½ cup **unsweetened coconut cream**
2 teaspoons **active dry yeast**
¼ cup **white granulated sugar**
2 **eggs**
4 cups **all-purpose flour**, plus more for dusting
1½ teaspoons **kosher salt**
6 tablespoons **unsalted butter**, softened

For the filling
¾ cup **dark brown sugar**
¼ cup **coconut sugar**
1 tablespoon ground **cinnamon**
¼ teaspoon ground **allspice**
¼ teaspoon ground **cloves**
½ teaspoon **kosher salt**
½ cup **unsalted butter**, room temperature

For the filling

Stir together the sugars, spices, and salt in a small bowl.

When ready to assemble, grease a 9-x-13-inch pan. Remove the dough from the refrigerator—it will be stiff and cold, which should make it easy to roll out. Dust your work surface and rolling pin lightly with flour, then roll the dough into an approximately 12-x-16-inch rectangle.

Spread the dough evenly with the butter, leaving a 1-inch border along one of the shorter edges. Sprinkle the filling mixture evenly over the butter and press down lightly to adhere.

Starting from the short edge with the butter all the way to the edge, roll the dough into a tight spiral. Gently pinch the long edge of the roll to seal, then trim ½ inch from each end of the spiral. Cut the roll in half crosswise, then cut each half into 4 even pieces. Place the rolls in the prepared baking dish, cover loosely with plastic wrap, and let rise in a warm place until pillowy and doubled in size. (Depending on how warm your kitchen is, this may take as little as 30 minutes or as long as 90 minutes.) While the rolls rise, heat oven to 350°F.

Bake the rolls until puffed and golden, 25 to 35 minutes. Transfer the baking dish to a cooling rack.

For the frosting

While the rolls bake, make the frosting: In the bowl of a stand mixer fitted with the paddle attachment (or in a large bowl with an electric hand mixer), beat the cream cheese, butter, sweet potato purée, and vanilla bean paste on medium until creamy and combined. Add half the powdered sugar and 1 tablespoon cream. Turn the mixer to low speed and gradually increase to medium; beat for 1 minute, then gradually add the remaining sugar and beat for 1 minute more, until fluffy and smooth. Add additional cream as needed to reach desired consistency.

Let the rolls cool for 5 minutes, then frost generously and serve warm.

For the frosting

4 ounces **cream cheese**, room temperature

4 tablespoons **unsalted butter**, room temperature

¼ cup canned **sweet potato purée**

2 teaspoons **vanilla bean paste**

2 cups **powdered sugar**

1–4 tablespoons **heavy cream**

Kosher salt, to taste

Sweet potato cinnamon rolls will keep in an airtight container in the refrigerator for up to 3 days. Warm slightly before serving.

SOURSOP GRANITA

This palette cleanser is a shout-out to my local icy-stand guy in the Bronx, whose name is lost to history but who was a fixture at the Bronx Park where I spent most of my summer afternoons as a kid. Shaved ice desserts, what I always called icies, are popular in the Dominican Republic and Puerto Rico and so, it follows, in the Bronx. The icy-stand guy isn't like a Mister Softee driver, who travels the boroughs blaring his infernal song on repeat. The only sound accompanying the icy man is the creak of his pushcart, the bell he rings, and the recitation—usually in Spanish—of his flavors: cherry, mango, tamarind, pineapple, and passion fruit. One icy cost twenty-five cents, which meant, as a kid, the dollar my mother gave me could stretch for an icy *and* a coco bread. Though soursop and its frozen pulp—in the Caribbean the fruit is called guanabana and in Brazil, paw paw—is available at most grocery stores, it isn't part of the traditional icy man repertoire. But the unique flavor, a sort of sour-tinged strawberry, along with the lime make this granita as bracing and refreshing a snack as what I remember from my childhood.

ORIGIN: The Bronx
YIELD: 6 to 8 servings

3½ cups **water**
One 14-ounce package **soursop pulp**, thawed if frozen
1⅓ cups **white granulated sugar**
½ cup + 2 tablespoons freshly squeezed **lime juice** (from 3 to 4 limes)
Lime zest, to serve

Granita may be made up to the point of shaving 1 week in advance. (If you're not going to serve it the day it's made, cover the pan tightly with plastic wrap or foil to keep the granita fresh-tasting.) Scrape into shavings just before serving.

Combine water, soursop pulp, and sugar in a large pot over medium-low heat. Stir until the sugar dissolves, then transfer to a blender. Purée until completely smooth, then refrigerate until completely chilled, 2 hours. Stir in the lime juice.

Pour into a 9-x-13-inch baking dish and transfer to the freezer. Freeze for 6 hours, then use a fork to scrape into shavings.

Scoop the shavings into bowls and serve garnished with lime zest.

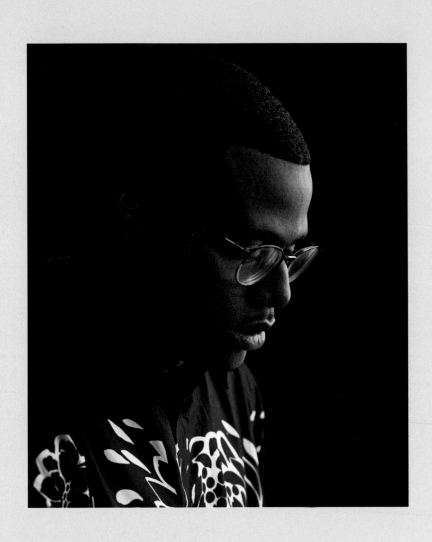

ACKNOWLEDGMENTS

From Kwame

I'd like to thank Paz, my main man who has been rocking with me since day one, from catering weddings in culinary school to doing events around the world. Thank you for trusting in my vision. To Taylor, who is such an important part of my life professionally and personally, you bring a smile to my face and keep me grounded. To Clay, who helped capture the amazing essence of this book. To Lori, who always has my best interest at heart, and whose laugh is infectious. I'd like to raise a non-alcoholic beverage for Tom for keeping everything on track. To Caroline, for all of the yummy samples while I was filming. And of course to Joshua, for trusting in my vision and capturing my voice so eloquently, I bestow on you as many thank-yous as you have tattoos.

From Joshua

As with *Notes*, my deepest gratitude goes to Kwame, who invited me to help tell these stories and to share these recipes. A huge debt of gratitude as well to the entire *My America* party, including Caroline Lange, our intrepid tester; Paz, keeper of all knowledge; and Taylor, keeper of all schedules. Praise be to Clay Williams, whose images bring these dishes to life. At Knopf, this work couldn't have been done without the guidance and trust of our extraordinary editor, Tom Pold; the too-often-unheralded copy editor Amy Stackhouse; and designers Cassandra Pappas and Kelly Blair, who gave us a book as beautiful as it is soulful. Finally, a big thank-you to my agent, David Black, for being my tireless advocate in all matters publishing.

INDEX

Page numbers in *italics* refer to illustrations.

A NOTE ABOUT THE AUTHORS

Kwame Onwuachi is a James Beard Award–winning chef and author of *Notes from a Young Black Chef*. He has been named one of *Food & Wine*'s Best New Chefs, *Esquire*'s 2019 Chef of the Year, a 30 Under 30 honoree by both *Zagat* and *Forbes*, and has been featured on *Time*'s 100 Next List. A former contestant and now a recurring judge on *Top Chef*, he currently serves as *Food & Wine*'s executive producer. Raised in New York City, Nigeria, and Louisiana, Onwuachi trained at the Culinary Institute of America in New York and opened five restaurants before turning thirty.

Joshua David Stein is a writer, editor, and illustrator. He is the co-author of *Notes from a Young Black Chef*, with Kwame Onwuachi; *The Nom Wah Cookbook*, with Wilson Tang; *Il Buco: Stories and Recipes*, with Donna Lennard; *Food & Beer*, with Jeppe Jarnit-Bjergsø and Daniel Burns; and *Vino: The Essential Guide to Italian Wine*, with Joe Campanale. He is the author of the cookbook *Cooking for Your Kids: At Home with the World's Greatest Chefs* and of many children's books including *Can I Eat That?*, *What's Cooking?*, and *Solitary Animals*. He lives in Brooklyn with his two young sons and a mutt named Hermione.